The Bermuda Triangle

Books by Gian Quasar

The Bermuda Triangle II
Scarlet Autumn: Jack the Ripper
Distant Horizons
A Passage to Oblivion
SOMA
Recasting Bigfoot
They Flew into Oblivion
Into the Bermuda Triangle

THE BERMUDA TRIANGLE

II

An Odyssey of the Sea

Gian J. Quasar

Brodwyn, Moor & Doane
2017

Cataloguing-in-Publication Data

Quasar, Gian Julius

THE BERMUDA TRIANGLE

1st *Edition*

ISBN
978-0-9888505-8-3

No part of this publication may be reproduced, broadcast, transmitted, distributed or displayed— except for brief quotations in reviews— without prior written permission.

Copyright © 2017 by Gian J. Quasar
All Rights Reserved

Contents

Chapter 1	The Bermuda Triangle: An Enduring Mystery	7
Chapter 2	A Saga of Disappearing Planes and Lost Ships	24
Chapter 3	Over a Past Horizon	72
Chapter 4	"Aircraft Damage and Injury Index Presumed"	89
Chapter 5	A Triangle of Today	119
Chapter 6	Electronic Fog: an Answer or a Symptom?	150
Chapter 7	Vortices, Space-Time-Continua and Electromagnetic Anomalies	171
Chapter 8	Worlds Above; Worlds Beneath	193
Chapter 9	Beyond Forgotten Tides	236
Chapter 10	A Saga of the Earth's Past	260

Bibliography

Chapter 1

The Bermuda Triangle: An Enduring Mystery

The covers of all world newspapers captivated readers when they detailed the puzzling facts behind the inexplicable disappearance of a huge Boeing 777 carrying 239 people on a routine flight over Malaysia. Such a chilling event, played out over hours, was declared to be contrived without obvious reason, cunningly executed and heinously premeditated. I am not trying to use an excessive number of adjectives to get your attention, but I want the reader to understand the gravity of such a scenario when it happens hundreds of times along the busiest coast in the USA, in the most crowded and guarded sea and airways, in circumstances that are even more incredible. For these disappearances are not just of people quietly taken off course without reason to a point over a huge ocean; they are the sudden and total disappearance of over a 1,000 people and the aircraft in which they were flying, or the yachts they were sailing, or even the great freighters they crewed. These are not just boats and planes lost on a big ocean. Their losses are as inexplicable as a person disappearing between their door and the corner of their street. Many have vanished just at the edge of the harbor, others while cruising around a peninsula; many aircraft were on radar, gone in a single sweep of the radarscope, and in some instances just moments from landing. They disappear as if suddenly plucked from safety, without any clue except brief and panicked Maydays.

Derelict vessels continue to turn up with distressing regularity. Crews are gone, snatched as if by the same hand of mystery, leaving behind them sound and stable ships yet completely minus any indication why they fled. Disappearances of this character have been puzzling annalists and historians since mankind first began sailing the waters of the New World, making this phenomenon an observed mystery for hundreds of years.

What has made the phenomenon so high profiled and excited so much interest in the last 50 years is the discovery that the disappearances are not random and spread throughout the entire North Atlantic Ocean, but that at a contrast they remain in a comparatively small part of it— a section off the southeast coast of the United States between the island of Bermuda, Miami, Florida, and the Caribbean island of Puerto Rico. This area, frequently known as the Bermuda Triangle, continues to see more disappearances than any other equally trafficked section of ocean on the Earth to this day. This is in spite of modern technology such as GPS, VORs, and the use of radio by which at the very least a pilot could give base stations an idea of what was going wrong.

When there is radio contact, rather than clarity the opposite predominates. Jumbled Maydays have related: "I don't know what is happening to me;" "a weird object is in my course;" "my compass has stopped working;" or messages indicating that visibility, which previously extended for miles, is now suddenly gone, replaced by a spontaneously appearing "fog" that surrounds the aircraft and forces the pilot to fly on instruments as if in normal meteorological conditions but in these instances the instruments are going "haywire." Gauges are erratic. The compass is spinning. GPS or LORAN readouts cease or clear to 8888. On some occasions the pilot is so consumed with trying to understand the circumstances that they are only able to say "I seem to be having instrument trouble" or just "instrument trouble" without being able to clarify it, repeating this until they vanish.

Normally the result of losing control is a wide debris field scattered over the ocean. But in the cases where a pilot was able to indicate the "electronic fog" before vanishing, little or no debris is found at all.

This area, though it is highly trafficked, does not, however, contain any significantly higher number of problems than those that ordinarily vex travelers in other sections of the Earth's oceans. Great hurricanes strike in the area of the Triangle, but the ships lost and the aircraft downed leave wreckage that is located, studied and upon which conclusions as to the cause of the accident can be drawn. In the regular course of events, traffic through the Triangle encounters the same vagaries of weather and human interaction. The Coast Guard answers the same type and near the same number of SOS calls as in any other heavily traveled tourist and commercial seas. Yet disappearances remain alarmingly disproportionate.

There is, however, one noteworthy difference in the area of the Bermuda Triangle than in other comparable trafficked areas. Its most heavily traveled seas are so shallow they are transparent or the bottom can be reached on a straight dive. It is precisely here, in the Triangle's southwest corner, where most of the disappearances in the Bermuda Triangle occur. This area covers the vast archipelago of the Bahamas, where over 700 islands, their ports and airfields, make for easier and safer island-hopping through to the Caribbean. In many places the sea bottom is only a few feet deep. The average depth is about 50 feet. Land and potential safety, even for a shipwrecked crew, is never far. Nevertheless, the disappearances continue without trace of wreckage on the beaches or any visible sign of or shadow of the sunken aircraft or vessel below the thin blanket of azure waters.

This last phenomenon extends even over time. Most any wreck in the shallow waters of the Bahamas will attract the growth of turtle grass. The result is an underwater oasis teeming with sea fauna. Such oases easily stand out from the surface as a marled dark green scar in the mirror-clean turquoise shallows. Local divers are very familiar with such locations, and it is not long before the exotic kaleidoscope of a new one attracts their curiosity. Yet though most of the disappearances have occurred over this archipelago, there are no such unexplained marled areas indicating the presence of uncatalogued wrecks. The most logical, or at least prosaic, explanation is that the aircraft or ships were completely obliterated before they hit the ocean or sank— the frequency of disappearances, however, would suggest anything but prosaic possibilities as the cause.

These are not the only mysteries attending the many disappearing ships and planes in the Bermuda Triangle. None has ever sent any ELT or EPIRB signal to base stations. These acronyms represent very powerful automatic alarms— Emergency Locator Transmitter and Emergency Position Indicating Radio Beacon— that are set in motion by the impacting of an aircraft or float free from a ship when it sinks. They continue to send their electronic Mayday for days. Passing aircraft, base stations, and even satellites can easily home-in on them. None of the missing, however, though the number must be in the hundreds that carried such devices, have ever sent a signal indicating they impacted (for aircraft) or sank (for ships) in any conventional sense of the word.

It is becoming more acceptable today to believe that the Bermuda Triangle, for whatever reasons, represents an exception to the way nature traditionally operates on this planet and interacts with travel. It may also be that there is something very different about this part of the planet. Among the disappearances there is an interesting proportion of travelers who survive unusual encounters and who continue to report odd electromagnetic phenomena and that strange "electronic fog" that envelops them and "fritzes" all electronic equipment including radio, VORS, LORAN, all gauges, and in addition drains battery power. Taken altogether, the entire enigma of the Bermuda Triangle may, if finally unraveled, help us to exploit the very real complex network of forces that surround us, cause this still mysterious orb to rotate, revolve, and interact with the greater and equally inescapable forces of time and space.

At the very least, the Bermuda Triangle represents a

challenge for our minds to grasp, one that over a thousand people have given their lives (presumably) unintentionally to reveal to us. Every year, and with every new case, as disappearances continue to defy every effort to prevent them or at least to forestall the sense of mystery attending them, the Triangle is slowly being drawn out of the clutches of the "paranormal fringe" and into the cold hard light of scientific acceptability. When thousands of tons of shipping and aircraft vanish it becomes increasingly hard to attribute the disappearances to the supernatural or flirt, however winsomely, with Saturday afternoon pulp theories.

Some may find it easier to dismiss the enigma of the Bermuda Triangle by pointing out that disappearances obviously do not happen over land. Looking beyond any prosaic cause such as "crash and sink" from pilot error or weather conditions is therefore merely the penchant of those trying to create mystery where it does not exist. And yet as true as this is, when it comes to the land versus sea argument anyway, it is equally true that the phenomenon of the "electronic fog" does not exist over land. Nor does this humbug attitude take into account that the sea itself is a very different medium than land, and that water is essential to conduct that world of electricity and therewith intensify that more dynamic and still mysterious world of electromagnetism. Nor do navigators on land, in any place, so frequently encounter odd redirections of their compass as if some unusual electromagnetic event is transiently occurring over the horizon but out of sight. It is so frequent in areas of the Bahamas that shipmasters have taken it for granted. When it occurs, invariably they will say, with the expected bemusement, "It's the Bermuda Triangle!" For pilots or strangers it is not so amusing an experience.

Such is the case with Simon Ludgate, a British documentary producer, in a TBM Avenger re-flying the course of Flight 19, the 5 Avengers which vanished in 1945 and whose mysterious loss is generally considered to have directed world attention to the area. When he noticed that their compass just stopped, before he could even react, they were almost immediately radioed by the chase plane filming them saying that their compass too had stopped. Such an event, occurring simultaneously, was enough to alarm the otherwise calm filmmaker.

Only 3 planes of space exist, and yet only 2 fields of energy are discovered—electricity and at a right angle to an electric current a magnetic field. Presupposing Dr. Albert Einstein to be correct, theorists believe a 3rd field of energy should exist. But so far none other has been discovered, whether it even exists to be discovered, and obviously there is no information how it must interact with the other two. Gravity is the only other "force" known. It exists though it was never truly discovered. It is merely "apparent" that it exists. Some believe it to be the 3rd field of energy, though established nomenclature considers it not a force but a "phenomenon," a word which almost seems to establish its mystery rather than clarify it. It is the most obvious "phenomenon" about us and yet paradoxically the most mysterious. All that is known is that Time itself can be affected by gravity. Since time and gravity are intertwined, if gravity is the 3rd and elusive field it must be affected by the other two and therewith the most mysterious world of space and time can be manipulated through electromagnetism.

Over the oceans, with their ability to help generate electromagnetism, would be the best place for unexplained and potentially dynamic electromagnetic phenomena to occur. Specific areas may be more prone to these phenomena, based on factors that offer all the right conditions, whether this is humidity, interaction of ocean currents, effects due to rotation of the Earth, or whatever, that allow them to come together to create the startling effects. Theorists, as we shall see, are more and more certain the Triangle represents one of these areas, and alarming potential may come about, foreshadowed by the erratic behavior of the boat or plane's electronic equipment.

Even if every missing ship and plane could logistically be explained as the result of some already known agent, the interest the Bermuda Triangle has created has led to the broadening of our knowledge about time, energy and mass.

Professor David Pares of the University of Nebraska has not been put off by the folkloric claims that surround the Triangle. Rather he has come to believe that the "electronic fog" at least is very real, and the details of one pilot, Bruce Gernon, who experienced its most intense manifestation and who set about to discover what caused him to move 100 miles in space and 30 minutes in time during the period he was enveloped in it, have convinced Pares that Gernon's experience is key to unraveling space and time travel.

Other scientists have risen to the challenge, both in the United States, South America, and even as far afield as Russia, where Dr. Oleg Mercheryakov, who has possibly solved the riddle of ball lightning, has attempted to explain the Triangle's infamous "electronic fog."

A more *in situ* attempt to crack at least one of the cases of the Triangle has inspired the daughter of a lost pilot to try and correlate his missing aircraft with one unaccounted underwater oasis called "The Eye" 55 miles east of the island of Bimini on the Great Bahama Bank. Pam Harrison lost her father over 35 years ago on a flight from the Bahamas to North Carolina. Her desire is to mount an expedition to finally clear the sea bottom off the still-unidentified wreck to see if its registration number matches that of the aircraft her father flew.

Another attempt to unravel some of the mystery of the Triangle is taken rather in a piecemeal effort. Dr. Greg Little has been diving in the Triangle for decades. No matter what the subject of the dive is, he makes a conscious effort to divert to any wreck to see if he can identify it with one of the many missing in the Bermuda Triangle.

Yet for every attempt to chip away at the legend of the Bermuda Triangle, a new mystery arises or an older one almost seems confirmed. American psychic Edgar Cayce's predictions about the last remnant of Atlantis being found in the waters of the Bermuda Triangle go hand-in-glove now with the enigma of unexplained megalithic ruins found underwater in the Triangle's most exotic corner of the Bahamas. Some individual stones and entire structures are cyclopean in size. Coincidently (or not so coincidently) they match colossal prehistoric architecture around the world. Naturally (albeit *very* unofficially) they are attributed to being Cayce's Atlantis, which he had described as having been a worldwide super-civilization, both technologically and in terms of mental powers, with its last surviving section having sunk exactly here 12,000 years ago. Furthermore, he declared this last remnant of the Atlantean civilization to hold the secret electromagnetic power sources of this vanished prehistoric age.

Caycean Atlantis and these cyclopean ruins are some of the most alluring components of the legend of the Triangle. Daily, tourists glide over massive stone foundations off Bimini, where Cayce had predicted (in 1933) such ruins would be found and where they indeed were (in 1968), and gaze through glass bottom boats. But nothing approximating a city or even advanced technology has (yet) been uncovered.

Admittedly the Atlantean theory ably resides with the fringe and paranormal crowd, who propose that these sunken power complexes, designed as they were, according to Cayce's trance readings, to operate on natural forces, could still be down on the sea bottom causing the electromagnetic aberrations in the Triangle that eventually lead to disappearances either by disintegration, by space-time shift and warps, or by creating the "electronic fog" that sends panicked pilots to their doom.

Although it is a theory easy to scorn, the idea of an ancient, even prehistoric sunken civilization in the area received startling interest from established circles, including the National Geographic, when Dr. Paulina Zelitsky's bottom scans finally located what appeared to be an ancient and complex city that had been plunged beneath the sea off Cuba long before recorded history. From tests of the surrounding geology, she placed its subsidence back, coincidently, to 12,000 years ago, the precise time that Cayce, in trances, said that the last remnant of a fabulous and advanced civilization sank in the Bahamas and Caribbean.

Taken on its own a sunken city is, of course, more of tangible rather than paranormal interest to the adventurer and investigator, who must keep a skeptical eye on such claims of prehistory for fear it is belief in Cayce rather than objective study that has set the time frame. It is to be noted that Mayan legends and stone glyphs tell of coming to Yucatan after the massive destruction of a city across the eastern sea, which must mean the Gulf of Mexico and Caribbean, and the sunken city off Cuba could therefore be to what these glyphs refer.

The discovery of a sunken city and its coincidence with psychic readings from 85 years ago is yet another of many coincidences in the Bermuda Triangle that cause us to gaze beyond that invisible horizon and wonder at our own mysterious prehistory.

This is not the only occasion where the legend of the Triangle has found some form of belated fulfillment in reality. As early as 1962 some form of electromagnetic aberration was suspected to be contributing to the disappearances. Such theorizing was inspired by what later were proven to be apocryphal words attributed by an imaginative writer to the pilots of Flight 19, the flight of 5 Navy Avenger torpedo bombers whose disappearance in 1945 is considered one of the greatest mysteries of aviation. These alarming phrases included: "The compass is going crazy. We don't know where we're at; even the sea doesn't look as it should." Although these words were later exploded as false, actual research has revealed historic references to just such reactions by pilots to strange electromagnetic phenomena and unexplained fogs that caused all their navigational gear to suddenly go erratic. Among the historic encounters is the entire crew of the British ship *Mohican* in 1904 and Charles Lindbergh in 1928 while flying *Spirit of St. Louis* from Havana. Modern reencounters with such electromagnetic fogs are documented since 1970, six years before Lindbergh would admit to his own encounter in the Triangle in his 1976 book *Autobiography of Values.*

There is nothing novel in old and new reconfirming aspects of the Bermuda Triangle's enigma, or the cart of legend coming before the horse of fact. Aircraft disappearances, for example, are fairly easy to document these days. Older incidents, though they prove tenuous to extract from the obscurity of old archives, reveal remarkable continuity and can seem to be little more than an earlier version of the latest case; all that is required is to adjust date and time.

This continuity is remarkable and it suggests that the vast

majority of disappearances have the same factors contributing to them. These, at least in the most sensational and inexplicable cases, revolve around sudden "fogs," electromagnetic phenomena, or such lightning-like disappearance it seems as if the aircraft simply "winked out" both visually and on radar.

Ultimately the answer to the mystery of the Triangle lies not just in unraveling and understanding the origins and potential of "electronic fog" but in delineating exactly what needs solving in the first place. When someone is asked "Do you believe in the Bermuda Triangle?" various giddy replies ensue, most often based on false impressions, urban legends, and kneejerk reactions to popular or even bizarre theories. In essence there can be no poignant answer to the question because the question itself has no parameters. What, in essence, constitutes the "Bermuda Triangle"? While as many theories as legends exist, no investigator can proceed to a solution without accepting that to "believe" in the Triangle can initially mean only two things: to believe in what seems obvious, that it is an actual geographic area (though the name is certainly unofficial); and, two, that to "believe in the Bermuda Triangle" means to accept its enigma, that is, that more ships and aircraft disappear in this area than in any other part of the world for as yet no readily explainable reason. If not these two basic points then otherwise the entire topic simply becomes an ouroboros feeding in a shallow pool of questionable theory.

History alone is the only parameter that can define the Bermuda Triangle inasmuch as it gives us context and in that it is also the clearest step to defining the geography of the phenomenon.

As early as 1887 the US Hydrographic Office set up a study of derelict vessels in the North Atlantic. Under the guidance of then-Commander Charles Sigsbee the study, which revolved around 1,628 abandoned vessels, concluded that the majority were to be found in the area around Bermuda to the southeast coast of the United States, the area today known as the Bermuda Triangle. Outside of this area the largest concentration was to be found in the seas north and south of the Sargasso Sea and west of the Azores. However, many of these derelict vessels found here could be explained by their subsequent drift in the powerful Gulf Stream currents that flow through the Triangle and then around the Sargasso Sea and back again to the Triangle, indicating that whatever befell the crews did so in the area delineated today for the Bermuda Triangle and the vessel, now deserted, continued to drift in the currents.

To this day, the majority of disappearances and occurrences of abandoned vessels in the entire North Atlantic happen within the Bermuda Triangle *and* within these currents that we collectively call The Gulf Stream. They do not occur in the heart of the Sargasso Sea, the very center of the North Atlantic. For that matter, the heart of the Triangle, which is nothing but the western approaches of the Sargasso Sea, is largely also devoid of disappearances, both then and now. This is actually at a contrast to the old sea legends. Ancient mariners in the days of sail dreaded and tried to avoid the Sargasso Sea because of its notorious calms. This is understandable since calms would delay a sailing ship. But the true area of disappearances and mystery and hence the true "triangle" is not the "damnable Sargasso Sea." It is really a long whip lashing out from the Gulf and snapping through the heart of the Atlantic before it comes back to the warm Caribbean.

It is not the drift of these powerful currents that has created the missing ships and planes by scattering the debris (the Coast Guard is well aware of the drift and takes this into account in any search), for tumultuous currents cannot make so many crews abandon their sound ship and plunge headlong into the very thing that has frightened them. Rather it is over these powerful currents and in these odd latitudes where sailors have thrown themselves over to an unforgiving and abiding Deep, or have been taken there unawares. Of his encounter, the Captain of the *Mohican* declared: "the vessel was enshrouded in a strange metallic vapor, which glowed like phosphorus. The entire vessel looked as if it were afire and the sailors flitted about the deck like glowing phantoms."

The largest number of encounters with "electronic fog" and transient electromagnetic phenomena are, probably not so

Marking only 100 cases of derelicts contained in Sigsbee's work highlights how the Bermuda Triangle has always been the center of deserted vessels. Arrows mark the drift of the currents.

coincidently, also encountered in this area of the Triangle; the difference between the Triangle and those areas around the Sargasso Sea being that the currents in the Triangle are the most powerful in all the collective Gulf Stream. Several theorists, including the late Ivan Sanderson, speculated that the powerful tangential currents played a key role in creating or exacerbating the electromagnetic aberrations.

In attempting to dismiss the Triangle's mystery or at least enigma, it has also been pondered quite out loud why this present writer, who is solely responsible for bringing the subject back to life, is obsessive in never referring to himself in the first person, and why he is not more critical of the theories especially in light of the fact that his other books are noted for investigation and critical analysis. Why, for example here, would he even refer to Ivan Sanderson, an investigator of whom he has been critical? "I" will answer by saying that in this case Sanderson, no matter what his other shortcomings were, may be quite correct, as we will later find out.

Of all the topics I have investigated, and about which I have written, none of them have been as complex as this one nor encompass so much. There is a difference between investigating a single event, serial killer, or quotient, and investigating hundreds of mysteries over centuries of time spread over hundreds of thousands of square miles of sea hard to personally investigate. No one attempting to educate can limit data based on personal preference. That is indoctrination and not education. Nor can anyone deprive the devil of his due. I present this subject as a reporter and commentator and not as the critic.

What I cannot solve or dismiss on evidence I must include. Personally I do not care for alien abduction theories and much of what and those who come with them. But that does not mean I can ignore Russian admirals, captains, and numerous other eyewitnesses, to such things as "flying saucers" that seem to make the Bermuda Triangle the center of their activity; nor the statements of credible witnesses, such as Simon Ludgate, whom I personally know, when he reports that during the same flight in which their compass froze and then spun he saw silver discs circling high overhead their aircraft.

The reader must decide to what extent of a role these objects, for they have certainly been seen out there, have played in the litany of missing craft.

The Bermuda Triangle is a tall and wide subject. It is not one man's theory. It is much more than disappearances. If I can conjure an old Kodachrome image of a *Flipper* serial, investigators shod in Van tennis shoes facing high seas adventure but with enough mentality to appreciate the chords of ominous music when a derelict boat is found, when a pilot's panicky voice crackles over the receiver about a weird object, of eyes that brighten with the prospects when they gaze through the kaleidoscope of dancing shallows at a cyclopean edifice, then I have served the subject well.

In continuing, one of the many arguments put forward to minimize the number of missing boats in the Triangle as being suggestive of anything out of the ordinary is to point out that the Triangle, at least in the Florida-Bahamas corner, is the pleasure boating capital of the world, and therefore the number of yachts that vanish is not by percentage out of proportion. Large numbers are merely statistically expected. On paper this may look correct, but in practice it is not. Florida has spiraled into that void that follows past glory. Economic decline has seen thousands upon thousands of boats abandoned. There is no mystery in these cases, however. Before the Great Recession the owners had been borderline boaters seldom taking out their boats and keeping them only in a state of repair necessary to maintain them at anchor.

Every county in Florida is now plagued by abandoned boats. Sailboats have sunk at anchor. Expensive old yachts and even Chris Craft or Browards slump with bilges that need pumping. Power boats are abandoned in lagoons. Conchers, scallopers, several types of fishermen lie deserted where they were left. To save on dock fees and eventually fines from special police who now give notices of a boat in danger of being considered a derelict, many have towed out their once prized boats and allowed them to drift away. Bermuda residents, 1,000 miles away, are complaining about the number that follow the Gulf Stream and drift by.

Over wide sections of the Triangle's most popular corner, in fact, it is becoming undeniably clear that the days of casual boating are bygone. Boats and parts of boats lie scattered as mementoes to a more opulent age, on beaches, sunk in coves, or hauled out and ravaged and a sort of curious and fun birdhouse to investigate on a quay's bank at low tide.

Interdicting drug running is almost a daily affair for the 7th Coast Guard. The boats and aircraft forced down are left where they are, each forming a contribution to a neglected open-air museum to crime and the progress of avionics and boating that many wilder parts of the Bermuda Triangle have become.

But nowhere amongst these can be found the missing, not even a fraction of them. Those vanished in the Triangle are gone. They vanished in large numbers before the days of modern piracy and boat hijacking and they continue despite all the law enforcement concentrated in this sensitive underbelly of a nation consumed with potential terrorism.

An Enduring Mystery

It is undeniable, however, that the number of disappearances in the Bermuda Triangle has drastically declined over the last decade. It is not because there is no more "electronic fog." Nor are GPS and more advanced navigational aids responsible by preventing mariners and pilots from getting lost (though no doubt this has helped in some cases), for such advancements cannot prevent the appearance of debris after an accident anyway. Besides, there are always a large number of perennially crude and miserly boaters who will not outfit their boats properly with EPIRBs and state of the art electronics. The existence of this group is never a secret since they are the ones who most noisily take offence when it is suggested that a bare minimum of safety must be legislated into effect. Although one might think that they're prime candidates for disappearing, fools go where angels fear to tread and invariably survive, though causing untold angst and frustration for the Coast Guard. No, the average boater is simply not transiting the seas anymore. Tens of thousands exist only on paper, and thousands more ride at anchor and are nearing the graveyard created by disuse. Logistics explain it. Sadly, it is not electronics or progress. Fewer travel far out, and thus fewer encounter an unchancy fate, whether this fate is natural or contrived.

Fear of encountering pirates and being hijacked is also

keeping boat owners in their safe harbor. Millions in cocaine and marijuana are being brought in along the Gulf side of Florida, into the Ten Thousands Islands area, where a battleship could get lost. The illicit trade is well organized and funded. Semi submersibles are even being used in order to reduce the radar target on a scope. Interdicting these is quite rare, and the first was intercepted only within the last few years. Gunplay between pirates may even explain some odd mysteries. On one occasion the Coast Guard picked up a lone bale of cocaine floating at sea. Since such illegal valuables are not stacked up on deck like crates of bananas and therefore not apt to fall overboard, such an article at sea testifies to some mystery which befell even a drug runner or to some violent clash between modern day pirates of the Caribbean.

Florida's east coast is one long beach and tourist mecca—not an environment conducive to the secretive rigors of smuggling. But its Gulf coast is dark, full of mangrove lagoons, desolate river mouths, secret blue bays of undisturbed conch; old rickety piers creep out cautiously from the jungles where boats can dock after coming in from Cuba. It is curious to note that it is on this side of Florida where a number of derelict vessels, having been crewed by only a single navigator, have been found, the owners completely vanished, victims perhaps of having been in the wrong place at the wrong time.

But the overall answer to the mysteries of the Bermuda Triangle lies elsewhere. It is not in economic woes and the reduced number of travelers. Reduced numbers are a clue, but they are at best only a temporary clue. Something is not being fed. Disappearances are increasingly happening closer to shore than ever before, on short runs where boats have seldom been touched before. Derelicts are turning up on closer runs more than ever before. Something is coming closer to shore; for most, something figurative. But for some who have been touched by it, something literally is coming closer to shore.

However true all the points raised here are, they nonetheless remain factoids. A solution to the Triangle cannot be found in only one point by reducing it to an abstract. As abstracts are impersonal, intellectual general overlays they can never be tempered by details. The truth of the Triangle's enigma can only be found in coming down to cases. Before we delve into the developing changes in the Triangle and the alarming possibilities they suggest, we must go back. We must relay the foundation and look into the vast litany of those lost. Without understanding these, the impact of the last decade cannot be fully appreciated.

Chapter 2

A Saga of Disappearing Planes and Lost Ships

Until 1945 the disappearance of planes and ships in the North Atlantic was generally not considered limited to any particular area. In fact, outside of World War II military training and patrol losses there were no previous reports of a missing aircraft. Disappearances of ships were the lamentable albeit intriguing hazard of traveling a big ocean. Without radio and wireless there was little ability to plot the locations of where ships had vanished along their far-flung courses, and after radio's invention the absence of a ship's routine position reports— indications it had vanished— only helped plot where it had vanished but not what had caused it to suddenly go missing. In this context it became noteworthy that certain courses seemed to lead to mystery, those specifically that traversed the seas off the southeast coast of the United States.

While radio distresses commonly reported foundering, breaking in twain, and the other gambols imposed by an untamed sea, those that had vanished had sent no word, a contrast that was beginning to spark curiosity back on land. No SOS, in fact, was far more commonplace, even the norm for ships that vanished.

During World War II cargo ships were in peril on every ocean, hunted sheep getting off whatever message they could before the German wolf packs sank them; those that couldn't get a message off left telltale flotsam that they had fallen victim to torpedo.

Had it not been for the rigors imposed by the war it might have been a greater source of comment, in the US military at least, that dozens of military planes were vanishing, not in the war zone but off Florida where the flights were engaged in nothing more hazardous than routine training and patrol, all relatively close to the coast. One may well suppose it was the lack of a radio distress indicating anything unusual, plus the fact there had previously never been much flight over the ocean in order to gauge what is a normal ratio of disappearances, that kept the number of disappearances and the lack of debris from being regarded as alarming.

Peacetime brought with it a significant factor to the equation. Frequent military flights continued unabated over the Triangle, before they would be discontinued by mass discharge of wartime personnel from the service. But peacetime meant unhampered press coverage, a factor absent during the war. It also meant the lack of a potential enemy to blame. Conditions were now right for the reporting of one of the most sensational disappearances in the annals of aviation and for the transcribing of radio messages that would set the standard for unusual communication from any pilot over the sea.

The incident was the disappearance of Flight 19 on December 5, 1945, a squadron of 5 large US Navy Avenger torpedo bombers with a combined crew of 14 men (pilot, radioman, gunner). They had taken off from their base of Fort Lauderdale, Florida, at 2:08 p.m. on an afternoon of fair weather and brisk trade winds. Their mission was a routine training flight over the Bahamas. At 3:40 p.m. when the first indications came back there was a problem, they were considerably less than an hour away from their base and safety. Somehow, despite the area being completely rung in by landmarks, without seeing any land, or noting the position of the westward setting sun, the entire squadron of 5 planes was drawn north into the open Atlantic.

Compass malfunction was the initial reason the flight got lost. This information was picked up incidentally by another pilot, Lt. Robert F. Cox, also flying a TBM, in his case just off the east coast of Florida near Fort Lauderdale. Over his radio he heard a pilot contacting another pilot, asking what his compass read. As it would turn out, this was the Flight Leader of Flight 19, Lt. Charles Taylor, asking one of his student pilots, Captain Ed Powers. Taylor then informed Powers that his own compasses weren't working. For Cox, this seemed harmless enough at first. The only training flights far out over the islands numbered at least 5 aircraft. One of the other pilots would be able to determine their position and continue to lead the flight.

However, as the radio communications continued Robert Cox overheard a discussion on compasses and directions, as though none of the pilots could agree. He intervened and was finally able to raise the Flight Leader, Lt. Taylor, in FT-28, the designated number of his TBM. Taylor reiterated that his compasses were not working and they were lost. Although Taylor did not mention whether the other pilots' compasses were not working, it was clear to Cox there remained no consensus amongst them, something that indicated more than one other pilot was unsure as well, a phenomenal coincidence in an entire squadron with 5 pilots and a combined 10 compasses (each plane had two compasses).

At the very least, something in Taylor's voice had motivated Cox to intervene. He offered to rendezvous with the squadron and lead them back. But Taylor now said he knew where he was. He believed he was in the Keys but didn't know how far down along the chain of islands, which extend over 200 miles from the south of Florida until they end in the open expanse of the Gulf of Mexico. However, the transcoastal highway connects the islands, like the string through a chain of beads, and it is very noticeable from the air at the flight's proscribed altitude of only 1,000 feet. Since Taylor did not mention this feature, it was unlikely he was in the Keys. Then Taylor mentioned that he had climbed to 2,300 feet— standard procedure in an attempt to find Fort Lauderdale Naval Air Station's homing beacon. Based on altitude, the homing beam was detectible at varying distances, the further out from the coast the higher a flight would have to ascend to pick it up. Taylor's present altitude indicated that he thought he was close to shore.

Put together this did not make sense. Nevertheless, Cox was prepared to fly south to the Keys to meet them and, in doing so, hopefully improve the spotty radio communication. So far, he was Flight 19's only link to the tower. Fort Lauderdale Naval Air Station could never raise Flight 19, and Taylor could never reach the tower but had to use Cox as a go-between.

Flight 19 continued on. Taylor was soon asking if Cox could obtain information from Fort Lauderdale's tower if they could pick him up on radar or detect his IFF signals. Both proved negative, indicating the flight was too far out, IFF being detectable 150 miles out.

Robert Cox was about to dart south to the Keys when by a peculiar coincidence his radio transmitter suddenly konked out. He returned to base. The last message he had heard was Taylor saying he was now over an isolated island that he believed was at the end of the Keys— in other words, far out into the Gulf of Mexico.

It was now between 4:05 and 4:15 p.m. Fortunately, Lt. Taylor was now in two-way contact with Port Everglades, a search and rescue base only a couple of miles from Fort Lauderdale. His messages were broken, sometimes strained, but sometimes they came in with surprising clarity. He repeated his belief he was over the Keys. Then one of the messages was alarming.

From the point of that isolated island Taylor had ordered the flight northeast and then direct east for 10 minutes, the hope being that they would be able to see the Gulf coast of Florida. This was yet another example of how he continued to believe the flight had gotten lost in the Florida Keys and had flown to its very terminus in the Gulf, a phenomenal deduction considering how far this area is from their own proscribed training flight over the Bahamas to the east of Florida.

This did not set well with Fort Lauderdale's tower staff, in particular the flight officer, Lt. Commander Don Poole. They had been picking up snippets between Port Everglades and Taylor, but were still unable to establish two-way radio contact with Taylor.

A quick check of the roster had revealed that the flight was on a very routine triangular run out of the base to Hen and Chicken Shoals, north of Bimini, about 56 miles from the coast. Their next target was Great Stirrup Cay in the Berry Islands, about 67 miles further out. This was the furthest they would be from base, about 123 miles or about an hour's flight time from Fort Lauderdale. After turning northwest, their next landmark should be Grand Bahama, itself one of the Bahamas' largest and most distinctive islands. Then after crossing Grand Bahama, the island of Great Sale Cay would mark their final point in the triangle. From there they would turn southwest and head straight into Fort Lauderdale on a True course of 241 degrees. This course was entirely east of Florida. They could never have been near the Florida Keys. The flight had taken off at 2:08 p.m., time enough to only be around Grand Bahama on their cross leg at 3:40 p.m. when Robert Cox had first heard Lt. Charles Taylor say his compasses weren't working.

Flight 19 had to be east of Florida, and the orders Taylor had just given would send the flight further eastward into the Atlantic. It was now past 5 p.m. Now almost two hours after they had gotten lost it was clear the flight was heading out to sea. Consequently, radio communication was getting fainter, and there were grounds to worry that Taylor was so confused he could no longer command.

Flight 19's triangular training course (A) was well within the Bahamas. Taylor believed he was at the Keys (C), but most likely was at the Bahama Cays (B) when in touch with Robert Cox.

Soon pilot voices were heard in a disagreement. Taylor was protesting that Powers had not led the flight far enough eastward. (Lt. Taylor had already agreed to let another pilot, the aforementioned Ed Powers, lead the flight; this did not mean giving up authority, only that the flight would follow his compass directions). The argument was settled quickly, with Taylor then informing Port Everglades that they were now headed west and would continue to fly this course "until they hit the beach or run out of gas."

Although the disagreement between the pilots was not overheard clearly by those listening at the bases, Powers had obviously won the argument handily. He appears to have been the pilot who earlier had expressed certainty that they must fly west. "Dammit, if we would just head west we would get home!" The tenor in which it was said is underscored by the fact it is one of the few times another of the pilots of Flight 19 had been overheard clearly at a base station. For a pilot to now overrule his commander in the field not only reflects Powers' previous certainty, the support of the other pilots, but also reflects to what extent he and perhaps some of the other pilots must have felt that Taylor's condition warranted it. The seriousness of this act can only be appreciated by the fact this now placed Powers on an unavoidable course to court martial.

At 5:50 p.m. a radio fix was developed by several base stations homing in and triangulating the flight's various radio messages. This placed the flight off the east coast of Florida in the Atlantic. This meant that Powers was right and that heading west, which they had been doing since 5:15 p.m., would solve the issue when the flight over-crossed the Florida coast and they found a base at which to land.

Communication had been essentially nonexistent after the disagreement about direction at 5:15 p.m., presumably because there was little reason for the pilots to discuss anything. The only reason why the direction finding stations were able to get a bearing on the flight at 5:50 p.m. was because Lt. Taylor had refused when asked by Port Everglades to switch to the distress frequency of 3000 kilocycles, which was monitored by all the bases in Florida. Port Everglades, the only SAR station in contact, was barely receiving anything from the flight. Unless Taylor switched to 3000 kilocycles, Flight 19, now close to 6 p.m., was on a very, *very* thin strand connecting them with shore and help. Nevertheless, he remained on the training frequency despite its limited range (it was primarily keyed into Fort Lauderdale). The exchange between he and Port Everglades allowed the high frequency stations to finally triangulate his position. Taylor's refusal to switch was due to the darkness. Night had fallen and it was likely that in switching in the darkness one pilot would not be able to find the frequency. "I cannot change frequency," he finally responded. "I must keep my planes intact."

Since the flight was now within an hour of the northern

coast of Florida, hopefully the issue would resolve itself soon. The exercise would prove a harrowing experience, and perhaps even jeopardize the careers of Taylor and Powers, but the mystery of just what had happened and why 5 pilots could not recognize they had been off course, before the fiasco even started at 3:40 p.m., would be answered.

However, this was not to be the case. Despite following the right westward course, the flight never made it to shore. Fuel estimates confirmed they had flight time for another couple of hours, to still be in flight between 8 and 9 p.m., more than enough time from their radio fix position off New Smyrna Beach to make the northern Florida east coast and one of the Navy bases.

All bases had lit up to the greatest possible extent, by orders from SAR, in order to aid the flight's safe return. This was now becoming a serious situation. Avengers had no landing lights, and a ditching at sea could prove fatal.

After 6 p.m., hundreds of miles further west, Pensacola, Florida, and Houma, Louisiana, both high frequency stations, began to pick up the flight. Alarmingly, Taylor was asserting that they must fly east, insisting once again that they were in the Gulf of Mexico and had to turn around in order to get to Florida. "We stand a better chance of being picked up closer to shore." Powers was not heard to acknowledge anymore.

Thereafter the only messages picked up were between the pilots; the base stations were merely an audience to broken and otherwise meaningless sentences. Through the static, Taylor's voice was growing increasingly desperate. At 7:04 p.m., Ensign Joe Bossi, one of the pilots, was overheard with surprising clarity, uttering Taylor's call letters "Fox Tare two-eight." Taylor was not heard to respond nor did Bossi respond to Port Everglades' challenge to respond to them.

By 9 p.m. the flight should have been down. Two hours had passed since Bossi's last brief message, a span of time in which the flight should have found some military base, each incandescent from its lights that the flight could hardly have failed to see it. Yet no messages or teletypes came into SAR or Fort Lauderdale from other bases informing them that their warbirds were safe and sound, albeit the pilots' faces red with embarrassment.

Hope held out that the flight had at least made land somewhere and the pilots were soon to be rescued. Since the flight had remained on their Fort Lauderdale frequency, which the northern bases did not regularly monitor, it was entirely possible that none of the bases had heard Flight 19 as they approached the coast and presently didn't know they were safe somewhere else, perhaps at a civilian airport.

Searches for the squadron had already begun around 5 p.m. when a Dumbo, the euphemistic nickname for a PBM Martin Mariner, had taken off from Dinner Key, Miami, to follow an eastward course in an attempt to raise the flight and act as a radio link between it and the search and rescue network. This effort was thwarted by a peculiar irony, becoming the first of many ironies that night that forestalled any attempt to rescue Flight 19 while still in the air. In this case, the Dumbo's radio antenna iced-up and they were unable to pick up the flight or report into the base, thus making the whereabouts of this PBM another source of worry for SAR until it safely returned to base hours later.

Permanent mystery, however, would shroud another one of the PBMs searching for the flight that night, forever dragging it into the same void that swallowed the "Lost Squadron."

At 7:30 p.m. two more PBMs had taken off, this time from Banana River Naval Air Station near Cape Canaveral. Soon afterwards the planes, which had been flying in tandem, split up off the coast, each taking a different heading to the 5:50 p.m. radio position fix. Training 49 took the route from the north whereas the other PBM, designated Training 32, took a more direct approach. Training 49, however, never sent any routine update reports and seemed to have vanished as well.

This mystery was added to later when a radar check brought back a response from the carrier USS *Solomons*.

Bee-lining for the coast as part of the search, her radar operator had detected an aircraft blip, presumably Training 49, vanish or fall from the scope. Further information came from a cargo vessel, the s.s. *Gaines Mill*, travelling this general area. At the precise time the radar target had fallen from the *Solomons*' scope the tanker's crew had observed a fireball in the sky overhead and what must have been an aircraft falling to sea. Diverting to search the impact location, the tanker nevertheless encountered no trace.

Next morning Fort Lauderdale NAS and the entire training command had to accept that 6 aircraft and 27 men (the PBM carried 13 crewmen) had utterly vanished the night before. For a week a huge search, averaging 200 aircraft per day from the combined military bases, scoured the sea and Florida swamps without discovering a shred of evidence as to what happened to an entire squadron.

While the Press continued to churn out stories, an inquiry had to be prepared to address all the details. This intensive and protracted Naval Board of Inquiry met over a period of weeks. When it adjourned it blamed Lt. Charles Taylor, in true military fashion, since he was the commander of the mission. Assessing the radar reports and the reports of the *Gaines Mill*, the Board had no choice but to conclude that the PBM Mariner totally disintegrated for unknown reasons, a disturbing coincidence on such a strange and tragic night.

Unfortunately, the Board never fully addressed all the circumstances it had uncovered in its laborious hearings into the disappearance of Flight 19. Blaming Taylor did not explain why the flight vanished. It didn't really even account for how the flight got lost. Taylor's radio communications plainly tell us that in the beginning he had thought the flight had gone off course. As a result he had taken the flight back to what he thought was the correct heading. Presumably, when a landmark did not appear he realized his compasses had been wrong and not the flight's original course. This consternation began the entire saga at 3:40 p.m. when Robert Cox overheard Powers and Taylor talking to each other.

Moreover, blaming Taylor alone does not address why the other pilots had not objected to a course change to begin with. Unless there was something truly wrong, all of their compasses should have read the same heading. When Taylor said they were off course and he was taking them to the right heading, all 4 should have objected. While in comment on the flight, Ensign Joe O'Brien, flying in Flight 22 that day, and intimately familiar with the basic course Flight 19 had flown, would later explain. Each student pilot navigated a leg of the flight, not Taylor who was largely only an observer of their progress. Each was equally responsible for monitoring and crosschecking the current leader of the leg. If the leader made a mistake, all were to blame for not catching it. The result would be that the entire flight "would get a down." When Taylor first took them off course, if each pilots' compasses read the same and correct heading, they should have objected in unison. Obviously none did.

Blame on Taylor also hinges on some of the questionable orders he gave, and then attempted to give, about heading eastward, but the condemnation of Taylor as solely guilty does not address that the flight, heading westward under Ed Powers' directions, still vanished. Nothing indicated the flight ever turned around. Nor does blame explain why none of the pilots before, during or immediately after they understood they had been flying an erred course, had not and still did not notice the position of the sun toward the west. The weather was clear. There was nothing *theoretically* that could block the sun, a fact confirmed by the other flights out that afternoon. It was only hazy toward the west, but late in the day the sun was visible on its decline to dusk.

The combination of these unanswered questions was so powerful that by 1961 a cloth of legend had developed that required these very same unanswered questions to be addressed. Alan W. Eckert either believed the following dialog or proposed it as a way of trying to account for the flight becoming completely lost in the Bahamas without ever re-orienting itself with a familiar landmark.

> Flight Leader: Calling Tower. This is an emergency. We seem to be off course. We cannot see land. . .Repeat. . . We cannot see land.
> Tower: What is your position?
> Flight Leader: We are not sure of our position. We cannot be sure just where we are. . .We seem to be lost.
> Tower: Assume bearing due west.
> Flight Leader: We don't know which way is west. Everything is wrong. . . Strange. . .We can't be sure of any direction— even the ocean doesn't look as it should. . .

Ironically, although the dialog was not really spoken by Taylor, the situation it presents was so far the only scenario that could account for the pilots not seeing the sun, the many distinctive islands, nor making heads of their compasses. Penned in popular *American Legion* magazine, this article naturally initiated broad discussion on what could have happened to Flight 19. Among the most significant theories, it introduced the probability that electromagnetic forces were somehow responsible.

Dale Titler noted in *Wings of Mystery* (1962) that no conventional theories could account for the mysterious disappearance "because every theory failed to account for the weird sky conditions described by the pilots and their failure to orient themselves." He speculated instead that "a magnetic disturbance from above" which has occurred in the past in "erratic, wavelike pulses" was to blame.

Vincent Gaddis, the author of the popular *Argosy* magazine article in 1964 that coined the term "Bermuda Triangle," also felt the dialog was crucial. "In all reports of this mystery, the importance of this last remark by the flight leader has been overlooked. The implications of an ocean that didn't appear 'as it should' are shocking. . .and chilling."

Gaddis continues: "Let's suppose that the patrol had run into a magnetic storm that caused deviations in their compasses. The sun was still above the western horizon. The Flyers could have ignored their compasses and flown west simply by visual observation of the sun. . .Apparently not only the sea looked strange, but the sun was invisible."

Altogether though the lines Eckert penned were apocryphal the situation that inspired them remains to be explained. Perhaps Eckert had been influenced to accept them (or pen them) as a paraphrase of what must have happened because of similar details in subsequent airplane disappearances. Flight 19's loss was followed by so many unbelievable disappearances nothing conventional seemed capable of explaining them and, with hindsight, the combined mystery they created attached itself to the already sensational and equally unbelievable disappearance of Flight 19.

Less than 2 years later the first large aircraft would vanish in the Triangle in peacetime. This was a MATS (Military Air Transport Service) C-54, the military designation of the civilian 4-engine DC-4, the largest airliner of the time. On July 3, 1947, it had taken off from Bermuda bound for West Palm Beach, Florida. When it did not arrive, search planes followed its course. Eventually, an oxygen bottle was sighted and retrieved, then tattered exposure suits and some cabin paneling and a "hell hatch" door.

In this case the aircraft was not strictly a disappearance, since this minimal debris could be identified as coming from it. However, a considerable component of mystery was uncovered in the investigation, one which indicated its compasses were not working properly and the crew was unaware of it. Plotting its radio position update reports revealed the aircraft had either never been on course or was making fatal course changes into a severe storm it would otherwise have avoided. In comment on this fact, the investigation stated: "There is no logical reason for the plotted courses . . ." LORAN position reports lined up with the correct track into West Palm Beach, but "If the navigator gave the corrections indicated on the plotted track the turn would have carried the aircraft north of course and directly into the frontal zone. This procedure would have been improbable for an experienced pilot, particularly with the large course change indicated on the plotted position reports."

The investigating board concluded, with an air of disbelief, that there had been no attempt by the very experienced pilot, Major R.B. Ward, to avoid the storm front, adding therewith unbelievable pilot error to an already improbable and unexplained navigational error.

Soon there would be a rash of airliner disappearances grouped within the span of only a year. Each would present far more challenging scenarios to comprehend, including disappearance in perfect weather conditions, the lack of transmitting a Mayday despite each being within recent contact with its local radio control, and from each case not a single shred of evidence would be found by exhaustive searches.

The first was British South American Airways airliner "Star Tiger," a new 4-engine Tudor IV aircraft, with hermetically sealed hull, wireless transmitter, telephony transmitter, and all the latest navigational aids. She was near the end of her long flight, en route from London via Lisbon, the Azores, and now in the early morning of January 30, 1948, just a couple of hours away from Bermuda. Coming in from the northeast the captain of the airliner, B.W. McMillan, had radioed a request for a bearing to follow in order to home in on the isolated island. At 3:15 a.m. he received a first class bearing of 72 degrees. He acknowledged it.

Coming closer to her destination, as the airliner was, Bermuda expected more routine transmissions and replies within the remaining two hours. However, none were ever received from "Star Tiger," and as its dawn ETA of 5:30 a.m. passed to early morning it was clear the aircraft was overdue. Facing the probability the airliner had suddenly crashed, a search was immediately launched.

Limited to a relatively small area of its track line (somewhere along the bearing), the search for the "Star Tiger" had been quick and literally to the point along the bearing northeast of the island. Absolutely no trace of the aircraft, however, was ever sighted.

Previously it had been quite a source of news comment when one BSAA aircraft had landed at Bermuda with only 100 gallons of fuel remaining, a reminder of the long trip from the Azores and the hazards of headwinds. In this case, in addition to the crew of 6 there were 25 passengers aboard, including World War II Air Marshal Sir Arthur Coningham, meaning international news coverage was quite intense.

A full investigation, headed by Hugh Pattison, Baron Macmillan, puzzled over what had happened. Concentrating its studies on the time period just after Star Tiger's last radio communication had been received, several key factors were quickly eliminated as contributing causes. With only two hours left in flight, it was impossible the airliner could have gotten lost because the radio bearing would have brought the airliner within sight of Bermuda's powerful marine lights. "On this basis, the aircraft could hardly have failed to find the island in a short time, in the conditions of visibility which prevailed." Minus the heavy weight of a full payload of fuel, the aircraft was unlikely to have fallen victim to any serious engine problems. "The failure of one engine is a possibility," the board concluded, "but this aircraft could fly entirely safely on three engines, and, indeed, at her weight at the relevant time, on two." It considers: "The possibility of a simultaneous, or an almost simultaneous failure, of two or more engines due to mechanical causes as so remote as to be almost inconceivable, having in mind the long record of high reliability possessed by engines of this general type."

Only one clue shed light on a sudden as opposed to a protracted nature of the airliner's loss. A message sent to it from Bermuda at 3:50 a.m., about an hour and a half before ETA, was never acknowledged. It thus had vanished within less than 45 minutes after the 3:15 a.m. contact, perhaps even just minutes after receiving the radio bearing.

Adding more to the mystery, Captain Griffin had been flying a cargo flight on the same route only an hour before

Star Tiger. Except for an increase in headwinds, he observed the weather was uneventful.

The board of investigation could not, in fact, even offer guesses as to what might have happened. Rather with stoic if not elegant language, their report concluded:

> In closing this Report it may truly be said that no more baffling problem has ever been presented for investigation. In the complete absence of any reliable evidence as to either the nature or the cause of the disaster to "Star Tiger" the Court has not been able to do more than suggest possibilities, none of which reaches the level even of probability. . .What happened in this case will never be known and the fate of "Star Tiger" must remain an unsolved mystery.

As if almost completing the delineation of the Bermuda Triangle's popular shape long before the term was coined, another airliner vanished that year, this a DC-3 with a full passenger compliment of 28 people. It had left one corner of the Triangle, San Juan, Puerto Rico, on December 28, 1948, bound for another corner, Miami, Florida. The circumstances were immeasurably more alarming than those ascertained in the loss of "Star Tiger" earlier in the year. The airliner had made its 1,000 mile journey uneventfully and its co-pilot, Ernest Hill, had just signaled they were 50 miles south of Miami. This position report would mean that at this moment captain Bob Lindquist, the pilot, was turning north to approach Miami Airport. At 4:13 a.m. the lights of Miami must have been visible in the distance. Below, the Florida Keys sparkled with lights from the settlements, and each island was surrounded by the shallows and their crystal clear waters, a factor that would only serve to heighten an already dramatic mystery.

For between this point and Miami the DC-3 and all its passengers and contents completely vanished; this included all the luggage, floatable seat cushions, paneling, and bodies. Nothing, not even a concentration of sharks, which usually mark a crash site at sea, was noticed. A full search also found no trace in the Everglades (taking into account the DC-3 may have veered off course suddenly). Its fuel reserves only gave it about a 45 minute window to go off course, so that the aircraft could not have gotten radically lost after it had signaled Miami, not beyond the shallow waters and the southern Everglades, that is.

Some concern was expressed that if the crew had attempted a Mayday it may not have been overheard. Before takeoff at San Juan International Airport the aircraft's radio had problems. It could receive, but due to a low battery its transmitter was not sending. San Juan had it topped off. Flight Control allowed the DC-3 to take off, but required that Lindquist circle the field until the battery was recharged enough so he could make contact. Although San Juan's tower did not receive the A-OK signal, the nearby CAA Communication did. Then NC16002, the DC-3's call numbers, broke its pattern and headed to Miami.

Transmitter problems could have returned, though it would have been a remarkable coincidence if they had. The long flight would have completely recharged the batteries by the time NC16002 sent its last message, so that something else would have to be blamed, at least theoretically, for the lack of a radio distress.

Any theory relying on a breakdown of the radio transmitter can only explain the lack of a Mayday. It cannot, of course, explain why the aircraft vanished and left no trace. The aircraft could not have gotten too lost after its last message, and there was no reason to dispute Bob Lindquist's statement they were 50 miles south of Miami. The sky was clear and the co-pilot Ernest Hill could have located them by taking an astral fix. In fact, it seems probable Lindquist's certainty was based on an astral fix. At this time the flight was only technically late by 10 minutes, and in all likelihood the pilots had verified their position rather than relying on dead-reckoning. If the aircraft had met some inexplicable fate, as it was quietly (and certainly unofficially) suspected in the case of "Star Tiger," the transmitter problems could not explain the lack of debris which should have been scattered over a fairly wide field at sea or in the Everglades, where the crash site would be instantly more recognizable from the air by a mown strip of jungle the aircraft would have created as it sliced through the trees before impact.

Curiously, NC16002's last radio message had been picked up by New Orleans 800 miles to the northwest, and not by Miami, reflecting a considerable jump in the transmission. While New Orleans had picked up Miami traffic before, it is curious in this case that it was the only station to pick up the last message. This "jump" in last radio messages will be noted in other disappearances as well.

Before the Civil Aeronautics Board had even begun to deliberate the findings in this case, on January 17, 1949, just about a week short of the anniversary of the disappearance of "Star Tiger," another new Tudor IV airliner, this one named "Star Ariel," silently vanished between Bermuda and Kingston, Jamaica.

Under the command of Captain J.C. McPhee the plane had taken off from Bermuda with 13 passengers and 7 crew. Only 150 miles south of Bermuda, McPhee informed Kindley Field he was switching channels to pick up Kingston. It was a little early in the flight, but Kindley rogered. However, Kingston never picked up "Star Ariel," and the flight never tried to contact Bermuda again, presuming it would after having failed to raise its next control. Again, we are reminded of narrow timespans indicating disappearances as opposed to accidents are lightning-like in nature.

In this case, the search was enormous. Judging from the lack of any radio message after the one above, the search area was narrowed down to the Sargasso Sea south of Bermuda, not long after Star Ariel had entered the Triangle. Joining the search was a flotilla of US naval ships on maneuvers in the area. This included the carriers *Leyte* and *Kearsage* and all of their aircraft. Despite the intensive search lasting over a week, no trace was found.

Over a span of 1 year, three mainline airliners had vanished, without an iota of wreckage, without any having had time to send a Mayday, no matter how terse, to give an impression of what had happened to them. To put this in even more disturbing perspective for today's audience, the disappearance of these three airliners is the equivalent to the disappearance of 3 Boeing 777, the mainline airliner of today, of which Malaysian Flight 370 is a notable (and only) example of one having vanished at sea. Attending that mystery in March 2014 was an unprecedented amount of worldwide comment and sensational theorizing, even by otherwise reserved heads of state, even though the circumstances were not as alarming as in 1948. It had vanished in mid-flight and not, like two of those back in 1948 which had vanished close to shore, in NC16002's case while it should have been in sight of its destination. For 3 Boeing airliners to have vanished between March 2014 and March 2015 would no doubt have given rise to even more sensational theories and perhaps even political assignations. After the controversy had died down, perhaps journalists would have looked into the past of the Indian Ocean to see if history revealed a pattern of disappearances. Doubtless they would have found some, but when journalists looked into the past of the Triangle the pattern became undeniable, the pattern continually being fed each year as more and more continued to vanish, some in unbelievable circumstances. No legend developed in the wake of Flight 370's loss because there really was no basis for any legend in the Indian Ocean. For the seas encompassing the Bermuda Triangle there was.

Considerable efforts were expended back in 1948-1949 to account for this rash of disappearances. There was little reason to cast suspicion on the design of the DC-3. It had been serving throughout the world, with thousands of units having formed the backbone of Allied aerial transport and paratrooper deployment in World War II where its widespread use earned it several designations— C-47 in the American Army Air Force, or Dakota in the RAF, and often just the humorous epigram "Gooney Bird." However, the Tudor IV was a relatively new design. Although no inadequacies could be found in it, it was removed from passenger service.

Over time the Tudor IV was adapted, most notably by Freddie Laker, who modified the aircraft for cargo service at low range altitude. To determine if it was feasible to begin with, Laker had a cargo door cut into the fuselage of one of the neglected airliners. Charles Martins, one of his engineers, was assigned the task. When cutting through the fuselage he had a chance to examine the inner construction of the Tudor. As far as he could tell the Tudor IV was "prone to explosive decompression due to metal fatigue." He came to the firm opinion that this was the cause of both Tudors' losses.

Modification of the aircraft for lower altitude flying eliminated any need for it to be hermetically sealed, and the fact that the Tudor IV, now back in service as the "Super Trader," had no more accidents only served to underline Martins' confidence in his theory that somehow there was a problem with the design at high altitudes and this is what had caused the "Star Tiger" and "Star Ariel" to disappear or, in his theory, to crash after exploding.

Explosive decompression would certainly destroy the aircraft, and this might explain the loss of "Star Ariel" since McPhee was at high altitude. But it could not have played a hand in the loss of "Stair Tiger," which was only flying at an altitude of 2,000 feet where there would be no effects of decompression. In neither case could the theory account for the lack of debris. And it obviously has no relevance in the case of NC16002.

Another possibility was put forward some years after the fact. Wing Commander M.O Ware, who became the first Civil Air Director for Bermuda, recalls that engineers came out from London to check on BSAA's Tudor IVs, now lined up on the side of Kindley's runway. Tests revealed that fuel had a tendency to accumulate in the engine farings of some of the aircraft. Taken to its obvious extreme, an explosion might have been capable of blowing a wing off the aircraft, a factor that would be catastrophic to an aircraft at any altitude.

It is nevertheless true that no Tudor IV was lost anywhere else around the world or on any other leg of British South American Airways route to South America. Only the leg from the Azores to Bermuda involved a part of the Triangle (toward the end), and then the entire route between Bermuda, Havana, and Jamaica. Only these areas lay in what would later be dubbed the Bermuda Triangle, thanks in no small part to the inexplicable disappearance of both aircraft. No losses occurred on the route to Lisbon, to the Azores, or from Kingston to the various ports of call to South America, which included long runs over the "green sea" of the Amazon, an even more impenetrable mass than the oceans. When headwinds were too strong between the Azores and Bermuda, BSAA pilots had to detour to Gander in New Foundland, a course through fairly harrowing skies in turbulent weather, and yet in each case they never encountered trouble. It is only "Star Tiger" and "Star Ariel" that had vanished, both in the Bermuda Triangle.

Aside from these disappearances contributing to the eventual enigma of the Bermuda Triangle, the natural and more expected result was that BSAA was finished and the Tudor IV was parked for years until Freddie Laker brought it back into service with complete lack of instability.

Weather presented no problems in any of the cases, none to account for sudden loss or the removal of all debris. The cases are linked only by total disappearance and within a year's time, with the DC-3 being the most alarming considering the rather startling circumstances.

There are those who would note that the DC-3 airliner was turning to come in for a landing and in such circumstances it may have encountered a sudden downdraft and plunged into the sea. But the causes of a crash are not what excite debate here. Causes for a total disappearance are the issue— disappearing meaning not an unexplained crash but a total lack of *any* indications there was a crash.

Furthermore, in what is an even more disquieting comparative, the MATS C-54 which had vanished on July 3, 1947, most likely encountered convective storm activity on its long flight to West Palm Beach from Bermuda; in this case, though the search had to follow its entire 1,000 miles course, pieces of debris were retrieved and identified as belonging to the large airliner. For those that vanished in fair weather there is little more that can be said but to "suggest possibilities, none of which reaches the level even of probability," as it was trenchantly expressed in the case of "Star Tiger."

Unusual happenings at sea at this time include the disappearance of the crew of the yacht *Evelyn K*, which was found abandoned off the bay side of the Florida Keys on March 5, 1948, near Craig Key. The three men aboard, including famed jockey Al Snider, had boarded their 13-foot dinghy for some nearby fishing. Heavy winds were thought to have come along and wiped the three men overboard. When found, however, the dinghy revealed a surprising element of mystery. Someone had tried to tie themselves down in the boat, but obviously had failed. The boat's bottom was cracked and the motor had been ripped off. A search of the Everglades revealed no clues. Nor were any footprints found on the many isolated beaches, indicating any of the men had gotten to shore.

A number of yachts vanished along the Bermuda to US east coast routes at this time. With the war's close, sport and casual boating had returned. Along with the postwar prosperity the hobby increased, perhaps one explanation for the frequency of disappearances now becoming noticeable to those who lived along the surrounding shores, though this does not explain *why* the yachts were disappearing now. Somewhat more interested in cases (due to the rash of sensational vanishings), the Press was more alert to any reports of overdue boats.

Ship disappearances were considerably more sensational because of their size, floating deckworks, and sometimes buoyant cargoes. The coastal freighter *Sandra*, with a cargo of DDT, vanished in June 1950 on her southward course after passing St. Augustine, Florida.

Further north *ostensibly* a more unusual disappearance

occurred on December 6, 1954. The *Southern Districts*, a wartime LST converted to cargo ship (carrying sulphur), of about 314 feet overall length and 3,337 tons, disappeared somewhere between its last sighting off Jupiter Inlet, Florida, on December 5, and 5:58 p.m. December 6, when the ship did not answer radio messages sent to it via Savanah, Georgia. The *Gulf Keys* was the last vessel to have sighted the *Southern Districts* as it passed her at Jupiter Inlet, on its way north. Because the *Gulf Keys* reported heavy seas that evening, it was assumed that the *Southern Districts* went down in foul weather with all 23 hands.

Three years before, her sister ship the *Southern Isles* had inexplicably plunged below the waves off the Carolinas, and would effectively have been posted missing if another nearby ship had not seen her running lights suddenly drop into the sea as if the vessel simply dropped into a pool of ink. Since *Southern Districts* and *Southern Isles* were LST conversions, suspicion was cast upon structural failure resulting from the conversion process.

Yet the mystery of the *Southern Districts* is not so simply solved. On January 2, 1955, the captain of the s.s. *Tullahoma* spotted a ring buoy with the *Southern Districts* name stenciled "very legible on it in block letters" plus a 2 by 8 foot gangplank and a gray life jacket. However, the debris was found floating off Sand Key in the Florida Straits, a location hundreds of miles *south* of Jupiter Inlet where the vessel was last sighted. Because the current in the Florida Straits is northbound the debris could not have floated against the current from where the vessel presumably vanished off Florida or Georgia.

Excuses to explain the debris often cite that the ring buoy alone was found and that it simply must have been tossed over because it was defective, an explanation also offered by the Marine Board without considering the other items found floating nearby.

No shred of evidence remained to explain away the disappearance of the 450-foot *Samkey* on or about February 1, 1948. The vessel was a wartime Liberty Ship, a type of vessel designed originally to haul cargos and not the result of conversion to accommodate postwar business. She was also a relatively new ship, only a few years old. She had passed the Azores, signaling "All well." Sometime thereafter, before her next 48 hour check-in time, she vanished; coincidently this would be in an area approaching the Triangle.

Although no clue was found, the British Marine Board of Inquiry dogmatically affixed a cause, declaring that her Thames ballast had shifted, resulting in the ship suddenly capsizing with all 43 hands aboard. One wonders if the phenomenon of the Bermuda Triangle had already been established whether the Board would have risked its reputation by dogmatically asserting any cause for a disappearance in fair weather.

Aircraft disappearances remain the most alarming since their routes are carefully monitored and their time en route is considerably less than seagoing freighters, amounting to only hours in flight over the Atlantic as opposed to a freighter's several days in passage. Comparatively speaking, aircraft obviously spend an even shorter time passing through the Bermuda Triangle since it occupies only a fraction of the expanse of the North Atlantic. Nevertheless, major aircraft disappearances are primarily concentrated over the Triangle.

A particularly baffling disappearance occurred on October 30, 1954, to Flight 441, a 4-engine Navy Super Constellation ferrying 42 passengers to the Azores, family of military personnel stationed overseas. Everything went fine in the flight after the aircraft had taken off from Patuxent River Naval Air Station in Maryland until, coincidently, when north of Bermuda, where afterwards it sent no more updates. It is relevant, in fact unavoidable, to note that the lack of the search finding any trace here is particularly strange, considering that the cargo consisted of paper cups, life jackets, and even large life rafts!

The lengthy and intense, though negative, search was called off, with cablegrams then sent to the surviving members of the families. The cablegram to the Pflager family is typical:

WITH DEEP REGRET I MUST TELL YOU THAT SEARCH OPERATIONS FOR THIS MISSING AIRCRAFT HAVE BEEN DISCONTINUED WITHOUT REVEALING A TRACE OF THE PLANE OR ANY INDICATION OF SURVIVORS X YOUR HUSBAND JAMES RICHARD PFLAGER IS NOW OFFICIALLY CONSIDERED TO HAVE LOST HIS LIFE IN THE SERVICE OF HIS COUNTRY IN THIS GREAT TRAGEDY X YOU WILL RECEIVE FURTHER DETAILS BY LETTER X I WISH TO ASSURE YOU OF EVERY POSSIBLE ASSISTANCE TOGETHER WITH MY SINCERE SYMPATHY IN YOUR GREAT LOSS X

More officiously the Navy commiserated with the families in a subsequent telegram. It is when elaborating on the search efforts that we get a vivid sense of the unbelievable nature of mystery in this disappearance. "The intensive phase of the 12 day search for the missing Navy Constellation. . .has not uncovered a trace of the aircraft or its passengers. During the search some 260 aircraft of the Navy, Air Force, and Coast Guard participated. In addition 27 surface vessels including 2 aircraft carriers participated directly in the coordinated search. A total of over 16,000 personnel participated in the search. Records indicate that this search is the greatest on record in scope and most intensive yet conducted. We must reluctantly conclude that it has established that there are no survivors."

North of Bermuda, in the same general area (about 300 miles), on November 9, 1956, a Martin Marlin, a large US Navy amphibian patrol plane, with a crew of 10, also vanished. In this case, the freighter *Captain Lyras* signaled that an airplane passed nearby and simply flew into the ocean— not crash it was stressed— just flew into the ocean 6 miles distant at a steady, even rate and angle of descent. The Marlin was capable of landing on the sea, but the angle was just enough that the aircraft hit the surface and exploded, without the pilots taking any evasive action. A Board of

Inquiry could only speculate that there was instrument malfunction. The report noted that an altimeter error of 300 feet existed in that area which, if the pilots did not compensate for it, they may have thought they were much higher when they flew into the ocean. This last surmise is surprising, considering they had just seen the lights of the *Captain Lyras* and could estimate thereby their altitude over the sea, at least enough to know they were fairly close. In light of developments in other cases, we would have to suspect that this could be yet another example of pilots who could not see out of their windows and moments in which instrument gauges simply did not work.

Again, in this general area north of Bermuda an 8-engine B-52 designated "Pogo 22" vanished on October 15, 1961. "Pogo 22" was last seen by its cell partner Pogo 13 as they, along with the other B-52s on this exercise (Sky-Shield II), separated to 10 mile lateral intervals and headed direct back to North Carolina and Seymour Johnson Air Force Base. "Pogo 22" simply never arrived, had sent no SOS, and a massive though fruitless search ended on a discordant note like in the other cases of missing aircraft.

Nothing reasonable can explain the simultaneous midair destruction of 2 KC-135 Stratotankers south of Bermuda on August 28, 1963. The KC-135 were Boeing 707s specially factory designed to be used for refueling in midair, a task they had jointly accomplished and now they were heading back in tandem to Bermuda. Without any indication of trouble, Kindley Field lost contact with them. A search soon discovered a debris field, which given the large size of both jetliners was surprisingly small. The conclusion of the Air Force investigating board was that the aircraft must have collided in midair, but nothing was advanced to logically explain how experienced pilots, supposedly not flying that close, could lose control and collide. It was as if the two jets simply hit an invisible brick wall at the same time and thus neither crew had time for a Mayday.

A particularly sensational disappearance occurred on the morning of March 18, 1960, to the lagging jet fighter in a squadron of 5 other F-104 Starfighters. Designated Polly Alpha, this set was the first group of 18 jets that would takeoff from Kindley Field, Bermuda, and head to Spain. The jet in question, Polly Alpha 4 under the command of Morris Larson, was tardy in climbing and joining his squadron. At a steep incline he entered the haze layer and vanished. No part of the jet was captured on radar as descending or falling to the sea. When it was realized the fighter was missing, the Scramble alarm was hit and several fighters and search craft were launched. Randy 12, one of the rescue choppers, scoured the sea north of Bermuda. Visibility was down to 500 feet from fog, but still enough to determine that the sea surface showed no sign of an impact. Search units raced up above the haze and cloud tops, thinking that Polly Alpha 4 was above and trying to link up with the squadron. Failing here, the search concentrated at sea level for days, and though still over the shallow Bermuda Banks no trace of the large jet fighter was ever found.

Minutes after leaving Dover, Delaware, on the night of May 27, 1962, a 4 engine MATS C-133 "Cargomaster" simply flew into a void. Radar and radio contact had been normal as the flight was directed to its cruising altitude. After the pilot confirmed reaching 17,000 feet, the plane vanished from the scope. It was assumed that the aircraft must have crashed, but a huge search uncovered only a tire and a tattered life raft. Such minimal debris created quite a chord of mystery considering that as the largest cargo plane of its time it carried 50,000 tons of assorted cargo. No fuel slick was reported, again a startling fact since most of its 85,000 gallons had not been spent yet. Examination of the tattered life raft revealed a cross section of the C-133 reduced to mere particles, including paint, glass, aluminum and an unidentified "minute magnetic particle."

A year later on September 22, 1963, another C-133 disappeared in the same area, but unlike its predecessor of the year before it occurred in what might be called steps, beginning with what seemed the masking of its electronic and radio signals until final physical disappearance from the

A Saga of Disappearing Planes and Lost Ships 51

radarscope. It had not long left the US east coast (also from Dover in Delaware) when it began to fade from the radarscope and its communications became weak. The pilot rogered the request to "indent," that is to send an electronic signal to assist in identification on the scope. Nevertheless, this "SIF" feature (Selective Identification Feature) did not appear. The operator immediately contacted the Cargomaster and told the pilots that their aircraft was only registering skin returns, that is, the actual radar wave echo off the fuselage of the aircraft. Radio replies were heard but proved to be weaker, the last being a faint "roger, roger" in response to reporting cruising altitude. Dover then lost the radar return. A radar plot from skin returns alone, not confirmed but most likely the C-133, continued to be tracked by New York for a few miles and then vanished between the next sweep of the radarscope's arm, though something unintelligible over the radio was heard later by Dover.

In this case a search found nothing in the location of the last "raw" radar return. It then naturally quickly expanded along the aircraft's flight track to Lajes in the Azores, but this still proved fruitless. In the end the Air Force investigators had to assume that the C-133 had vanished only 25 miles off the coast and left no trace. Failure at finding a trace in this area inspired a sonar grid search, which also found no trace on the bottom, including any clue of the C-133 which presumably had crashed here the year before.

Given they vanished each within 25 miles of the coast, and that the searches were prompt, the lack of debris and the lack of a fuel or oil slick is particularly intriguing.

On a much longer run, but essentially the same course as the Cargomasters were intending to fly (to Lajes in the Azores), a KB-50 aerial tanker "Tyler 41" vanished on January 8, 1962. From radio messages, it was last known to have been north of Bermuda, on its eastbound course from Langley AFB in Virginia. The lack of any trace of this aircraft was so frustrating that five Coast Guard vessels searched its entire course from its last reported position north of Bermuda to the Azores but found nothing, a huge area of sea estimated at 440,820 square miles. The Air Force ventured no guess. The report concluded: "No trace of any survivors or wreckage was ever found, thus preventing the accident Board from obtaining any physical evidence upon which to base their investigation."

A considerably less area of sea had to be searched for the *Marine Sulphur Queen* the next year, a T-2 tanker bound from Beaumont, Texas, to Norfolk, Virginia, due to the fact that radio messages indicated the 502-foot tanker had vanished between February 2 and February 4, 1963, the time between a message sent but return message not acknowledged. The ship also failed to make its routine reports thereafter.

Initially a huge search had turned up no clue or bodies of its 39 crew. Then, tardily, 20 miles southwest of Key West, Florida, several pieces of debris were sighted, retrieved and easily identified as belonging to the *MSQ* because part of her signboard, the part remaining only containing the letters "arine Sulph," was floating within the debris, the tattered nature of it indicating some unusual destruction that, taken together with the lack of an SOS, must have been spontaneous and without warning. Breaking in twain was suspected, since T2 tankers had shown that tendency, but the *MSQ* had been modified to carry liquid sulphur, which entailed installing a 300 foot tank down the center of the ship, something that was thought, along with the necessary alternations in the bulkheads to accommodate it, would prevent the ship from splitting asunder as regular T2 tankers had done. A mere breaking in half could not explain, however, why the signboard should have been so tattered.

Explosion of her liquid cargo was ruled out. Fires in the ship, completely independent of the cargo, were a possibility. The ship had suffered a fire before. Nevertheless, it was still hard to explain why there was no SOS.

From the looks of two of the life rings retrieved, it seemed they had been attacked by sharks, indicating two men had survived. These were speculated to have been worn by the men on watch, who alone of the crew had time to get into the sea when, presumably, the ship ignited and quickly plunged.

While these cases above were major disappearances, most of which attracted news coverage to some extent, within this time frame small aircraft and many yachts were vanishing or, in the case of some yachts, being found strangely deserted with no sign of their crew.

The schooner *Home Sweet Home* had not long left Bermuda, January 13, 1955, traveling south into the Triangle when Bermuda Radio received a call from the vessel. The time was 9:30 a.m. The captain (presumably) was merely initiating contact in a calm, steady voice, as one would while studying an observation, saying only "Bermuda, this is the HSH." Before Bermuda could reply, the yacht must have vanished. Hails went unanswered. What motivated the captain to hail Bermuda was not betrayed by his calm voice. But the possibility he was observing something peculiar becomes intriguing considering the vessel vanished before he could elaborate.

Exactly what happened to the *Sno' Boy* is still a subject of wonder. Searchers found no trace of the 63-foot converted PT-Boat or any of the 40 persons aboard, each bound for an overnight fishing trip on July 4, 1963, to nearby Pedro Banks south of Kingston, Jamaica. Searchers, however, eventually found numerous fishing poles and even the dinghy, though empty yet floating upright. When the fishing charter had left Kingston she appeared quite overloaded to those at the marina. Nevertheless, the vessel had the latest radio equipment and the lifeboat, in which none of its passengers and crew were apparently able to get in, or remain in for long if they had.

Circumstances appeared so unbelievable in the disappearance of a C-119 "Flying Boxcar," a military cargo flight on a routine cargo run to Grand Turk Island, on June 5, 1965, that when it was discovered that astronaut James McDivitt, while in orbit in Gemini IV, had seen a UFO beneath them over the Caribbean the day before, attempts were made by the International UFO Bureau to link the two occurrences, despite thousands of miles separating the "UFO" at orbital heights and the C-119 at its altitude of 9,000 feet over the Bahamas— theorists pointing out that this is a mere matter of seconds difference for a UFO in terms of travel time.

Radar had long captured the presence of UFOs zooming through scopes at thousands of miles per hour and making right angled turns, among other seemingly impossible maneuvers, that purely testified the object was not manmade in origin. When McDivitt reported the sun glinting off a silver object below, his report was stretched to become a clue to a disappearance which otherwise had no clue.

The C-119 had taken off from Homestead Air Force Base with a crew of 10. Its course was simple. It need only follow the "Yankee Route," a well-guarded air highway between southern Florida, over the Bahamas, and straight to Grand Turk. At 11 p.m., only 45 minutes from ETA, Major Giuntoli, the pilot, sent the routine report. "There was no indication of trouble, and nothing has been heard from them since," reported the Coast Guard spokesman in Miami. A Homestead AFB crewman added some intriguing inference when he carefully observed: "It's strange that the planes that go down in the Bahamas never leave a trace." The search was reputed to have found a dramatic clue— a wheel chock from the aircraft bearing its number stenciled thereon, although the accident report does not allude to this discovery at all.

Consideration of the radio and radar controls of the "Yankee Route" would seem apt here (see map on following page), as it sheds light on the surveillance of a route that many aircraft have traveled and disappeared on both before and after the C-119. It appears at first glance to be a very outback course, but it is one that is amply covered in radio communication controls, considerably more today than in 1965, though this has not aided in explaining the disappearances but only served to heighten the mystery of what

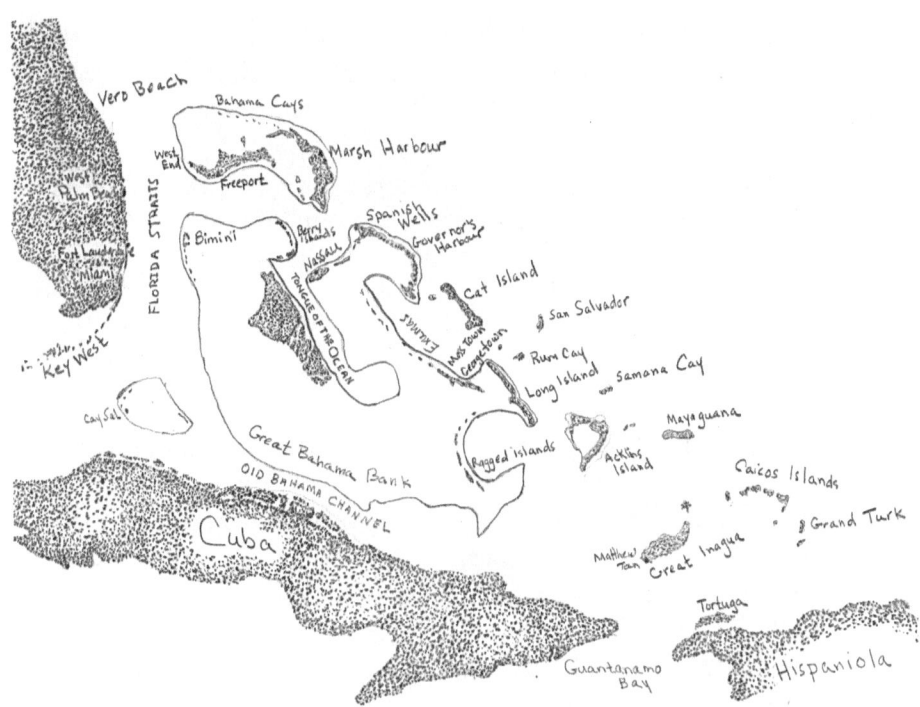

Although far more dangerous and outback for the boater, for an aircraft the Bahamas are transited in only hours and have many radio controls. The shallow Bahama banks are marked in outline.

has happened to so many planes along here.

Along this same route on April 5, 1966, another military airplane vanished. However, in this case the classic B-25 had been converted to a civilian cargo plane, the treasured prize of pilot Gene Nattress. In addition to hauling a cargo of frozen chicken parts, eggs, and spare aircraft parts, he was taking bush pilot company owner George Golas, and 17 year old Ken Pekin, to Aruba, Dutch West Indies. The flight was last known to be somewhere over the Tongue of the Ocean, a deep and unnatural looking underwater gorge in the shallow Great Bahama Bank, itself the most visible geologic oddity of the Bahamas. The disappearance of this aircraft was particularly mysterious considering this air corridor parallels the Bahamas' largest island of Andros on one side and the long chain of the Exumas on the other—

popular halfway points for yachters who readily notice the drone of aircraft overhead as the Yankee Route is the main route to the Caribbean. Yet none noticed the heavy drone of Nattress' B-25 suddenly fall silent.

In addition to the traffic in the area, the restricted secret weapons testing and development base AUTEC is located on the east coast of Andros Island, a strategic location in order to take advantage of the depths of the ominous Tongue of the Ocean for testing of underwater missiles and revolutionary military undersea submersibles. As one might imagine for a highly sensitive base, it closely monitors airspace and radio frequencies; yet it too was another base that had no contact with the B-25.

Considerable amount of mystery surrounds the discovering of a barge, floating intact and undisturbed, but which had been in tow behind the tug *Southern Cities* when it had left Freeport, Texas, on October 29, 1966, for Tuxpan, Mexico. While the barge and its cable, including the attaching end to the tug, remained intact and undamaged, there was no sign of the *Southern Cities*. The unusual nature of this disappearance is what has caused the case to be commented on and often linked with the other disappearances in the Bermuda Triangle despite the fact that it had vanished near Mexico; the similarities being the obvious indications that the crew and their vessel rather than their cargo appeared to be of interest to the cause or force (officially "mishap") that mysteriously swept them away during their routine voyage.

Taking into account this case prompted author John Wallace Spencer, the first to write a book solely devoted to the Triangle incidents (*Limbo of the Lost,* 1969), to extend the reaches of the Bermuda Triangle into the Gulf of Mexico and speculate on alien abduction, a cause that obviously did not require the disappearances to be limited to the "strict" Triangle. He proposed that the actual area of danger to ships and planes extended around Bermuda, through the Caribbean islands and taking in, apparently, the entire Gulf of Mexico, hence his reticence to refer to it as anything but a "limbo."

It is implicit in Spencer's theory that the "danger zone" centered on the traditional Triangle between Bermuda, Miami, and Puerto Rico, but especially in the Bahamas, where disappearances were most concentrated. His theory would later be added to by naturalist Ivan Sanderson, who proposed that the Bahamas' unique underwater terrain made it an ideal base for UFOs and their underwater counterparts, USOs. According to either view, whatever would be considered "raiding" territory within easy reach from this location would make it technically the "danger zone." However *outré* the theory sounds, later happenings in these precise areas, including a disappearance following the report of a UFO, with the Mayday of the panicking pilot describing the "weird object" recorded by a base station, requires that elements of the disquieting theory be taken into serious consideration later.

Others have speculated on the exact or, for some, more viable shape and location of the Triangle. Unlike John Spencer's "limbo," however, these other shapes and sizes are based on the location of the greatest concentration of missing vessels and aircraft rather than using such an area for a base and then accepting every other disappearance relatively nearby, except each takes into consideration rare incidents in outlaying waters, such as the C-133s or the *Southern Cities*.

By the time of the *Southern Cities* disappearance, the name "Bermuda Triangle" had been coined. It had first been put forward in the February 1964 edition of *Argosy* magazine in an article written by Vincent Gaddis. The title "The Deadly Bermuda Triangle" had merely clarified the earlier and somewhat colloquial expression "Deadly Triangle" for the area, but this was not the first time a triangular shape had been suggested. It was first proposed in an October 1952 *Fate* magazine article in which the author, George X. Sand, dubbed the area a "watery triangle," a name that with time could hold a double meaning considering the shape of the Triangle is rather fluid.

Puerto Rico, Bermuda, and Miami, had emerged quickly in 1948 as the nodal points between which the rash of airliners had vanished, and within this same triangle Flight 19 had been flying in 1945. Continuing disappearances always highlighted these nodal points, with the southwest corner off Florida noteworthy for the heaviest concentration of unexplained disappearances. Freighters that had vanished were also sailing toward it or through it when last heard from, or, from computations of their speed or from lack of subsequent and expected routine position reports, were estimated to have entered the area but not to have emerged.

Sailing south to Miami, for example, the 150 foot schooner *Enchantress* was approaching the "strict triangle" off South Carolina when something struck so quickly there was only time for a short SOS, in which the captain Count Christopher de Gebrowski said they were heeling over. *Evangeline* was sailing to the Bahamas from nearby Miami in 1962 and vanished. Between the Bahamas and North Carolina the *Callista III* was last reported and then was never seen again after leaving on April 25, 1961. Cruising along the Keys heading to Miami, the disappearance of the schooner *Revonoc* on New Year's Eve 1958 was so unbelievable because of both the all-weather design of the champion racer and the ability of its master, Harvey Conover, that fellow yachtsmen speculated that a freighter had run down the schooner without knowing it. On the short routes between Miami and the Bahamas, the sailboat *Bounty* vanished around July 1956. George Boston left Miami in his houseboat *El Gato* voyaging to the next corner of the Triangle, San Juan, Puerto Rico, put in at Georgetown, Exuma, Bahamas, and then left there for Great Inagua on October 28, 1965, and then vanished sometime thereafter.

Before the moniker Bermuda Triangle was born, the concept of an "area of danger" showed how each disappearance subsequent to Flight 19 continued to inspire curiosity, not just because of the circumstances but because of the location. By the time Gaddis' article presented "Bermuda Triangle" for the reader the name just seemed to stick. "Deadly Triangle" was good enough locally, but "Bermuda Triangle" brought with it instant geographic recognition for a world increasingly interested in the area's unusual enigma.

Coupled with the new catchy and handy moniker, the phenomenon easily crystalized in the public mind. Continuing disappearances were easy to fit into the Bermuda Triangle concept, at least geographically, and with the enigma of those that had vanished in these seas before. Each new case was now given considerably more Press coverage and popular speculation and comment.

Within a week's time in January 1967 three smaller aircraft vanished, something that was becoming more commonplace, especially in the Miami/Bahamas corner of the Triangle, because small aircraft were the travel of choice to access the nearby Florida Keys and Bahamian vacation ports, though three in one week was cause for alarm. Heading toward nearby Bimini from Miami a Chase YC-122 in cargo for an Ivan Tors movie shoot vanished on January 11, 1967, although minimal debris was later found. In the next case, one is reminded of the DC-3 in 1948 and the mystery of the lack of debris. With 4 people aboard, a twin Beechcraft had taken off from Miami on January 14, 1967, and headed south to Key Largo and then along the Keys, a route entirely over shallow water and broken keys along the intercoastal highway. Yet like Linquist's DC-3 it utterly vanished. Reminding us of the shape of the Triangle yet again, a Piper Apache with 3 aboard had left from San Juan, Puerto Rico, on January 17, 1967, for an hour flight to St. Thomas in the nearby Virgin Islands, only to disappear.

Even if the litany of missing ships and planes should include a few incidents far removed from the traditional triangle, yet in the adjacent waters, it should be obvious the nodal points of the Bermuda Triangle were aptly chosen.

The extent to which small aircraft were mysteriously disappearing was not appreciable until decades later when

The location of major disappearances until 1980— missing planes numbered in triangles whereas missing vessels are marked in squares. Consult the index beginning on page 101.

this present observer had a computer database search done of the records of the National Transportation Safety Board. Starting with the year 1962, the results uncovered the alarming average of 4 airplanes per year, each missing in fair weather, each diligently searched for, and many equipped with ELTs (the acronym for Emergency Locater Transmitter), an electronic SOS which is launched from the fuselage upon impact and is traceable by other aircraft and base stations (and later even by satellites) so that the precise area of the accident can be pinpointed quickly and rescuers directed with accuracy. Each nevertheless vanished without any indication they ever crashed into the ocean, the event that would commence the signal.

Speculation on what forces are at work, for lack of a better word, in the Bermuda Triangle added to the exciting discussions of the subject during the heyday of Triangle fever in the 1970s. In addition to John Spencer's theory of alien abduction, each new book and radio or TV program added more intriguing suggestions, each based on plenty of newer disappearances to discuss, including surprising discoveries made through pertinacious research from those deeply committed to uncovering what was happening to so many people, ships and planes. For instance, it was in 1973 that the International UFO Bureau made so much about a possible link between the disappearance of the C-119 Flying Boxcar on June 5, 1965, and a UFO reported by astronaut James McDivitt the day before while in orbit over the Caribbean in Gemini IV.

The latest disappearances added to the increasing momentum of interest in the subject, such as the disappearance of Navion N5126K on May 25, 1973. Pilot Bob Corner had taken friend Reno Rigon along for a flight to Freeport, Grand Bahama, a short run from Miami. Midway over the Gulf Stream he was contacted by Palm Beach radio control and warned that heavy weather lay between him and his destination. Along with another aircraft on the same route (about 10 minutes behind him) Corner was rerouted to the south around the heavy weather. He duly acknowledged, and this was the last heard from him.

Alerts that Corner's plane had not come in for a landing were radioed quickly. Close to landing, the plane traveling behind him turned around and crisscrossed over the route in an effort to find him. This pilot, though having flown just behind the Navion, had experienced no trouble of any kind. Considering its speed of near 200 miles per hour, it was only minutes behind Corner. Yet no Mayday message had been received or intercepted. There was no indication on the surface that there had been a crash. Rescue operations were soon augmented by Coast Guard cutters and aircraft, though once again the search proved fruitless. Because there was a plane traveling the same route behind Corner, it was easy for investigators to get a firsthand description of the weather. The rerouting had taken the flights completely out of harm's way, and there was simply no accounting for why or how the Navion had vanished.

Despite the popularity of the Bermuda Triangle concept at this time, most disappearances simply did not become public knowledge. Except for major disappearances few were contained in the books and magazine articles, which were themselves largely based only on newspaper accounts rather than official investigative reports and statistics maintained by such bureaus as the National Transportation Safety Board.

Scant information and often errored reportorial accounts allowed for some initially successful attempts to debunk the very idea the number of missing aircraft and ships was unusual let alone that the circumstances of the disappearances cause for concern. The most notable attempt culminated in a book in 1975 whose title *The Bermuda Triangle Mystery— Solved* garnered the book more publicity than its contents deserved. Taking only a selective number of cases (57 in all), the author claimed to have solved the phenomenon, usually by using newspaper articles that indicated there had been some rough weather or a delayed search. For those articles that did not conveniently mention foul weather, he speculated on some prosaic cause, though he admitted that the "big" cases— i.e. the most famous and inexplicable— remained baffling.

Research since that time, however, has revealed that between 1962 and 1980, as many as 57 aircraft had vanished, of which *no author*, proponent of the Triangle or otherwise, had been aware. In essence, for every case the author claimed to have solved more than 10 could be added to the litany of those missing— considerably more now if we take the statistics and cases of the last 40 years into the equation (to be discussed in Chapter 4).

Moreover, in 1977 *Miami Herald* journalist Carl Hiasson obtained a US Coast Guard database search of missing vessels between 1971 and 1977. He was inspired by the continuing and disturbing number of reports coming back from the local marinas and harbors which he, of course, as a local newsman had been continually hearing about. Yachts simply never came back or never arrived at their intended port of call. Over the period of 1971 to 1977, the Coast Guard listed 44 vessels missing. While piracy was suspected in a number of them, for 17 of these vessels the Coast Guard would not even speculate as to the cause.

Clandestine drug smuggling required getting fast power yachts in order to make the runs between the islands, often Cuba, into the sequestered Gulf coast of Florida feasible. Unsuspecting yacht owners were usually the target. It had been a long and accepted tradition in the area that when students came south and needed (or wanted) to get to the nearby Bahamas, a yachtsman already intending to go would take them free or even use them for crew on a more extended trip (such as a few days to Nassau to attend the local festival the Junkanoo). By the mid-1970s, however, this was the exact means by which pirates were getting passage. Once at sea, they would take over the ship at gunpoint (weapons would be concealed in their duffle), kill the occupants, cast the bodies over, and use the yacht for a limited time as a drug runner before sinking it and repeating their pattern with their next intended victims.

One notable example of possible piracy is that of the 54-foot luxury yacht *Saba Bank*, which vanished in April 1974 with 4 men from New Jersey aboard. No trace was ever found of the yacht after it had departed Nassau. Rumors indicated they may have taken help aboard, being that none of them were familiar with the unique currents and sandbars of the Bahamas, or because each preferred to spend their long-planned vacation partying on a sun drenched teak deck without diversion to the cumbersome details of navigation.

Extending over only a period of 7 years, the Coast Guard readout constitutes the mere tip of the iceberg, so to speak, for the 1970s, and even more so for the decades before and afterwards. Remaining completely unrecorded, over the period of 1978 and 1979, a mere two years, over 20 aircraft would vanish, a few in circumstances that tempt rational explanations, and this represents only a fraction of what has now transpired in the last 39 years since this phenomenal two year crisis.

Of those vessels on Hiasson's list whose disappearance the Coast Guard could (or would) ascribe to piracy, even theoretically, they may have only used a tenuous or presumptive criterion; for example, reasons such as the power and endurance of the yacht. Reasons for hesitation to include a vessel may have been that it was too slow, such as a sailboat or motor sailor, large languishing yachts not capable of the fast cruising speed of power and luxury yachts. Considering that powerful yachts have vanished in sensational circumstances in which piracy could not have played a factor, there is room to doubt whether the disappearance of large and faster yachts were all due to piracy, at least merely because of this factor.

The unusual, to say the least, circumstances involved in the disappearance of the 24-foot cabin cruiser *Witchcraft* are an example of those that defy logic. The cabin cruiser was most definitely alone until it hit an unidentified and unexplained object underneath it at the entrance to Miami's safe harbor, about only 1 mile from shore, on the night of December 22, 1967. Owner Dan Burack had taken his friend, Father Padraig Horgan, out to see the Christmas lights of Miami. The vantage from Buoy 7 by Government Cut was ideal. It is from this point, close to 9 p.m., that Burack contacted the Coast Guard and said he had hit something below. Fearing he might have bent his propeller, he asked for a tow.

In only 19 minutes the Coast Guard rescue boat was slicing its beam of searchlight through the darkness and, though the beam crisscrossed Buoy 7 several times, there was no trace of Burack's *Witchcraft*. The search soon expanded and took in 1,200 square miles of sea, mostly to the north of Miami, assuming that the cabin cruiser could have gotten sucked out into the fast northbound current of the Gulf Stream after a squall had hit later that night.

The complete disappearance of the *Witchcraft* was some cause for discussion. Burack was an outspoken proponent of boating safety. He had outfitted his cabin cruiser with the latest flotation devices, including life rings, floatable cushions and rafts. Secondly, *Witchcraft* itself had built-in floatation and was for all intents and purposes unsinkable. Buoyancy may not have remained, but some part of the boat would remain languishing above the surface. Without any trace having been found, we are left to speculate on the last words he reportedly had spoken through his microphone. Looking down into the dark ocean, he observed lights or mentioned that something was down there.

Another unlikely candidate for piracy is the 338-foot coastal freighter *El Caribe*, which had vanished with all 28 crew sometime between October 10 and 14, 1971, while in passage between Barranquilla to Santo Domingo, with nothing more valuable than a cargo of cement clinkers. In this case there was a conspicuous postscript of mystery. She had been outfitted with the new electronic EPIRB. It never signaled, indicating the ship had not sunk. For this reason alone piracy was at first feared, but with continuing investigation it seemed little likely.

In 1971 an aircraft disappeared in circumstances that once again highlight the unusual. This was a supersonic Phantom II F-4E Air Force jet. At the time of its disappearance it was south of Florida (from its base at Homestead AFB), in routine maneuvers. Its pilot Norm Northrup was practicing under the guidance of Top Gun pilot Harry Romero. Homestead Vector Control ("Blissful Control") noted that the SIF (Selective Identification Feature) of this aircraft was fading— something that reminds us of one of the missing C-133s. They contacted the flight in order to make sure it was the one they were tracking at the border of Alpha Six sector. Northrup responded: "Roger, I am in a port turn at this time"— and then the aircraft vanished. Other Phantom II's in the area were redirected to the spot. Only one saw an area of "water discoloration" that was 200 feet long and 100 feet wide and oblong in shape, with one end above the water and the other end underneath. The Coast Guard cutter *Steadfast* was 5 miles distance and by the time it arrived there was no oblong shape to see.

The exact nature of this oblong discoloration must have been clarified by the pilot, or at least speculated upon, but the next paragraph in the released report was redacted, meaning there was nothing but a huge square cut into the page where the paragraph otherwise would have been.

In order to set the record straight it is necessary to go back and touch on a few cases. For instance, the mystery in the disappearance of the *Home Sweet Home* in January 1955 was also later minimized by noting that a hurricane had struck on its course through the Triangle. However, in a fair gesture Captain John Waters, once head of Coast Guard Search and Rescue, wrote how he visited the vessel and crew the night before they left. He warned them of approaching foul weather, and several expressed concern and even that they wanted to go back to the US east coast instead. When the *H.S.H.* contacted Bermuda the next morning, therefore, we may wonder if the captain's voice was calm because he was merely informing Bermuda of their new course back to the US and away from the storm, though why they then vanished still remains intriguing.

Considerable mystery should still surround *Connemara IV*, a 70-foot yacht found derelict 150 miles southeast of Bermuda on September 26, 1955, by the freighter *Olympic Cloud*. Attempts to minimize the unusual circumstances of the discovery of the deserted yacht remind us that 4 successive hurricanes had struck the fringes of that area. Thus, taking the argument to its logical conclusion the crew must have one by one or altogether thrown themselves over, each being incapable of enduring the incessant rough weather. However, it is equally apparent by the helmless vessel's survival of the hurricanes that the yacht could have been abandoned before the storms even hit and then breasted them on its own. Ivan Sanderson pertinently observed that any deserted boat should be taken as quite an intriguing mystery, noting that "even an inexperienced or leaderless crew seldom if ever abandons ship because of storm. To do so is obviously asinine, because if the ship won't hold up, no yawl, gig or small lifeboat can do so."

Waves of derelict vessels are obviously a particularly alarming occurrence. Taking one grouping in 1969 off the Azores as reflecting a cross section, a number of causes can be put forward. A capsized 36-foot sailboat was found drifting between Bermuda and the Azores on July 13, its position explained by the strong North Atlantic Drift which would carry any vessel deserted in the Triangle or north of Bermuda to a point off the southwest coast of the island group. Probably more than one explanation can account for at least 3 other sightings, one on July 12 when what appeared a deserted 35-foot yacht on automatic steering was sighted heading eastward in "mid Atlantic." On course for Australia from Stockholm, Peter Wallin had vanished and his deserted sailboat *Vagabond* was found shipshape off the Azores. Of most interest is the case of the *Teignmouth Electron* found about 200 miles distant from the *Vagabond* (700 miles southwest of the Azores) on July 10. The trimaran had been captained by Donald Crowhurst, a contestant in the Golden Globe 'round the world race, who seems to have gone barking mad, judging by entries in his log where he is speaking to God. At last no longer in possession of himself he stepped over into the sea.

Another grouping occurred over August, September, and October 1972 off Puerto Rico concurrent with the "Adjuntas Flap," the name given to a rash of UFO sightings that radiated out from the mountainous village of Adjuntas to the west coast of Puerto Rico, around Cabo Rojo and Aguadilla, precisely where the deserted vessels were later found. Although the flap was unusual, the sighting of UFOs is not a rarity in this area off Puerto Rico, as we will later find out in this volume. In comment on how frequently UFOs are seen in the area, particularly in Laguna Cartagena, Frederico Cruz, director of Civil Aviation in Lajes, has confessed, albeit to his chagrin: "We have seen brightly colored ovoid and round objects as they overfly the area, making right-angled turns, and sometimes they enter the lagoon and disappear underwater."

Those listed as missing according to the Coast Guard list (prepared for Carl Hiasson) include the 20-foot sailboat *Saintois Flean*, Monserrate to Martinique with 4 persons aboard, February 1971; *Playmate*, a 24-foot cabin cruiser, Martinique to Guadeloupe, March 1971, with 3 crew; the 65-foot motor sailor *Princess*, Gulf of Mexico, with 3 crew on board also in March 1971; *Reborn*, a 22-foot cabin cruiser off Barbados, April 1971 with 2 men aboard on a local trip. A particularly curious disappearance is that of *Joven Serena*, a 74-foot yacht on a short trip from Miami to Orange Cay, Bahamas, with only the skipper aboard in June of 1971. A 33-foot schooner from Montauk, with the humorous name of *Red Jack* (Jack the Ripper's nickname), vanished in the Bermuda Triangle en route to Bermuda and then to the Virgin Islands, in December 1971; only the skipper was aboard.

Weather is not always listed in such long printouts, and as time has passed the facility and even, to be honest, the effort cannot be mounted to find every detail in these old cases. It thus does not serve any useful purpose to recount an old list of vessels and the vagueness of their circumstances. However, a few more merit some attention due to their short routes or type of boat which made it unlikely they were the object of piracy. Such is the case of *Miss Scottie II*, a 29 foot cabin cruiser which left Miami for Freeport, Grand Bahama, in October 1972, with 2 crew. The *Tecumseh* was a 75-foot trawler which vanished before arriving at Grand Cayman Island, also in October, with her crew aboard. The 45-foot ketch *Silver Dawn* disappeared between New Hampshire and Bermuda, with 3 crew aboard in January 1973.

More details exist for the 73-foot shrimper *Dawn*, which vanished off Key West sometime after April 22, 1975, when a passing boat saw her anchored 10 miles northwest of Smith Shoals Light. A large search found no trace or any of the bodies of the three men known to have been aboard. Then there is the case of 53-foot yacht *Ixtapa*, which must have been annihilated somewhere near here around

A Saga of Disappearing Planes and Lost Ships 69

Christmastime 1971, on her voyage from Cozumel to Marathon in the Keys. On December 28 part of her cabin was found awash in the Gulf Stream, and finally towed to port. Since there was no indication of explosion, one excited theorist offered that "spacemen" had to remove the cabin in order to "get at the hiding crew."

Searches by the Coast Guard were prompt for most of these cases, but those that vanished without filing any boat plan simply eventually end up as statistics. Comprehensive searches included radio sweeps, following the track line, taking into account the drift, involved grid searches by multiple aircraft and cutters, and alerts to all civilian traffic to be on the lookout.

Comment was frequent and lively on radio and television around the Florida coast each time a new disappearance was reported. Naturally the most vocal were those ready to offer a new theory or observe, as in the case of the *Ixtapa* and other disappearances, that only alien intelligences can account for the missing crews, an opinion essentially based on the fact that the cases were becoming more inexplicable despite our own technological advances which still could not prevent disappearances or explain how such little trace had been found from so many ships. But one far less esoteric observation has proven pertinent over time. It was noted that most of the disappearances, at least those that beggar the imagination, occurred during the holiday months, that is, November through January, giving rise to the term "Christmastime Hex."

Radio personality Robie Yonge proposed that a boat be rented and manned with dummies. Aboard would be cameras and monitoring equipment. Thus if/or when anything untoward happened there would be a visually recorded account of it. This is presuming, of course, that before the vessel or the dummies vanished the live feed would not be discontinued by any electromagnetic disruption, a phenomenon frequently associated with the appearance of UFOs, and one noted by those who have survived unusual encounters with "electronic fog" in the Triangle.

An unusual interruption both in terms of phone callers and electronic phone line switches occurred live on the air to WFtL late night radio host Ray Smithers on April 13, 1975, when he was conducting a hotline show on the Triangle. This event, preserved as the "Creepy Caller" episode, still remains unexplained to this day. After finding each line on his in-studio phone dead, though each line's light was blinking indicating a caller was waiting in queue, Smithers finally got a live connection. On the other end a voice spoke:

Smithers: WFtL, hello, you're on the air.
Caller: There's one of you on the program who'll understand what I am going to say. In every living thing on this planet has an aura. It is its communication with the Millionth Council who governs this planet. The area that you are discussing now is the aura of this planet. It is the communicative channel through which the Millionth Council governs this planet.
Smithers: Which council, sir?
Caller: The Millionth Council.
Smithers: The Millionth?
Caller: Millionth. . . Anyone going into the area when the communicative channels is open do not disappear, but they are in the timeless void. They're all perfectly alive and well. It is the only area through which the council can communicate with this planet.
Call cuts off.

Recorded and preserved, the voice print was analyzed and studied, indicating that the caller was not hoaxing. Stress at certain words indicated he fully believed what he was saying.

Almost as a dramatic postscript to this strange call, on April 22, 1975, just over a week later there would be no trace of the shrimper *Dawn* off Key West. Only a week later on April 30 an outboard Magnum was found deserted and motor still running off West End, Grand Bahama.

Continuing disappearances that year would include a

number of sailing vessels en route to Bermuda (two in June), an oceangoing tug with the exuberant name of *Boundless* in December and a coaster off the Leeward Islands, to name only a few. Each was an exclamation point, in its way, for about any theory proposed about the Triangle. As we will see in future chapters, dozens of aircraft would join their ranks in the 1970s.

For all intents and purposes the 1970s would see the Triangle both flower in terms of popularity and eventually wither under the assaults of debunkers who insisted based on the paltry number of cases in the public forum or recorded and discussed in books and magazines that the subject was merely the result of inaccurate and sensationalistic reporting. Until this present observer would rejuvenate the subject 20 years later, with over a hundred additional disappearances, the subject essentially went into the Deep Six itself, the metaphoric end for all those listed as missing in "Davey Jones' Locker."

Worldwide interest in the Bermuda Triangle had brought forth a valuable clue, however. Historical research uncovered many disappearances and even, more intriguing, the repeating theme of deserted vessels found in the area. Nothing underscores the reality of the Bermuda Triangle enigma as does an abandoned ship— a unique type of mystery in the history of travel. Until the advent of wireless in the 19th century only one thing was capable of pinpointing any location of mystery— the discovery of something as inexplicable as the ship itself, deserted but shipshape. With currents and drift computed, each ghostly hulk testified that it had sailed through the area today delineated for the Bermuda Triangle.

Before we continue to the present time, we must take a look at what history has uncovered for us over a considerably longer span of time than a few decades.

Chapter 3

Over a Past Horizon

Since centuries have passed from the time the New World has been discovered and hence the seas of the Bermuda Triangle have first been sailed, one might assume that the number of ships that have gone missing in that infinitely larger span of time by comparison to the last few decades would be enormous. While this may be true, the lack of record keeping, and the conditions under which existing records were originally made, only afford us a glimpse, perhaps at only a few footprints, of what we must assume is a longer trail.

Even if records were easily attainable, the data to make them worthwhile to the modern compiler could only have come from the existence of wireless and radio on the ships so that some idea of their last reported position could be fitted with some precision to the location of the modern Triangle. This obviously was not the case. Those accounts of missing ships that come down to us prior to radio or wireless are those that were preserved in independent written histories. Many of these cases are quite intriguing, as you might imagine, since the very reason they were preserved in literary sources is because some element in them had stood out and was deemed worthy of comment; meaning, the most bizarre cases are those that are preserved, but also the very ones suspect to having fallen victim to embellishment. This, of course, makes it problematic when using their details to fit them into any theory.

On its own a mere litany of Triangle cases only serves to impress upon us how frequently the unusual *might* strike. This is because in most cases there are simply no real details to confirm or deny anything but total disappearance. The expression of such an attitude does not minimize the tragedy that is presumed in all these cases. It is merely a fact that without any details it is impossible to draw any definite conclusions other than those that accept general location and total disappearance, neither of which are enough to fit the cases into a greater mosaic that may serve to reveal a common cause.

There is one exception within the annals of shipping that allows the biographer of this sea to set a greater degree of certainty as to the level of the unusual and as to the location where a vessel met its mysterious fate or, more accurately in this instance, where the crew met mystery. This is the phenomenon of derelict vessels. Short of radio and wireless, this was the only way in the days of tall ships and stout lads that one could firmly attach a location to the point where an ominous fate had intervened.

The 222 ton French frigate *Rosalie* is reasonably the first derelict to be documented as a mystery ship in the Triangle. This, of course, was due to the fact that she was one of those cases that stood out, plus the fact that a reporter was close at hand when the vessel was towed into Havana. It wasn't long before the account reached London and there appeared the following in the *London Times* in August of 1840.

> A singular fact has taken place within the last few days. A large French vessel, bound from Hamburgh to Havannah, was met by one of our small coasters, and was discovered to be completely abandoned. The greater part of her sails were set, and she did not appear to have sustained any damage. The cargo, com-

posed of wines, fruits, silks, etc., was of a very considerable value, and was in a most perfect condition. The captain's papers were all secure in their proper place. . .The only living beings found on board were a cat, some fowls, and several canaries half dead with hunger. The cabins of the officers and passengers were very elegantly furnished, and everything indicated that they had only recently been deserted. In one of them were found several articles belonging to a lady's toilette, together with a quantity of ladies' wearing apparel thrown hastily aside, but not a human being was to be found on board. The vessel, which must have been left within a very few hours, contained several bales of goods addressed to different merchants in Havannah. She is very large, recently built, and called the Rosalie. Of her crew no intelligence has been received.

Attempts have failed to link the *Rosalie* as being the *Rossini*, a derelict that was not-so-mysterious after all since she had gone aground in Cuba and her crew had rowed to shore. When the actual records were uncovered detailing the construction of the *Rosalie* and her launching in 1838 it was confirmed they were two different ships.

Instinctively it would strike the observer as a phenomenal coincidence that two derelict vessels could be found near the same area of ocean (near Cuba in this instance) at the same time, but as more data has surfaced from the 19th century the likelihood of several derelicts being found in the same area does not seem so remote a prospect anymore.

This data comes from the study of abandoned vessels done under the aegis of the US Hydrographic Office. Headed by Commander Charles Sigsbee, of the US Navy, the research concentrated on derelict vessels of the North Atlantic. Over the 7 year period (1887-1893) the study extended, the data it had gathered not only revealed the large number of deserted vessels that were afloat at any given month of the period in question, but the study was the first to note that the epicenter for deserted vessels was the area delineated today for the Bermuda Triangle.

In order to fully appreciate Sigsbee's work in context to the modern Triangle and its intriguing ramifications we must first draw our attention to the North Atlantic. At its center is the Sargasso Sea, a warm body of water largely created by the interlocking and swift currents of the combined Gulf Stream. This sea is essentially elliptical in shape and occupies the central North Atlantic Ocean between 20° to 35° North Latitude and 30° to 72° West Longitude— roughly starting a few hundred miles off the US east coast and extending into the eastern Atlantic.

Ever since the Spanish treasure armadas, ships have used this surrounding powerful Gulf Stream and its associated currents— The North Atlantic Drift, Canary Current, North Equatorial Current, and Antilles Current— to hasten their journey back to Spain or Europe (Gulf Stream, North Atlantic Drift) and back again to the New World (North Equatorial Current, Antilles Current). Experience, however, taught them to avoid the Sargasso Sea, for it was a place of unexplained calms and weak, indolent currents. Before discovering its starkly different features as compared to the surrounding currents, the Spanish fell victim to the deadly calms. Today this area is still called the Horse Latitudes because the Spanish conquistadores, becalmed for weeks, had to cast over their war horses in order to conserve water as they prayed for the wind to return and guide them out. These seas are also called the Doldrums, from which we developed the word for an inert, heavy depression.

The Sargasso Sea remains one of nature's greatest oddities, for while the North Atlantic is cold and tempestuous the Sargasso Sea is largely an immobile body of warm water. Its relative calmness may largely be the result of the surrounding and inter-locking currents. But these currents have not created the Sargasso Sea's most visible oddity. A unique form of seaweed grows over its surface called *sargassum*, from which this sea gets its name. In no other place in the world does this particular seaweed grow. It floats because of little grape-like pods on its stems. Bunches float idly with the soulful stillness of the lazy swells. Huge mats can cover acres. It doesn't venture oft into the conveyor belt of currents around the sea. Rarely are clumps of it found in other parts of the ocean or washed upon windward shores. It grows here and remains in its native environment.

The "damnable" Sargasso Sea occupies the heart of the North Atlantic Ocean. Sailing ships eventually used the currents around it rather than sailing through it.

Picturesque stories tell us of deserted ships found idling throughout its realm. Becalmed, their fate was to forever remain in its limbo until the crew died and rotted and the vessels became eternal ghost ships. Paintings show ancient galleons next to rusted old steamers. Such paintings are wonderful metaphors, but they are not entirely false. They are artistic distillations. They condense the Sargasso Sea's enduring aura into one powerful image. Doubtless galleons did not remain until the days of steam, but it is not fancy that every form of ship known to us has been found drifting in the Sargasso Sea's eerie solitudes at one time or another.

Paradoxically, however, as famous as the Sargasso Sea has become in sea lore, Sigsbee's work reveals that much of its legendary aura is stolen. Derelict vessels, especially during the heyday of sail, were actually more common outside of it. Over the 7 years which *Wrecks and Derelicts of the North Atlantic* was compiled by Commander Sigsbee, 1,146 unidentified derelicts were reported and 482 identified vessels. The sum total for only those 7 years was 1,628. In noting the location of these vessels, Sigsbee declared: "Pilot Charts show that most of the derelicts are sighted in the Gulf Stream off the United States coast, north of 30 degrees north latitude, and west of 60 degrees west longitude. The number gradually decreases to the eastward along the transatlantic steamer routes. A number of those which remain afloat the longest time make the circuit of the Sargasso Sea. The majority of the derelicts were vessels which were abandoned near the United States coasts."— a better delineation for the heart of the Bermuda Triangle cannot be imagined.

Ironically, the Triangle's modern reputation grew out of journalistic embellishment of only 50 or so missing ships and about 20 missing aircraft. This number, paltry compared to actual statistics, was enough to excite the world on the prospects of an eerie area of ocean where unexplained disappearances predominated. We have conceived theories of alien abductions and wistfully contemplated supernatural explanations. But the Bermuda Triangle, if defined solely as a place where more disappearances of ships and crews occur, has its origins squarely rooted in fact. If only 5 percent of the derelicts in Sigsbee's study were truly caused by some unknown agent, then the crews of 80 vessels must be added to the Triangle's litany of victims for just those 7 years.

While the 19th century statistics on derelicts do not address the cause in each case, they do justify the modern Triangle's enigma as a place of mystery. Even if the vast majority of these 1,628 derelicts have a known cause, where crew and captain escaped to tell their tale, it is still amazing that it is here where seamen forgot their senses and abandoned a sound ship more than any other place in the North Atlantic. Out of all the vast North Atlantic it is here where crews leapt from their vessels or mysteriously vanished. Either they flung caution and experience to the wind here more than other places or some mysterious fate befell them. It is interesting to note that Sigsbee's breakdown of derelicts by flag reveals that although American and British ships were the higher percentage (160 and 134 respectively) some 95 Norwegian ships, 24 German, 20 Italian, 11 French, 10 Swedish and even 9 Russian ships, among other nationalities, join the list of vessels where their crews fled safe ship for treacherous waters.

Since some 316 ships were reported floating keel over, we can tentatively reduce the number of ghostly sailing ships. However, we cannot be sure if some of these capsized hulks were derelicts that were later keeled-over by storm. Therefore it is not certain whether the ships were abandoned and drifted sometime before storm later capsized them.

Sigsbee notes that the number of derelicts increased over the 7 years of research. "This increase is probably not so much the increased number of derelicts, but it is due to the fact that this office has gradually increased the efficiency of its ocean patrol through its constantly increasing number of voluntary cooperating observers. This feature is exemplified by the fact that in 1893 there were 312 unidentified and 106 known derelicts; or a total of 418, and an average of 35 per month; and since the average length of time a derelict remains afloat is one month, it is evident that there must be 19 derelicts constantly afloat on the North Atlantic. Prior to 1893 this was estimated at 16, but fuller reports are received now than in former years." This minor increase indicates that Sigsbee's work is fairly reflective of the actual number of derelicts in the Atlantic for those decades before and after. The evolving efficiency of Sigsbee's office also indicates that many times the crews must never have been heard from again else reports would have been more consistently recorded and obtainable from some source regardless of the Hydrographic Office's personal network of observers.

An example of how accurately Sigsbee's calculations must extend backward in time can be found in the transatlantic encounters of the bark *Abd-el-Kader*. On March 8, 1873, just north of the Sargasso Sea, she came upon the abandoned *Robert C. Winthrop*. Captain Sparrow boarded with a prize crew and discovered all sails set except the main topsail, which had been blown away. Four feet of water was in the bilge (determined by sounding the ship) and the boats were gone. Yet Sparrow reported the ship was perfectly fine and manageable. Before he could determine whether he wanted to put a prize crew on board and sail her to their destination (Boston) a gale arose and they returned to the *Kader*, leaving the *Winthrop* to her ghostly fate in the storm. Nearing Boston, the *Abd-el-Kader* then encountered the tern (three-masted schooner) *Kate Brigham*, perfectly sound but deserted. She was bound from New York to La Havre with a cargo of petroleum. Sparrow docked on the 24th, reporting two mysteries of the sea.

Exasperated by such abandonments, the *New York Times* reporter denounced them on March 31. "What can be the matter with the crews of American vessels that they thus abandon their ships and vanish into the unknown? Their vessels were not abandoned because they could no longer protect their crews from the elements. Neither could the motive of their abandonment have been the desire to defraud the insurance companies, for in that case the vessels would have been scuttled. Can it be that the *Flying Dutchman* has crossed the equator in search of forced recruits for his venerable crew?" (According to Lloyd's, the crews from both vessels were actually saved.)

A far more eerie encounter supposedly befell the *Ellen Austin* in 1881, when she came upon the same derelict *twice*. The first time she encountered the nameless vessel she was north of the Sargasso Sea. Her master placed a prize crew aboard and in tandem both vessels sailed on to New York. About 2 days later the *Ellen Austin* and the nameless schooner were parted by a squall. When the squall dissipated, the schooner had vanished along with the *Ellen Austin's* prize crew. No trace was ever found of the vessel. The *Ellen Austin* crew, teeming with superstition, sailed on for New York. Another retelling has the *Austin* finding the nameless schooner again. This time the schooner was sailing erratically. When they boarded her again, they found the prize crew had also vanished as had the original crew. There they left the cursed drifter to rot at sea. The vessel floated away, a ghostly portal to another world.

It is very possible that the publicized affair of the *Abd-el-Kader* influenced the story of the *Ellen Austin*. Yet as we know, it would not have been impossible, even unlikely, for a ship to have encountered 2 derelicts on this route, much less the same one twice. As a London to New York packet, the *Ellen Austin* most definitely sailed the sea lanes attributed to her in the legend, and was frequently in a position north of the Sargasso Sea to encounter the many derelicts that drifted out of the Bermuda Triangle.

In the 19th century the Sargasso Sea's reputation essentially only fed off the crumbs of the as-yet-unnamed Bermuda Triangle. A fraction of the many derelicts found drifting in the currents from the Triangle had funneled into its stagnant clutches. There they sat, some perhaps for years, helping to build the legend of a "Sea of Lost Ships" or "Port of Missing Vessels."

Few ghost ships ever drifted out of the Sargasso Sea to make a real port on their own. However, this is the case with the bark *Vincenzo Perotta*. She was first spotted northeast of Bermuda on September 17, 1887. She thereafter drifted 2,950 miles over 536 days to finally end up at Watling Island in the Bahamas. In that time 27 ships reported her, and each carried a tale of mystery to some foreign port.

Few ships ever drifted out of the clutches of the currents. Legends of eternal and cursed drifters have a basis in fact. The legends are probably partially based on the actual drift of the tern *Fannie E. Wolston*. She was first reported derelict on October 15, 1891, west of Bermuda in the Gulf Stream, and last reported, as of the publishing of the Hydrographic Office's 1894 wreck report, on February 20, 1894, just a little southwest of that position *up current* from where she had been reported before. She had not remained in a void and drifted against the powerful current. Reports by other ships in those intervening years make it clear that the tern had drifted in the currents around the Sargasso Sea and had come back to the place where she was first sighted (or abandoned). Sigsbee writes: "She has, therefore, been a derelict for 850 days, during which she drifted 7,025 miles, the longest track of the kind on record; and, as she is supposed to be afloat yet, her track will probably be still further extended." Published reports, such as the aforementioned Hydrographic Office report (*Wrecks and Derelicts of the North Atlantic, 1887 to 1893 Inclusive*) were few and far between. How many times was the ghostly tern sighted thereafter? How many years did she continue to haunt the Atlantic? Did she make yet another complete orbit of the huge Sargasso Sea? Was she in limbo for many more years?

Obviously, the legends of ghostly derelicts are quite real. Maybe the *Fannie Wolston* is not so dramatic, but she is a worthy inspiration for eerie elaboration. Three and half, perhaps four or more, years drifting at sea being sighted by countless ships (34 ships by the time of the report) is enough to inspire a great and substantive sea yarn. As her legend grew, as more and more ships reported the vessel still miraculously afloat and never re-boarded or hauled to port, how many ships started to give her a wide berth? She earned the reputation as a damned ship, and for this reason she was never towed to port so that any master might dine from her bones in the court of salvage. She continued on until...until judgment day buried her and her clues.

One alarming incident gives us an idea of what might frighten men from a sound ship in the seas west of Bermuda. It was on the cusp of the Sargasso Sea in 1904, in the precise area where most derelicts had been sighted, that the British ship *Mohican* had a bizarre encounter. It was reported by the New York *Times* and the Philadelphia *Enquirer* on July 31, 1904.

ELECTRIC CLOUD ENVELOPED SHIP

Caused Mohicans's Sailors to Become like Animated Magnets

Compass Was Set A-Spinning and Iron Chains Could Not Be Lifted From the Deck

When the British steamer *Mohican*, from Ibraila, Roumania, which reached this port on Saturday, was making for the Delaware Breakwater, it had a most remarkable experience which terrorized the crew, played havoc with the ship's compass and brought the vessel to a standstill for nearly a half hour.

For that length of time the vessel was enshrouded in a strange metallic vapor, which glowed like phosphorus. The entire vessel looked as if it were afire and the sailors flitted about the deck like glowing phantoms. The cloud had a strange magnetic effect on the vessel, for the needle of the compass revolved with the speed of an electric motor and the sailors were unable to raise pieces of steel from the magnetized decks. Captain Urquhart described the thrilling experience and his story is vouched for by every man of the crew.

"It was shortly after the sun had gone," he said, "and we were in latitude 37 degrees 16 minutes and longitude 72 degrees 48 minutes. The sea was almost as level as a parlor carpet and scarcely a breeze ruffled the water. It was slowly growing dark when the lookout saw a strange gray cloud in the southeast. At first it appeared as a speck on the horizon, but it rapidly came nearer and was soon as large as [a] balloon."

Ship in Shining Cloud

"It had a peculiar gray tinge, and as it bore down upon us, we saw bright glowing spots in its mass. A mile away we perceived that it rose several hundred feet above the level of the sea and was almost that broad. It rolled over the sea toward us, the glowing spots becoming more and more vivid. Suddenly the cloud enveloped the ship, and the most remarkable phenomena took place. The Mohican suddenly blazed forth like a ship on fire, and from stem to stern and topmast to keel everything was tinged with the strange glow. The seamen were in terror when they found themselves looking as if they had been immersed in hell fire. Their hair stood straight on end, not from the fright so much as from the magnetic power of the cloud.

"They rushed about the deck in consternation, and the more they rushed about, the more excited they became. I tried to calm them, but the situation was beyond me. I looked at the [compass] needle and it was flying around like an electric fan. I ordered several of the crew to move some iron chains that were lying on the deck, thinking that it would distract their attention. But what was the surprise to find that the sailors could not budge the chains, although they did not weigh more than seventy five pounds each. Everything was magnetized, and chains, bolts, spikes and bars were as tight on the deck as if they had been riveted there."

Hair on Heads Stood Out

"The cloud was so dense that it was impossible for the vessel to proceed. I could not see beyond the decks, and it appeared as if the whole world was a mass of glowing fire. The frightened sailors fell on the decks and prayed. I never saw anything so terrifying in the years I have been at sea. The hair on our heads and in our beards stuck out like bristles on a pig. After we had been in the cloud for about ten minutes, we noticed that it became difficult to move our arms and legs, in fact, all the joints of the body seemed to stiffen.

"Then it was that my sea legs began to fail me for the first time. I've heard of phantom ships and stories about the needle running wild, but shiver me if I had ever seen the like of that. For a half hour we were enveloped in that mysterious vapor. And for nearly all that time, after the sailors' first cries of fright had subsided, there was a great silence over everything that only added to the terror. I tried to talk, but the words refused to leave my lips. The density of the cloud was so great that it would not carry sound.

"Suddenly the cloud began to lift. The phosphorescent glow of the ship and the crew began to fade. It gradually died away and, at the same time, the stiffness left the hair. In a few minutes the cloud had passed over the vessel and we saw it moving off over the sea. It loomed above the water as a great, gray mass, spotted like a leopard's back with the bright, glowing patches.

"The crew gradually regained their composure and whispered to one another. I went among them, telling that all danger was past and they slowly went about their work. When I ordered them to move the iron chains for the second time, the men had no trouble in lifting them from the deck and tossing them about. Then I took a look at the needle and it was pointing steadily toward the north, as it (sic—if) nothing had occurred. I have sailed the seas for many years, but I never encountered a cloud like that. It must have been composed of some magnetized substance, which at the same time was combined with phosphorus."

Lying buried in the archives until it was rediscovered in the early 21st century, this story of the sea gives us a disturbing foreshadow of what in the 1970s would be termed the "electronic fog;" this latter era a time in which the *Mohican* report, though startlingly suggestive, was inaccessible and could not have provided any inspiration for imaginative storytellers. In the early 21st century the *Mohican* account continued to gain recognition because it was oddly similar to these recent and independent accounts of survivors of unusual encounters in the Bermuda Triangle; each of them speaking about weird "electronic fog," strange lenticular clouds with magnetic properties, and unexplained periods where compass needles went haywire or "crazy." Unlike with the *Mohican*'s strange encounter, the sum total of modern data has been pointing to far more alarming potential for travelers than a brief interlude with a strange phenomenon. In *Without a Trace*, compiled in 1977, Charles Berlitz noted: "On a few occasions when a ship or plane has been seen to disappear (a paradoxical expression at best), it has first been covered by what appears to be an electromagnetic fog or, in the case of planes, a cloud into which planes fly but from which they do not exit."

Among the disappearance of large vessels, the case of the *Cyclops* is particularly striking. At 520 feet in length and with a crew of 309 men aboard, the total disappearance of this US Navy auxiliary cargo vessel constitutes the number one tragedy, in terms of life lost (presumed), in the Bermuda Triangle. The vessel had last touched port unexpectedly at Barbados in the West Indies and from there left on March 4, 1918, for Baltimore. The weather was excellent, but the vessel never arrived and no trace was found in a protracted search conducted by the US Navy. All the elements come together in this last voyage to rank it with the greatest sea tales. Her master, Captain Worley, was more hated by his own crew than William Bligh was hated amongst those of the *Bounty*. Furthermore, he was known to be pro-German, and to even keep a pro-German clique about him on the ship. He was abusive, cruel, and even given to drunkenness. The plot that played out may have less to do with the Triangle and more to do with the Navy's original fear that mutiny or treason had occurred (see *A Passage to Oblivion*).

Between the wars, ships that vanished included the *Cotopaxi*, last heard from off Florida on December 1, 1925, reporting she had water in her hold. In March 1926 the freighter *Suduffco* disappeared on a course from Port Newark to the Panama Canal. The tramp freighter *Anglo-Australian* was last passing the Azores in March 1938 when she signaled "All well" and thereafter, like the *Samkey*, was never seen again. Battered but unsinkable due to her lumber cargo, the freighter/schooner *Gloria Colita* was found abandoned in the Gulf of Mexico in February 1940 and towed to Mobile, Alabama, by the Coast Guard.

With the advent of WWII the cruel sport of war dominated the North Atlantic. Unexpected debris would signal not mystery to the crew of a passing freighter but the present dangers of a surface raider or U-boats. It is with a new phenomenon—the disappearance of aircraft— that we can be more certain of mystery rather than the effects of war as the cause for inexplicable loss. The training and patrol requirements of the US war effort created the perfect environment for close-to-shore flights, many of them based in Florida, far from the dangers of the war zone.

The disappearance of an O47B is particularly intriguing for the circumstantial similarities to Flight 19 inasmuch as it had pilot (Lt. Marsh Hemenway) and 2 crew, the weather was nearly identical (a southwest trade wind up to 35 knots), unusual radio interference occurred to *both planes* in the patrol, and the fact that as one of two patrol aircraft which had taken off from Key West on the morning of February 15, 1942, to patrol the Dry Tortugas, a limited area, it seems to have been selectively taken without any warning except that both planes experienced a draining of their radio transmitters.

About 9:10 a.m. the companion patrol airplane, piloted by Lt. John Tuite, had its last visual contact with Lt. Hemenway's patrol aircraft. It was 10 miles distant heading northeast 030 degrees from the Dry Tortugas. In a rather nebulous entry in the report, it is then stated: "Lt. Tuite and Lawley [radioman] reported that at this time they sighted what they thought might be a suspicious circumstance existed and proceeded to return to companion ship." However, Lt. Hemenway's aircraft was no longer visible.

Tuite's radioman, Lt. Lawley, now contacted Hemenway's aircraft in order to ask Hemenway to take up a heading of 90 degrees so that their paths would cross and they could rejoin. However, Lawley noted that his radio transmission and reception were weak. This was unsettling because the same thing had happened earlier to Hemenway's aircraft. Lawley had overheard Hemenway's radioman, Lt. Kelley, report to Key West that his radio transmission and reception were weak— so now Lawley's weak reception seemed more than an odd coincidence. It was so weak that when Kelley now responded to Lawley's request, all that Lawley could hear was a very weak "Roger." This was the last heard from Hemenway's patrol aircraft.

> Companion ship circled navigation buoy East of Dry Tortugas for some time and also circled Marquesas Key in an attempt to relocate the missing plane but no visual contact was made. Ship circled Key West Airport as well and landed at Key West at 10:15 a.m. During this time Lt. Lawley reports that his radio failed to operate, and he had no contact with the missing plane or ground station. Upon arrival at Key West he used the radio of another plane to ask the ground station to contact 2YZ [Hemenway] and report his arrival at Key West.

The response was also negative, not so surprising considering that Lt. Kelley, Hemenway's radio operator, had earlier also reported his radio was getting weaker. Both aircraft encountering this is a rather unusual coincidence, if it was, and if it was not then it is an indication of some electromagnetic drain, a particularly alarming element when one of them then vanishes.

What prompted Tuite and Lawley to interpret some event as "suspicious" and warranting both aircraft to join up is not clarified, but they never pursued whatever it had been. The rest of their patrol was taken up trying to locate Hemenway. As would become the norm, a full search never found a trace, despite the aircraft having a very limited patrol area.

On June 21, 1943, a Navy Ventura, a 2 engine light bomber with 5 crew, took off from Boca Chica, Key West, at 12:50 p.m. for a practice bombing run off shore. After it headed into the exact area where Hemenway had vanished, it must have disappeared. The flight was to be quite short. They were due back by 2:30 p.m. The practice bombs were only basic water-filled bombs. An "exhaustive search" was commenced within the hour without finding a trace.

Officially, all aboard were declared to have drowned, although in a confidential memo from the Judge Advocate General's Office to Naval Operations the assistant JAG stated cautiously: "While there is [sic] possibility that the plane crashed and all aboard were killed, there is no definite evidence to that effect." The only recommendation was an officious one: that the pilots and crew be declared missing for 12 months and then declared dead, which was done on June 22, 1944.

A B-24 "Liberator" bomber was a considerably larger aircraft, with 4 engines and 8 crew. One in RAF service departed Nassau on April 24, 1944, bound for Key West. Jack Burgess, who knew the pilot, Ken Cameron, participated in the search for the aircraft and later wrote an article about his experience. He observed that the plane and "crew were never seen or heard of again. They never reached Key West, and although they carried instructors including a fully qualified and experienced wireless operator instructor, no signal or message was ever received by the many ships, aircraft or agencies who would have been listening out for them and others. Along with other crews, we looked for any sign of wreckage or dinghies for nine hour searches over the next few days." Although the Bermuda Triangle was not a term in effect yet, after the 5 Avengers of Flight 19 vanished in 1945 Burgess came to feel that what had happened to his friend and the B-24 could only be explained by the same phenomenon. He considered this incident "our first taste of losing an aircraft and crew in strange, mysterious circumstances in such splendid peaceful conditions."

In a sense we have come full circle again, back to peacetime and December of 1945 when there was no hindrance to reporting the disappearance of aircraft and all that attended their vanishings no matter how unusual. There is, however, a limit of what we can learn from the past, especially from the muster of lost ships on long voyages. Aircraft, on the other hand, are closely monitored and are, relatively speaking, only a short time in transit. It is the disappearance of aircraft that essentially gave us the shape and concept of the Bermuda Triangle. Advances in radar, radio communication, flight plans, and automatic alarms, give us details impossible to glean from any ship disappearance, some perhaps unwelcome in their implications. The continuing disappearance of aircraft in the modern era has revealed to us the unusual circumstances in disappearances that cannot seemingly be explained by pilot error, structural failure, or foul weather. In other words, there are no easy answers to these missing aircraft.

Chapter 4

"Aircraft Damage
and
Injury Index Presumed"

Prior to the index year of 1978 the records of the National Transportation Safety Board hold very little, and database searches will give only the barest of information regarding missing aircraft. Called a "Brief," this information essentially includes location, course, some hint of weather conditions, the number of those aboard, and the type of aircraft. A brief summary may also be at the bottom of the one-page chit if there is more specific information available to summarize. Redundant information is not recorded, such as the extent of what was, for a disappearance anyway, obviously a fruitless search. Altogether the "Brief" lives up to its name. With or without a summary, the incident is always concluded with officious terseness: "Aircraft Damage and Injury Index Presumed." Considering that a disappearance is being summarized there is little more that can be deduced with certainty.

Prior to the index year of 1962 there is nothing to even form a dot matrix printout. Although the Civil Aeronautics Board, the precursor to the National Transportation Safety Board, investigated the accidents to small, private aircraft under the heading "General Aviation," the reports were eventually thrown out or remain lost in boxes in a warehouse, the likes of which is probably best illustrated at the ending of the movie *Raiders of the Lost Ark* where even the holy ark of the covenant could be conveniently lost amongst all that the Federal Government owned and carelessly stored.

Averaging missing aircraft statistics during the span covered by extant records, however, can provide one with relative certainty as to how many must have vanished in the time prior. Between 1962 and 1977, 4 aircraft on an average vanished each year. This does *not* include those where heavy weather was listed, though we must keep in mind that those that vanished in heavy weather may not necessarily have vanished because of those conditions. From 1945 to 1962, it is safe to say that the average remained fairly even. Despite the lack of readily accessible official reports, supposedly 9 aircraft vanished in 1949 alone, the unexpected number being the reason the figure was preserved in popular journals.

The number of airplanes lost in unusual circumstances in the 1950s must be staggering, comparable to the 40 aircraft that vanished between 1962 and 1977. It should be noted, however, that the 1960s was the dawn of the golden age of the weekend wing flyer, with perhaps many more small aircraft flying the Bahamas than in the 1950s, thus perhaps providing a greater average for missing aircraft.

As one might imagine, those cases that are preserved for us in newspaper accounts are those wherein there is the quality of the unusual and unexpected. Such is the case of the disappearance of a Maryland couple, George and Margaret Dickson, who on January 27, 1960, were returning to the US from their honeymoon vacation in Puerto Rico. Nearing the Caicos Islands in their Cessna light plane, Dickson sent radio messages indicating that he was lost and couldn't find the island group. Overhearing him and acting as a link with base stations was a military C-54. For 20 minutes the pilot tried to home-in on Dickson's messages, yet without success, before the radio waves fell silent. No trace was ever found of the plane or the life rafts and life vests it carried aboard. "It is believed that a faulty radio magnetic compass may have caused the couple to overshoot their destination and then ditch the Cessna 180 when it ran out of gas" presents a frustrating conclusion because of the lack of clarity whether Dickson stated he believed his compass was faulty or whether the pilot of the C-54 merely deduced this in the absence of being able to make out what the actual problems were. As we will see, pilots who encountered electromagnetic aberrations, including the "electronic fog," have still been able on occasion to use their radios, though the communication is weaker than normal and their words confusing to others trying to listen in.

The disappearance of Pompano Beach nurse Carolyn Coscio and her boyfriend, Richard Rosen, on June 6, 1969, appears almost identical to the Dickson disappearance. She too was flying in the same general vicinity, in this instance trying to find Grand Turk just south of the Caicos Islands. Coscio indicated she too was lost but was circling two islands "with nothing down there." Meanwhile, guests at the Ambergris Cay Hotel were annoyed by her light Cessna 172 repeatedly circling overhead. Finally, it dashed off into the sunset; if Cosco's plane, such a foolhardy act was her final attempt to find Grand Turk. No explanation exists for why she thought she was circling a deserted island. No trace of Coscio and her aircraft were ever found. While a further discussion of this incident is reserved for later, it is interesting to note here no reason could be discerned why she was lost, just as in Dickson's case, whether it was her compass or the malfunction of any other equipment.

Details were scant but provocative for the disappearance on February 10, 1974, of a charter twin engine Britten-Norman Islander which vanished precisely at 7:31 p.m. while in the remarkable circumstances of coming in for a landing at Harry S. Truman Airport on St. Thomas, US Virgin Islands. This incident was known to this present observer only through the Brief and its intriguing summation: "CLRD TO LND ST THOMAS, FAILED TO ARRIVE, PRESUMED LOST AT SEA"—a provocative enough statement in itself. Later, however, far more sensational details emerged. Noted Baltimore attorney

Harry Ezratty approached and elaborated on his experience with an odd disappearance while a young attorney for a charter airline. It quickly became obvious he was speaking of this same incident only glibly preserved in the Brief summary.

At the time of the incident he and the company's president flew out of New York for St. Thomas to help in the search and to try and understand what had happened. He retained a clear and firsthand memory of the events.

> I was legal counsel for North Cay airways, a commuter airline. In 1973 (I believe) we were flying Norman Islanders, a 9-seater (plus pilot) plane. We had a charter to St. Croix, but could not carry their luggage in such a small plane.
>
> A second Norman Islander with pilot and luggage handler took the baggage.
>
> In those days, Virgin Island airports closed at sunset. Since the baggage plane left after the passengers and it was late, the decision was made to fly to St. Thomas, the shorter flight, before the airport closed down. It would go on the next day to St. Croix.
>
> The plane was on course and on radar for landing in St. Thomas. Another commuter airliner (Prinair) was following the North Cay flight. Prinair acknowledged visual sighting of the plane and requested instructions for landing.
>
> Just before landing, the tower and Prinair pilot lost sight of the North Cay flight. No noise or water disturbance was heard. The plane had disappeared.
>
> The next morning I received notice of the event and with the CEO flew to St. Thomas. Since the event occurred in the landing path, we could not linger over the site. The waters off St. Thomas, as I'm sure you know, are as clear as water from the tap. Despite divers and aerial visuals (we landed and took off several times so that we could fly over the area), there was no wreckage of the plane, no floating luggage, nothing.
>
> A bizarre sidelight of this encounter was that the widow of the pilot filed for death benefits under Workman's Compensation. The Labor Board had a hard time handling the claim because she couldn't prove his death.

Another attorney took over the case for Ezratty in the Southern District of New York and finished it in 1980, but it was doubtful whether he still had the paperwork and original report from the National Transportation Safety Board. Another lead could provide more details. This would be the compensation records. Ezratty recalls that the widow of the pilot took things in hand and finally got an "expert in compensation claims" and somewhere the report might exist in his work or in viable depositions contained therein.

Startling examples of similar inexplicable circumstances can be found in the accident reports on other missing aircraft. From 1978 to the present all reports are still available. Actually, over the first 4 years of available reports there are over 30 aircraft disappearances, with at least one in each year suggesting incredible circumstances; one involving the participation of "electronic fog;" another indicating time-space displacement; a blatant encounter with UFO interference; and, most notably in 1978, the very first year of available records, an incident almost identical to the disappearance of the Norman Islander in February 1974, except in this case the details are carefully preserved in the accident report narrative and no less incredible than those recalled by Harry Ezratty.

This disappearance also involved a twin engine charter. This was a Piper Navajo, also coming from St. Croix at night and so close to landing at Harry S. Truman Airport that its landing light was being watched by the tower controller, William Kittinger. The circumstances are more unbelievable because, essentially, this is the only case in the Triangle in which an aircraft was observed, in the form of its landing light, to suddenly vanish before the eyes of a witness. He had cleared the twin Piper Navajo for landing and was presently watching its landing light steadying in line with Runway 9. He shifted his glance to the radarscope to follow a Herron DH-114 presently taking off from a parallel runway. Here he noticed that the scope only showed a single blip—the Herron taking off. He quickly looked back out the window of the tower and there was no more landing light from the Navajo. Within the span of shifting glances from the window to the scope—the Biblical "twinkle of an eye"— the Piper Navajo had vanished.

Immediately alerted to a possible down aircraft, a Cessna 172 in the landing circle diverted and overflew the approach, but sighted nothing. An intensive search over the days following found no trace, nor did it sight anything in the "tap water" clear shallows which comprise the ocean over the approach route. Moreover, the Navajo was equipped with an ELT, but there was no signal ever picked up, and the incident remains one of the most peculiar in the Triangle to this day.

Reports from 1978 through the present have also provided enough details to determine that over 120 aircraft have carried ELTs. Nevertheless, each one vanished without a trace of a signal having been picked up by other planes, base stations, or tracked on the satellite tracking network.

More aircraft disappeared in 1978 than in any other year in the history of the Bermuda Triangle. While it does not behoove the present observer to detail them all since they can be found already published (*Into the Bermuda Triangle*, McGraw-Hill, 2003), it is worthwhile to discuss some of those that have vanished on radar or within radio communication with airfields or other aircraft, since it is precisely these circumstances which give us clues to the unusual, to say the least, last moments of the flights, and the possible forces that may be at work in their disappearances, before they flew into what can only be said to be oblivion.

All sorts of circumstances have been captured on radar, which has given rise to a whole new field of evidentiary interpretation. A solitary blip, indicating the target, has on the next sweep of the scope's arm suddenly become more than one blip, a sure indication that the aircraft imploded during convective storm activity. Spatial disorientation has been captured preceding loss on radar, evident by an erratic course, many times followed by a 360 turn to lower altitude before radar coverage is discontinued by what is obviously the crash of the aircraft, altogether this recording the sequence of a "dead man's spiral" into the sea. Wreckage is found in each scenario, but for those that leave no trace at sea indicating a crash, coincidently, or possibly not so coincidently, radar shows that they just had "winked out." One turn of the radarscope they are there. The next it is blank.

Within this scenario there is the disappearance of a DC-3 airliner on September 21, 1978, one of the 11 disappearances of aircraft that year. Along with the sudden "blotting out" of the Piper Navajo coming in for a landing this incident makes that year one of the most provocative in the history of the Bermuda Triangle. N407D was over the Florida Straits en route to Havana with a special clearance, when it veered to one side, as if avoiding something, and then it was gone. The search was immediate, one that included Cuban rescue forces as well.

Often the excuse, whether truly believed or chosen out of conformity, that aircraft disappear because of tardy searches, meaning that the sea had enough time to disperse the debris, is not applicable here and in many other disappearances. No trace was found despite an immediate search directed by the last radar return. To the observer, it seems impossible to not be struck by the irony presented in all the cases, most notable here when compared with those where weeks later, as in the case of *Southern Districts* or *Marine Sulphur Queen*, debris of some sort is located over a vast ocean, but in the case of N407D, and others, there is to telltale clue whatsoever despite immediate and coordinated searches pinpointed by radar. All of its seat cushions, blue in color (over 30 of them), were floatable. There was much cabin paneling, etc., and yet no trace of this aircraft could be found. If one does not reach out to consider some exceptional cause in this and other similarly missing aircraft, one is left with nothing more than trying to explain them away. In this case, explanations would also need to include trying to account for why no ELT signal was picked up.

What may be the only time that such an ELT signal was picked up was on April 27, 1978, when a Ted Smith 601 was en route to Panama City, Florida, from Pompano Beach. The aircraft had vanished but later a brief, indeed fleeting, ELT signal was heard, so short that it could not be traced.

In all, 11 aircraft vanished over 1978, a number that had not been approached since 1949, though now one would have imagined that with better radios, navigation equipment, ELTs, plus quicker search craft, it should be considered far more phenomenal than in 1949, if not impossible under natural circumstances. If viewing these as only crashes, the searches, better vectored now, should have at least picked up some shred of flotsam.

Actual stats on missing airplanes may increase with the discovery of details on stolen aircraft for these decades. These cases are often not investigated by the NTSB and therefore there is no reflection of the flight's loss in their records. Without any entry for the registration number, even a database search yields no clue to the mishap. Rentals or borrowed aircraft are invariably the ones classified as stolen if they should disappear, the only legal way the owner can collect his insurance.

It was via this method that decades after-the-fact the disappearance of Kenneth Brodacki came to light. Along with a friend he had taken off in a large Beech Queen Air in March 1979 and headed out into the Triangle, possibly eventually to South America. On the whole, this is all that is known. He was later listed with the Doe Network and the aircraft appeared on insurance lists but never in the database of the National Transportation Safety Board.

The "two years crisis" of 1978-1979 would seem bad enough with 20 aircraft missing in those two years alone, but with the addition of Brodacki's flight it brings the tally of 1979 to 10 planes, almost equal to 1978's total number at least insofar as it is known.

The same classification of "stolen" kept the disappearance of Steve Harrison Sr. out of the records for close to 30 years. With his own light twin Cessna 310 in the shop in North Carolina, he rented a Cessna 310 and flew his friend to the Bahamas. He phoned his wife the night before his return trip, and somewhere over the Bahamas he vanished. Lawsuits later followed over insurance issues, as the owner of the aircraft had no choice but to declare the aircraft stolen despite the circumstances. Steve Sr.'s daughter Pam Harrison would begin the first detailed search for her father 30 years later, in this case one that tried to reconcile unidentified wrecks in the Bahamas with the registration number of the missing aircraft.

No study of missing aircraft in the Bermuda Triangle can fail to accept the significance of one stunning disappearance. This is the disappearance on June 28, 1980, of N3808H, an Ercoupe 415D, off the west coast of Puerto Rico, after a panicked Mayday in which the pilot, Jose Torres, is reporting he is taking evasive action to try and escape a "weird object" bearing down on him and at times trying to prevent him from making the safety of the nearby coastline. In the background his passenger, Jose Santos, can be heard to say "Look, look!" in somewhat awed tone.

Iberia Flight 976 intercepted the Mayday and acted as a link with San Juan International. At the same time Atlantic Weapons Radar was tracking Torres' aircraft until, that is, it mysteriously vanished from the scope, though being a military base their comments did not add whether there was another blip on the scope indicating the "weird object" that Torres was so alarmed by. However, after the Ercoupe vanished a blip soon returned on the scope, presumably the Ercoupe. Proceeding at a different angle from where the Ercoupe had last vanished, the blip then vanished again. Within this timespan, if this was Torres and Santos, neither sent a message elaborating on their current circumstances.

A fuller discussion of this disturbing incident is reserved for later, including parts of the transcription of the Mayday which was recorded and preserved. However, it should be noted here that this is not the only occasion in which radar helped confirm unusual events independent of the pilot's last message, sometimes very terse, which nevertheless shed little light on circumstances before the plane vanished from the scope.

In another case, after the aircraft had vanished a blip indicating the plane returned to the scope, also tracking in another direction, but the pilot still sent no more messages. This was on February 22, 1978, when a Navy KA-6 attack bomber vanished after the pilot alerted the carrier *Kennedy*, its destination, to "Standby," which was soon followed by the co-pilot stating "Standby, we have a problem" without time for either to clarify the problem. The aircraft, only 100 miles distant off North Carolina, then disappeared from the radarscope before another "return" registered but headed in a different direction.

On February 11, 1980, stranger communication preceded the disappearance of N9027Q, a twin Beech Baron, than that which preceded Torres and Santos' disappearance. Although no "weird object" was mentioned, the pilot, Peter Jensen, reported he was off Miami, lost and disoriented in clouds at only 150 feet altitude. He was out of fuel, he declared, and going down. Search operations off Miami reported nothing but perfect weather, and no trace was ever found. This proved to be only one of the mysteries. Miami had never heard Jensen. Jetliners around Bermuda 1,000 miles away had actually intercepted the messages and had relayed his Mayday to Miami.

Even stranger than the displacement of the radio Maydays, which can be explained by rare through freak bounces in the atmosphere, there is the report from the tower of Caicos Island, which is about 600 miles distant from Miami. Later that night after searches off Miami had been secured, specifically six hours after Jensen's last message indicating he was out of fuel and ditching, they distinctly heard the call letters of Jensen's aircraft N9027Q spoken by "a young voice." This fit Jensen perfectly. (He was only 16, though a student in the Civil Air Patrol). This voice stated he was only 10 minutes out and requested permission to land. Given permission by the tower, he nevertheless did not arrive. Jensen and the Baron are still listed as missing to this day, though no explanation can be given for the radio messages that came in 6 hours after fuel starvation and 600 miles from where he had last reported himself disoriented in "clouds" off the stunningly clear Miami coast.

Freak and delayed radio messages were received after the disappearance on January 6, 1981, of a Beechcraft Bonanza with 4 persons on board, piloted by "Robert Spector," a rather ominous name in light of events. The 4 were headed to Nassau to answer charges on illegal gun possession. About 20 minutes past their Nassau ETA (11:41 a.m.), the first Mayday was picked up by a pilot over the Exumas. The message was faint and did not include a call sign. Hours later, now past the time of Spector's estimated fuel exhaustion, another pilot over the Exumas heard more than one Mayday, this time with Spector's call numbers spoken. This indicated the aircraft was lost for unknown reasons.

While it is easy to believe they staged their own disappearance instead of facing the consequences of a Bahamian court, the mystery extends beyond what one would think could be manipulated by human ingenuity. The last radio message was picked up at least 30 minutes after fuel starvation would have happened. Despite an aircraft remaining in the vicinity to act as a Good Samaritan between the tower and "Spector," the messages could not be homed-in on and the Good Samaritan pilot could not get the messages in louder or prompt a more concise answer from "Spector."

It could be suggested that the faintness of the messages could indicate the aircraft had landed in Cuba, though this does not explain why no other aircraft except those 2 in the vicinity of the Exumas had overheard the Maydays; nor does it explain why "Spector" would continue to transmit from a secret airfield runway after the time of his fuel exhaustion, which would only tend to create suspicion he was faking the messages in order to fake his own demise at sea.

Investigation only clouded things more. It turned out "Spector" was completely unknown at Opa Locka Airport, where the plane was based.

It is inexplicable that there was no warning message preceding the disappearance on March 31, 1984, of a beefy Cessna 402B en route to Bimini from Fort Lauderdale considering that the Cessna was tracked on radar, which showed it suddenly slow to a dangerously low airspeed of 90 knots and then after maintaining this for a brief span plunged off the scope. No trace of the aircraft was found in an immediate search. The only clue at sea level didn't fit. Two witnesses saw an aircraft or a tall splash indicative of a plane impact into the shallow waters east of Bimini about 35 miles from where the Cessna 402B had vanished off the scope. There was no other aircraft missing that day, and searches and dives failed to find a trace where the witnesses saw the splash in the water, which was only 18 feet deep and therefore should have easily revealed aircraft wreckage below.

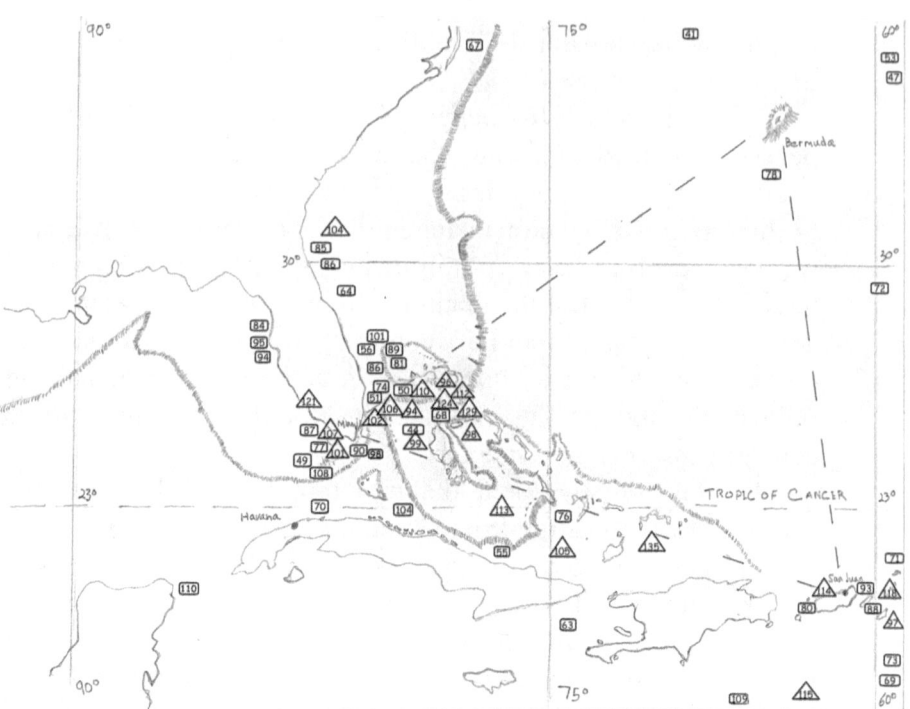

Aircraft disappearances are marked in triangles and ships in ovals; those above record the major disappearances between 1980 and today. See the list beginning on page 101.

Although radar did not confirm unexplained or even alarming events preceding the disappearance for many of those aircraft lost over the 1980s and 1990s, mystery is overwhelmingly associated with the aftermath of their losses. Not only was the total lack of any flotsam in the immediate searches a cause for comment, but this mystery remains to the present time. Many were flying over the shallow Bahama banks, almost unavoidable for the airways in the southwest corner of the Bermuda Triangle. Over time no unidentified wreck site has formed on the shallow bottoms. Each site should easily stand out as a green scar in contrast to the soft azure colors of the sandy bottom. This marled area is the result of the turtle grass and other undersea growth that thrives in the shallows on wrecks but not otherwise in the miles of sandy bottom.

Colloquially, these are called "eyes" because they stand

out vividly as little circles of vegetation or oases in the otherwise desert-like bottom sands. They are dived frequently, especially when a new one shows up, because they indicate wreckage, the object of so many curious divers in the tropic Bahamas.

None of the dozens of aircraft that vanished over the shallow banks, and none of those that vanished close to shore, ever left wreckage to be located on the beaches or retrieved by the heavy yacht traffic over the archipelago. And now with time the mystery extends beyond time to include no indication that they crashed into the shallow bottom and their wreckage lies below forming little oases of turtle grass.

Rather than re-detailing each of these cases for which the reader can consult *Into the Bermuda Triangle*, the list below helps to convey the extent of the mystery that is involved here. The list below, though by no means complete, nevertheless represents the most complete listing of missing aircraft there is.

Missing Aircraft in the Bermuda Triangle

1942, February 15: 047B on patrol near Dry Tortugas; 3.
1942, June 5: PBY Catalina in Gulf of Mexico.
1943, March 7: Douglas Dauntless, off Norfolk; 3.
1943, June 21: Ventura near Marqueses Keys; 5.
1943, July 10: Ventura; from Guantanamo, Cuba; 5.
1943, August 7: Ventura on patrol; blamed on sub; 5
1943, September 7: Ventura on search mission; 5.
1943, October 2: PBY Catalina, Gulf of Mexico.
1943, November 13: Ventura; convoy duty off Trinidad; 6.
1944, February 21: PBY Catalina off St. Augustine, FL.
1944, April 24: B-24 Liberator—Bahamas to Keys; 8.
1944, July 27: PBY Catalina off Norfolk; 9 Free French.
1944, September 11: Dauntless off Miami.
1945, February 7: B-24 "Liberator" near Bermuda.
1945, March 6: Dauntless east of Fort Lauderdale, FL.
1945, July 10: PBM Mariner, over Bahamas on night patrol.
1945, July 18: Navy Privateer on patrol over Bahamas.

1. 1945, December 5: The entire training flight of five Navy TBM Avengers; Crew: 14
2. 1945, December 5: PBM Martin Mariner. Off Banana River, Florida at 28° 59' NL 80° 25' WL. Crew: 13.
3. 1947, July 3: a C-54 Douglas en route from Bermuda to Miami in cargo service. Crew: 7.
4. 1948, January 30: BSAAC Tudor IV Airliner *Star Tiger* GAHNP near Bermuda; 29 aboard.
5. 1948, December 28: NC-16002, Douglas DC-3; south of Miami on approach to the airport. Persons aboard: 31.
6. 1949, January 17: Tudor IV *Star Ariel* GAGRE (sister of *Star Tiger*) Bermuda for Kingston, Jamaica; 19 aboard.
7. 1950, September 11: F9F-2 Panther; Atlantic Ocean.
8. 1950, November 27: Grumman Hellcat off Key West, FL.
9. 1952, December 21: Curtis C-46 in cargo; 3 crew.
10. 1953, December 5: Lockheed Texan; Atlantic Ocean.
11. 1954, October 30: Super Constellation; Maryland for Lajes, Azores. Crew and passengers: 42.
12. 1956, November 9: Martin Marlin amphibious patrol plane, about 350 miles north of Bermuda. Crew: 10.
13. 1960, January 27: Cessna 180 near Caicos Island; 2.
14. 1960, March 18: F-104C Starfighter, missing from squadron off Bermuda.
15. 1961, October 15: an 8 engine SAC B-52 "Pogo 22" north of Bermuda. Crew: 8
16. 1962, January 8: Air Force KB-50 Aerial tanker. North Carolina to Lajes, Azores. Crew: 8.
17. 1962, May 27: a C-133 Cargomaster, between Dover and Lajes, Azores. Crew: 10.
18. 1963, August 28: 2 KC-135 Stratotanker jets disintegrate over the Sargasso Sea. Crew: 10.
19. 1963, September 22: another C-133 Cargomaster; Dover for the Azores. Crew: 10.
20. 1964, February 8: Piper Apache N2157P between Grand Bahama and West Palm Beach, Florida; 4.
21. 1964, December 5: Cessna 140 N81089 with 2 persons; off New Smyrna Beach, Florida.
22. 1965, June 5: a C-119; Miami to Grand Turk. Crew: 10.

23. 1965, September 15: Beechcraft c18s N8063H, with 3 persons, near St. Thomas, VI, around 7:26 P.M.
24. 1965, October 31: Cessna 182 N4010D somewhere between Marathon Key and Key West, Florida; 2.
25. 1965, December 6: Ercoupe N99660; between Fort Lauderdale and Grand Bahama; 2.
26. 1965, December 29: Piper Cherokee N6077P; South Caicos for San Juan; 3.
27. 1966, April 5: converted cargo B-25 N92877; Fort Lauderdale to Aruba.
28. 1966, September 20: Tampa to Baton Rouge N7090P; Piper Comanche; 2.
29. 1967, January 11: Chase YC-122 N122E; between Fort Lauderdale and Bimini in the Bahamas; 4.
30. 1967, January 14: Bonanza N7210B near Key Largo; 4.
31. 1967, January 17: Piper Cherokee N4129P en route St. Thomas from San Juan.
32. 1967, July 2: near Mayaguez, PR, Cherokee N5100W. 4.
33. 1967, August 6: between Miami & Bimini; Piper Cherokee N8165W; 3.
34. 1967, October 3: Cherokee N3775K; Great Inagua for San Juan.
35. 1967, November 8: Cessna 182 N7121E; George Town, Great Exuma and Nassau; 4.
36. 1967, November 22: Cherokee N9443J near Cat Island, Bahamas; 4.
37. 1968, May 29: Cessna 172 N1483F near Grand Turk.
38. 1968, July 8: between Grand Bahama & West Palm Beach; Cessna 180 N944MH; 2.
39. 1969, January 5: Piper Comanche N8653P between Pompano Beach, FL & North Carolina; 2.
40. 1969, February 15: Beechcraft 95-c55 N9490S en route Miami from Georgia.
41. 1969, March 22: a Beechcraft N609R between Kingston, Jamaica & Nassau; 2.
42. 1969, June 6: Cessna 172 N8040L between Grand Turk & Caicos Island; 2.
43. 1969, June 29: a B-95 Beechcraft Executive N590T;

Great Inagua for San Juan.

44. 1969, August 3: Piper PA-22 N8971C; West Palm Beach to Albion, New Jersey; 2.

45. 1969, October 11: Pilattus-Brittan-Norman Islander N852JA; Great Inagua for Puerto Rico; 2.

46. 1970, January 17: Piper Comanche N9078P; between Nassau & Opa Locka, FL; 2.

47. 1970, July 3: between Maiquetia, Venezuela & San Juan, PR. Cessna 310G N1166T; 6.

48. 1970, November 23: Piper Comanche N9346P between West Palm Beach & Kingston, Jamaica; 3.

49. 1971, March 20: a Cessna 177b N30844 with pilot en route Andros Island from Miami at 3:18 p.m.

50. 1971, July 26: Piper (rental); near Barbados; 4.

51. 1971, September 10: Phantom II F-4E Jet; on routine maneuvers 82 miles south of Miami; 2.

52. 1971, December 21: Cessna 150j N61155 with pilot after leaving Pompano Beach; destination unknown.

53. 1972, October 10: Super Constellation N564E between Miami & Santo Domingo; 4.

54. 1973, March 28: Cessna 172 N7050T after leaving West Palm Beach, FL, with pilot.

55. 1973, May 25: a Navion A16 N5126K between Freeport and West Palm Beach; 2.

56. 1973, August 10: Beechcraft Bonanza N7956K; Fort Lauderdale to Marsh Harbour, Bahamas; 4.

57. 1973, August 26: after departing Viaquez, PR; Cessna 150 N50143; 3.

58. 1973, December 20: a Lake Amphibian N39385 between Nassau and Bimini; 3.

59. 1974, February 10: pilot and his Cessna 414 N8103Q vanish after leaving Treasure Cay, Bahamas.

60. 1974, February 10: Brittan-Norman Islander N864JA with pilot at 7:31 p.m. on approach St. Thomas.

61. 1974, July 13: Piper PA-32 N83CA between West Palm Beach & Walker Cay, Bahamas.

62. 1974, August 11: Beech K35 Bonanza N632Q; Pompano Beach, FL. for Philadelphia; 2.

63.	1975, February 25: Piper PA-30 N414DG; Greensboro, NC., to Freeport, GBI; pilot only.
64.	1975, May 2: Cessna "Skymaster" N86011; Fort Lauderdale area.
65.	1975, July 28: Cessna 172 N8936V; vicinity Fort Lauderdale. 1
66.	1975, December 9: Cessna 172 N5182R; St. Croix to St. Kitts. 1.
67.	1976, June 4: Beech D50 N1157; Pahokee, FL., to Dominican Republic; 2.
68.	1976, August 8: Piper PA-28 N6377J; Vera Cruz, Mexico to Brownsville, TX; 1.
69.	1976, October 24: Beech E-50 N5665D; Opa Locka, FL. to Grand Turk Island.
70.	1976, December 28: Piper PA-23 N4573P; Anguilla to Beef Island; 6.
71.	1978, February 22: a KA-6 Navy attack bomber vanished from radar 100 miles off Norfolk en route U.S.S. *John F. Kennedy*; 2.
72.	1978, March 25: Aero Commander 680 N128C; Opa Locka-Imokalee, FL. to Freeport, Grand Bahama; 2.
73.	1978, April 27: Ted Smith 601 N555BU; Pompano Beach to Panama City, FL.; 1.
74.	1978, April 30: Cessna 172 N1GH; Atlantic Ocean; 1.
75.	1978, May 19: Piper PA-28 N47910; Fort Pierce to Nassau; 4.
76.	1978, May 26: Beech 65 N809Q; Haiti to Bahamas; 2.
77.	1978, July 18: Piper PA-31 N689WW; Santa Marta, Col. to Port-au- Prince; 2.
78.	1978, September 21: Douglas DC-3 N407D; Fort Lauderdale to Havana; 4.
79.	1978, November 3: Piper PA-31 N59912; St. Croix to St. Thomas; 1. (right off St. Thomas)
80.	1978, November 20: Piper PA-23 N54615; De Funiak Springs to Gainsville, FL.; 4.
81.	1979, January 11: Beech N925RZ; Miami-St. Thomas; 2.
82.	1979, March: Beechcraft Queen Air N7959R; 2
83.	1979, April 2: Beech E18s N4442; Fort Lauderdale to Cat

Island, Bahamas; 1.
84. 1979, April 24: Piper PA-28R N7480J; Fort Lauderdale to Nassau; 4.
85. 1979, June 30: Cessna 150J N60936; St. Croix to St. Thomas; 2.
86. 1979, September 9: Cessna 182 N2183R; New Orleans to Pensacola, Florida; 3.
87. 1979, October 4: Aero Commander 500 N3815C; Andros Island to West Palm Beach, FL.; pilot;
88. 1979, October 27: Piper PA-23 N13986; Montego Bay, Jamaica to Nassau; pilot.
89. 1979, November 19: Beech D50b N1706; Delray Beach, FL to Key West; 1.
89. 1979, December 21: Piper PA-23 N1435P; Aguadilla to South Caicos Island; 4.
90. 1980, February 11: Beech 58 N9027Q; St. Thomas to unknown; only pilot aboard; reported stolen.
91. 1980, April: Steve Harrison Sr. in a rented Cessna 310.
92. 1980, May 19: Lear Jet N25NE; West Palm Beach to New Orleans; 2.
93. 1980, June 28; Erco 415-D N3808H; Santo Domingo, DR., to San Juan, PR; 2 persons. Pilot reported UFO before disappearing.
94. 1981, January 6: Beech c35 N5805C; Bimini to Nassau.
95. 1982, July 5: Piper PA-28R-201T N505HP; Nashville to Venice, FL.; 4.
96. 1982, September 28: Beech H35 N5999; Marsh Harbour to Fort Pierce, FL.; 2.
97. 1982, October 20: Piper PA-31 N777AA; Anguilla to St. Thomas, VI; 8.
98. 1982, November 5: Beech 65-B80 N1HQ; Fort Lauderdale to Eleuthera Island, Bahamas; 3.
99. 1983, October 4: a Cessna T-210-J N2284R; Andros Town, Bahamas to Fort Pierce, FL.; 3.
100. 1983, November 20: Cessna 340A N85JK disappeared near Orangeville, Fl.; pilot.
101. 1984, March 12: a Piper N39677 between Key West and Clearwater, Florida; 4.

102. 1984, March 31: Cessna 402b N44NC between Fort Lauderdale and Bimini; 6.
103. 1984, December 23: Aeronca 7AC N81947 between Cross City, Florida and Alabama; pilot.
104. 1985, January 14: a Cessna 337 N505CX in Atlantic northeast of Jacksonville; 4.
105. 1985, May 8: Cessna 210k N9465M; Miami to Port-au-Prince, Haiti; pilot.
106. 1985, July 12: Piper N8341L; Nassau to Miami.
107. 1985, August 3: a Cessna 172; somewhere near Fort Meyers, FL.; pilot.
108. 1985, September 8: a Piper N5488W northeast of Key West at 10:08 P.M. en route from Fort Lauderdale;
109. 1985, October 31: Piper N24MS at 8:29 a.m.; between Sarasota, FL. and Columbus, Georgia; pilot.
110. 1986, March 26: a Piper N3527E en route from Miami to West End or Freeport, GBI.; 6.
111. 1986, August 3: A Twin Otter; around St. Vincent; 13.
   1987, April 27: Cessna 337 N25195; Cozumel to Boca Raton, Fl.; 2.
112. 1987, May 27: a Cessna 402c N2652B; Palm Beach, FL. and Marsh Harbour, Great Abaco, Bahamas; 1.
113. 1987, June 3: a Cessna 401 N7896F; Freeport to Crooked Island; 4.
114. 1987, December 2: Cessna 152 N757EQ; La Romana to San Juan; pilot.
115. 1988, February 7: a Beech N844G; Caribbean Sea; 4.
116. 1989, February 6: a Piper N6834J; after departing Jacksonville, Florida; pilot despondent. 1.
117. 1990, January 24: Cessna 152 N4802B on instructional flight; near West Palm Beach, FL.; 2.
118. 1990, June 5: Piper N7202F; St. Maarten to St. Croix.
119. 1990, August 10: Piper N6946D; Sebastian, FL. to Freeport, GBI.; 4. Body found off Virginia.
120. 1991, April 24: Piper Comanche N8938P; off Florida; 1.
121. 1991, May 30: near Long Boat Key; Piper N6376P signaled directional gyro not working; spun into ocean; 2.
122. 1991, October 31: Grumman Cougar N24WJ jet; over

	Gulf of Mexico; vanished on ascent while on radar; 2.
123.	1993, September 30: Within Miami sector; Cessna 152 N93261, with only pilot on board.
124.	1994, August 28: Piper PA-32 N69118; Treasure Cay, Bahamas to Fort Pierce; 2 persons.
125.	1994, September 19: Piper PA-23 N6844Y; Caribbean; 5.
126.	1994, December 25: Piper PA-28 N5916V; unknown; over Florida; pilot.
127.	1996, May 2: Aero Commander N50GV; Atlantic/Caribbean; vanished with 3 in charter service.
128.	1998, August 19: Piper PA-28 N25626; Caribbean; 4.
129.	1999. May 12, Aero Commander N6138X; near Nassau only pilot aboard.
130.	2001, October 27, Cessna 172, after leaving Winterhaven, Florida; only pilot aboard.
131.	2002, September 6, Piper Pawnee N59684, southeast of Nassua, Bahamas; 1.
132.	2003, November 13, a Piper PA-32-300 N8224C went missing after leaving Staniel Cay, Exumas; 1.
133.	2005, June 20: Piper PA-23 N6886Y, Between Treasure Cay, BI, to Fort Pierce, FL.; 3.
134.	2007, April 10: Piper PA-46-310P N444JH, near Berry Islands. Only pilot aboard.
135.	2008, December 15: A Britten-Norman Islander N650LP; Caicos Islands; 11.
136.	2009, December 15: Cirrus SR22 N723LI; GOM; 1.
137.	2012, March 1: 23 miles southeast Boca Raton, FL.; Cessna 182; suicide suspected; 1.

Missing Vessels in the Bermuda Triangle

1.	1917, March, the 1,579 gross ton freighter *Timandra*, bound for Buenos Aires from Norfolk in cargo of coal. 21 crew under Captain Lee.
2.	1918, after March 6: collier U.S.S. *Cyclops* after leaving Barbados for Baltimore; 309 crew and passengers under Lt. Comm. George Worley.
3.	1925, December 1: steamer *Cotopaxi*; 32 crew under

Captain Meyers; Charleston, SC, for Havana, Cuba.

4. 1926, March: freighter *Suduffco*; New York to Los Angeles with 4,000 tons of assorted cargo; 29 crew.

5. 1938, March: 426-foot, 5,500 ton British freighter *Anglo Australian* from Cardiff, Wales, for British Columbia; 38 crew under Captain Parslow. Last reported herself off the Azores: "Passing Fayal this afternoon. All well."

6. 1940, February 4: Schooner *Gloria Colita*, Gulf of Mexico, found derelict and awash.

7. 1948, February: 416-foot, 7,219 ton British freighter *Samkey* reported herself at 41° 48' N longitude, 24° W latitude on January 31. "All well." Crew of 43.

8. 1948, March 6: yacht *Evelyn K.* is found deserted in the Florida Keys; 3 persons missing

9. 1950, April 5: the 185-foot coaster *Sandra*, with a cargo of DDT, disappears in passage to Puerto Cabello, Venezuela, from Savannah, Georgia.

10. 1955, January 13: yacht *H.S.H.*; Bermuda to Antigua.

11. 1955, September 26: yacht *Connemara IV* found derelict 150 miles southeast of Bermuda.

12. 1956, July: schooner *Bounty*; between Bimini and Miami.

13. 1958, January 1: 44-foot yawl *Revonoc* vanished between Key West and Miami; 4 crew.

14. 1960, April 16, yacht *Ethel C.*, missing off Virginia.

15. 1961, April 5: yacht *Callista III*, Norfolk to Bahamas.

16. 1962, November: *Windfall*, a 56-foot schooner left Mystic, Conn. for Bermuda; 5 crew.

17. 1963, February 4: the 504-foot T-2 Tanker *Marine Sulphur Queen*, near Florida Straits; 39 crew.

18. 1963, July 2: fishing vessel *Sno Boy*, between Kingston to Northeast Cay.

19. 1964: 36-foot ketch *Dancing Feathers*, en route Bahamas from North Carolina.

20. 1964, January 14: 58-foot *Enchantress*, 150 miles southeast of Charleston, South Carolina.

21. 1965, October 28: *El Gato*, near Great Inagua, Bahamas.

22. 1967, December 10: *Speed Artist*; Windward Islands.

23. 1967, December 22: cabin cruiser *Witchcraft*; Miami

Harbor; 2 persons
24. 1969, July 4: in the Sargasso Sea freighter *Cotopaxi* sees derelict power yacht on automatic pilot.
25. 1969, July 12: yacht *Vagabond* found derelict on edge of Sargasso Sea.
26. 1969, August: the 2 lighthouse keepers from Great Isaac's Rock lighthouse, near Bimini, missing from their posts without reason.
27. 1969, November 2: cabin cruiser *Southern Cross* found deserted off Cape May.
28. 1971, October 10: 339-foot cargo vessel *El Caribe*, missing in Caribbean Sea.
29. 1971, October 27: fishing yacht *Lucky Edur* found derelict of New Jersey; 3
30. 1971, Christmas-time: something annihilates 53-foot yacht *Ixtapa*, near Florida Keys.
31. 1973, March 21: 541-foot collier s.s. *Anita* vanished in building hurricane off Norfolk en route to Germany.
32. 1973, March 23: 88-foot yacht *Defiance*, derelict, near Cap du Mole, St. Nicholas, Haiti; 4
33. 1974, March: 54-foot luxury yacht *Saba Bank* disappears while cruising Bahamas; 4 crew.
34. 1974, July 24: *Dutch Treat*, Miami to Bahamas.
35. 1975, April 22: 73-foot shrimper *Dawn*, near Smith Shoals, Key West.
36. 1975, June 24: yacht *Meridian*; Bermuda from Norfolk.
37. 1975, December 2: tug *Boundless*; Bahamas.
38. 1976, April: *High Flight;* between Bimini & Miami
39. 1976, October: the 590-foot ore carrier *Sylvia L. Ossa*, about 140 miles west of Bermuda; crew of 37.
40. 1976, December 16: 40-foot sloop with 17 people between St. Kitts and Dominica.
41. 1977, November 20: *L'Avenir*; Maryland to Bermuda.
42. 1979, January 2: tug *King Co-bra*, near Cape Henlopen.
43. 1980, January 12: *Sea Quest* sends mysterious call, navigational equipment not working. Missing with 11 crew.
44. 1980, April: 43-foot luxury yacht *Polymer III*, while cruising Bahamas; 2.

45. 1980, July 26: 38-foot sailboat *Kalia III* found derelict in the Exumas, Bahamas.
46. 1980, October 26: the 520-foot s.s. *Poet*, in cargo of corn, Cape Henlopen, Dl., to Port Said, Egypt.
47. 1982, July 26: American yacht *Penetration* found deserted north of Sargasso Sea.
48. 1982, August 17: British yacht found deserted in Atlantic.
49. 1983, February 26: 44-foot *Sea Lure*, in group of other fishing vessels while headed toward Dry Tortugas. Later found derelict.
50. 1984, November 5\6: the 32-foot sport fishing boat *Real Fine*, Freeport to Fort Lauderdale. 3 persons.
51. 1985, February 22: 25-foot pleasure boat with 2 Canadians aboard; Freeport, to West Palm Beach.
52. 1985, May 3: 6 persons disappear in an outboard off Surf City, North Carolina.
53. 1992, October 27: fishing vessel *Mae Doris*, with 4 crew, south of Cape May.
54. 1996, March 4: 22-foot sailboat; Key West.
55. 1995, March 20: *Jamanic K.*, Motor Vessel of 357 gross tons; Cape Haitien to Miami.
56. 1996, October 14: 65-foot yacht *Intrepid*, 30 miles off Fort Pierce, FL; 16 missing after quick Mayday.
57. 1997, July 14: 25-foot *Atlantic Runner*, North Atlantic.
58. 1997, December: 23-foot *Robalo*, off Virginia Beach.
59. 1998, January 2: fishing vessel *Grumpy* found derelict.
60. 1998, May 1: 35-foot converted sport fisher *Miss Charlotte* hit off North Carolina by force that sucked everything off deck, then sunk; crew survived.
61. 1998, August 10: the *Erica Lynn*.
62. 1998, November: the *Carolina*, off Cape May.
63. 1998, November: 74-foot *Interlude* disappeared during cruise to Cayman Islands.
64. 1999, April 15: *Miss Fernandina*, 85-foot shrimp trawler off Flagler Beach, FL.
65. 1999, April 23: Motor Vessel *Genesis*, 196 gross tons, sailed Port of Spain in cargo of 465 tons brick, water tanks and concrete slabs; at 5:30 bespoke M/V *Survivor*.

Search for vessel was 33,100 sqm.
66. 1999, August 5: 18-foot day cruiser found derelict except for the dog; off North Carolina.
67. 1999, November 15: 2 persons in a 22-foot day cruiser between Frying Pan Shoals and Frying Pan Light.
68. 1999, December 27, *Alyson Selene* found derelict 7 miles northeast of Andros, Bahamas.
69. 2000, April, 228-foot freighter *Gran Rio R* disappears off West Indies.
70. 2000, August 14, fishing vessel *Hemmingway* is found deserted; missing crew and captain.
71. 2001, June 22, 2001, *Tropic Bird;* derelict off Antigua.
72. 2001, *Sophia* derelict Sargasso Sea.
73. 2002, September 23, freighter *Fiona R* missing off West Indies en route to St. Vincent.
74. 2003, June 18: Frank and Romina Leone of West Palm Beach, Fl. vanish with their 16 foot boat off Florida.
75. 2003, August 3: sailing yacht *Windhome*; Beaufort, NC, for Azores June 24. Overdue and reported missing.
76. 2003, August 25, three men vanish with a 32-foot sleek-go-fast white fiberglass vessel in the Bahamas between Exumas and Mayaguana.
77. 2003, October-November: the fishing boat *What's Left?*
78. 2003, November 25: *Peanuts Too*; deserted south of Bermuda.
79. 2004, March 23: the missing 19-foot fishing boat owned by Glenn Jamison is found by fishing vessel *Chummer* about 32 miles west of Egmont Key, Florida. No trace is found of Jamison.
80. 2004, December 21: fishing yola is found abandoned off Puerto Rico, nets deployed and anchored; 1
81. 2006, January 2: James Trindade disappears from his pleasure craft while en route to the US from Bahamas.
82. 2006, June: Cuban fishing vessel *La Curra* is found recently abandoned.
83. 2006, September 18: a partially submerged 18 foot pleasure boat found 9 miles east of Clearwater Beach, with fishing poles, cooler, and life jackets aboard.

84. 2007, September 20: Lindsay Forde vanishes off 45-foot *Extra Labor*.
85. 2007, March 15: 25-foot boat, derelict 27 miles northeast of St. Augustine. Steve Senecal went day fishing.
86. 2007, October 19: *Tranquility* (37-foot) sighted adrift and abandoned 65 miles west of Johns Pass, Florida.
87. 2008, March 16: a 28 foot Wellcraft missing with 3 fishermen between Everglades City and Tampa.
88. 2008, April 17: the 27-foot *Don Chepo* is missing en route from St. Johns, Virgin Islands, for Vieques, Puerto Rico.
89. 2008, May 24: *Holo Ki Ki*, a 36-foot sailboat is found derelict 20 miles north of West End, Grand Bahama.
90. 2008, June 17: Marcos Arguelles disappears from his 22-foot pleasure craft near Soldier Key, Florida.
92. 2009, March: 40-foot gaff Ketch *Lili-oh-La-La* headed to Bahamas from South Carolina is reported overdue.
93. 2009, June 22: Coast Guard suspends search for 3 missing fishermen off Pinones, Puerto Rico. They had departed in a 22-foot beige Grady White fishing boat.
94. 2009, August 17: the 22-foot boat of Mark Portus is found abandoned on the north end of Anclote Key.
95. 2009, September 20: a small 16-foot vessel is found abandoned near Anclote Key. Pet dog remains aboard.
96. 2009, October 11: off Mayaguez, PR; 18-foot Mako; 3
97. 2009, December 13: two men vanish in a 17-foot Largo pleasure craft en route to Bimini.
98. 2010, May: 46-foot *Genesis*.
99. 2010, July 1: *Head or Tails*; derelict Myrtle Beach, FL.
100. 2011, September 15: 36-foot *Know Patience*; off Cape Canaveral, FL.
101. 2012, January 19: *Joy B.* derelict Bahamas; 1
102. 2012, July 8: 23-foot sailboat; derelict off Marathon, Florida Keys.
00. 2012, December 33: *Jeri*; ABC Islands.
103. 2013, January 2: *Galilean*, derelict; Elliot Key; 1
104. 2013, January: sailboat *Blondie*; Florida to Jamaica; 2.
105. 2013, May 14: 39-foot trimaran derelict off Key West.
106. 2013, December 20: *Happy Day Tree*— off Juno Beach.

107.   2014, April 18: *Poker Face* 27-foot Gib found derelict; 1.
108.   2014, May 4: 28-foot *Miss Juliette*; 1.
109.   2015, January 18: *Pelengina II*; north of ABC islands.
110.   2016, March 30: *Anastacia*; Yucatan Channel; 5.

It was in 1990 that the present observer became interested in pursuing the subject of the Bermuda Triangle. It had been 13 years since any book had been published on the subject, the dearth of knowledge amounting to a blackout on the entire topic. Any mention of the Triangle was a recital of old and classic cases, and these usually went hand-in-hand with the statement that the Triangle was an urban myth and the product of poor or sensational reporting.

Yet if there was any basis of truth to the subject, and therefore any relevance for the many theories put forward to try and explain what seemed like inexplicable mysteries, the disappearances should still be continuing, their circumstances still drawing our attention to intriguing albeit frustrating clues. The result of my interest lies above. Dozens upon dozens vanished in the 1980s and 1990s. Disappearances had not abated in those silent years. Indeed, they had increased. Bizarre circumstances were far better documented, but left silently in storage boxes. It is now 13 years after the first publication of these incidents (*Into the Bermuda Triangle*, McGraw-Hill, 2003). Disappearances have continued in the last 13 years. Some provide surprising themes while at the same time others present some peculiar patterns that don't fit with the consistency of the previous decades.

A TBM Avenger bearing Fort Lauderdale NAS's markings. (NARA)

A BSAA Tudor IV; from the collection of J.C. McPhee. (Joan Beckett)

The DC-3 is one of the most reliable aircraft ever built. NC16002 vanished in 1948. N407D, below, vanished in 1978. (Alexander Avrane)

The crew of Sky Shield II's Pogo 22, a large B-52 which vanished without trace. Below, left, one of the crewmen, Helmut Christ (Karl Christ). Right, Steve Harrison Sr, whose disappearance in 1980 did not appear in the records. (Pam Harrison)

An F-104 Starfighter similar to the one that vanished in 1960 off Bermuda. Below, the Marine Sulphur Queen. (NARA)

Chapter 5

A Triangle of Today

Disappearances within the Bermuda Triangle in the last decade have basically been concentrated in the same sections of it as those over the century before, that is, in the southwest corner off Miami, amidst the Florida Keys, and within the Bahamas. Except for an emphasis on boats rather than aircraft, the same general circumstances have prevailed— none transmitted any clear Maydays nor, except in one possible incident, was an EPIRB signal picked up by any base station. While piracy can explain the incidents, both in terms of location and the utter silence of the victims, it should be noted that few of the missing boats were valuable to piracy. Pirates hijack large, fast cruisers which are the only models that make drug running viable. Sailboats, small day cruisers and sport craft do not, and yet these are precisely the kinds that have vanished most quantitatively over the last decade.

Unexplained disappearances near shore in the past have been very limited. The disappearance within a span of only 19 minutes of the cabin cruiser *Witchcraft* in 1967 was the most sensational whereas for aircraft the two disappearances while coming in for a landing at St. Thomas are the most inexplicable. Until recent years the *Witchcraft*'s loss was the closest to land much less to a harbor that any boat has vanished in the Triangle, one of four principle elements that make it the most sensational nautical disappearance. The other contributing elements are the short time span, the fact something was below the boat that either Burack hit or it hit Burack, and the fact that the cabin cruiser had built-in floatation.

To underscore the inherent mystery in the case of the *Witchcraft*, especially in an unsinkable boat, it would be wise to contrast this case with a more recent and tragic loss at sea. This is the disappearance (initially) of the 25-foot *What's Left?* near the Bay of Florida on October 17, 2002, and its reappearance two weeks later on November 3 capsized and beached at Cape Canaveral, an estimated distance of 400 miles. Presumably, it had drifted the entire time without being noticed by a massive Coast Guard search. Inside the cabin was the body of Gary Lisk, the owner. He seems to have been caught off guard in a lightning-like moment, with one shoe on and the other off, an indication that whatever happened caught him between dressing or undressing. The whereabouts of the other two aboard, Neil Eddleman and his son Neil Jr., remain unknown. Given the circumstances, it seems Lisk was preparing to come topside, perhaps even called by Eddleman, when the boat was capsized or something else happened that took the Eddlemans' off the boat. The Coast Guard speculated that the boat had drifted capsized; the reason why it had not been visually sighted was its aqua painted bottom, although the boat may have capsized in the surf as it came into shore with the breakers.

Yet by contrast the *Witchcraft*, at harbor's mouth, totally vanished and did so in a brief interim between the call for assistance at 9:03 p.m. and the arrival of the cutter at 9:21 p.m. If one does not accept the extraordinary, then the only other possibility is criminal, intentional disappearance, an unlikely fit for the successful Dan Burack and his friend, Father Horgan.

Standing on its own, considerable mystery surrounds the *What's Left?* The trio's destination was the wreck of the California about 65 miles southwest of Marco Island but still within the Gulf. This location cannot explain how it drifted into the swift Gulf Stream current in order for it to drift around Florida into the Atlantic. Nor can the speed of the drift be understood. It drifted 400 miles in only two weeks, a speed hard to imagine if it was capsized the entire time. One clue suggests the boat was trying to escape something. The throttles were found fully engaged. Why then was the skipper, Lisk, inside the cabin and not manning the helm? No water was in his lungs, so he was dead before the boat capsized. Yet his spine had been transected, which could not have happened from capsizing. An alternate explanation is that the Eddlemans were no longer aboard and Lisk, below, was hiding, unconscious or dead as the hydrosport sped on until it reached the Gulf Stream on its own. Such a scenario will repeat itself with derelict boats, though it doesn't explain in this case why Lisk would remain ensconced in the cabin below; or how he got a broken back.

Similarly, on August 17, 2009, a 22-foot fishing boat was found hard aground on a sandbar near the northern tip of Anclote Key, its throttles engaged and engine still running. The owner, Mark Portus, had gone fishing near the key early in the morning, some 12 hours before it was found at 7:30 p.m.

During the last decade a number of abandoned boats turned up in unusual circumstances along the same track line between the Keys and along the Gulf coast, with a disturbing concentration around Anclote Key.

A month later on September 20, 2009, the 16-foot sport craft of Paula Migliorini was found drifting deserted about 3 miles north of Anclote Key. Her pet dog was still aboard, so were the keys and her towel. Although her body was later found off Hudson Beach, there is an element of mystery here because this was one of several other incidents in the same area where boats were being found deserted and the bodies later found near Hudson Beach, proof they had fallen or bene pulled over.

Only the week before, on September 13, 2009, a boat grounded near Boca Chica, Florida. The Coast Guard discovered it belonged to David Schermerhorn and that he had been diving near Middle Sambo, a reef 5 miles south of Key West. During the Coast Guard search, the remains of a body where found, with legs gone, but it was not clearly identifiable if the remains were Schermerhorn's. The condition of the boat indicated Schermerhorn was about to dive when something came along and ripped it free, presumably throwing him into the water. The dive flag was up and 100 feet of anchor line was extended, though the end was frayed and the anchor no longer attached. His clothes, cellphone, and wallet were aboard.

Some clues do not add up. Chris Macquarrie left Siesta Key on July 12, 2010, to go snorkeling, a shallow water sport, and he was due back by 8:30 p.m. that night. Yet on July 16 his boat was found deserted 38 miles west of Sanibel Island, in deep water. This makes for quite a drift from the area of Sarasota, Florida, about 60 miles away. The only conclusion was that the boat drifted there and was not seen by anyone, including the Coast Guard, until then.

In almost the precise location where *What's Left?* was bound, about 30 miles north of Key West, at 4:13 a.m., an EPIRB briefly sounded on May 14, 2013, indicating trouble. It was registered to Jay Rydberg for his *3/4 Time*, a 39-foot trimaran. He had left Fort Myers the day before for a leisurely cruise to Key West. Before Coast Guard units could overfly the area, the signal was quickly extinguished. The boat was soon declared missing. Strangely, however, at the end of the month the trimaran was found beached in Cuba. Attached to it at the end of a line was Rydberg, dead apparently from drowning. Although it is common for a single-handed sailor to attach a "lifeline" to himself while sailing alone, there is no explanation for how the EPIRB had been triggered and why, on the face of it, Rydberg had fallen over, jumped, been knocked over or had been pulled over.

On May 04, 2014, Robert Garcia departed Key West, Florida, for a day fishing in his 28-foot *Miss Juliette* (white hull with a distinctive yellow stripe along the side). The weather was perfect; the trip should have been uneventful. No trace was found, even by fast response cutters like the *Margaret Norvell*.

Unlike with the previous decades, closer-to-shore disappearance of vessels and, far more intriguing, closer-to-shore

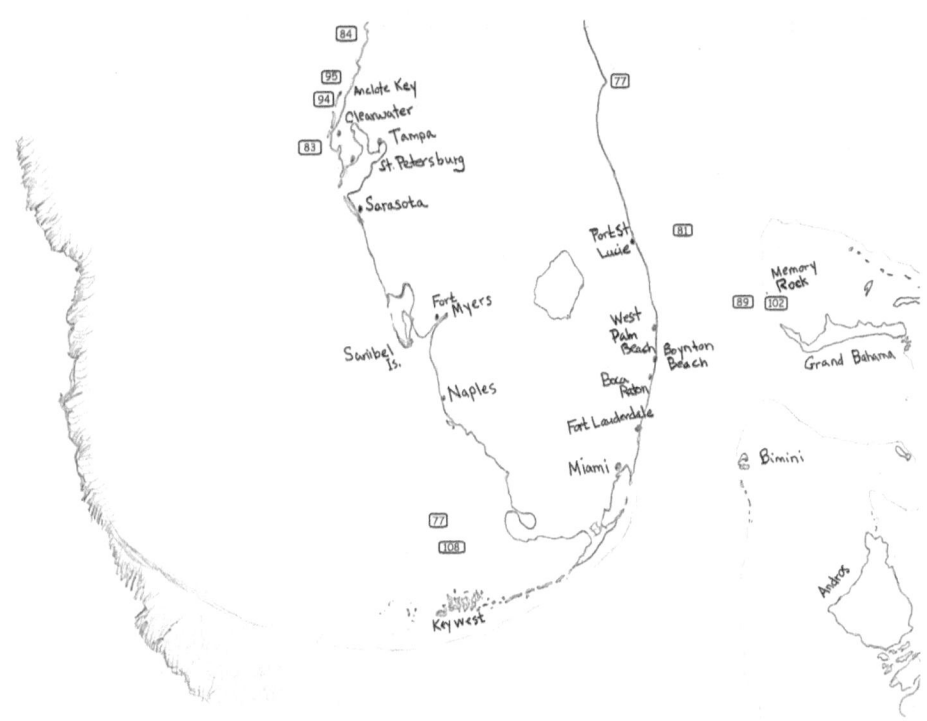

Locations of some of the more curious cases of disappearances or derelicts. Refer to index beginning on page 101.

disappearance of crews from sound boats, has almost become the norm in the 21st century.

Among these cases is the disappearance of Dominic Porcaro on December 20, 2013, from his 26-foot cuddy cabin cruiser *Happy Day Tree*. He had taken it for a cruise in Jupiter Inlet, north of West Palm Beach. The vessel was later found shipshape but grounded near Juno Beach in the Atlantic. An extensive Coast Guard search at sea, which included helicopters and fixed wing aircraft, failed to find any trace of his body.

The case was mysterious enough that organized crime was ephemerally blamed. Dominic's brother, John, had been accused of having been a part of the Gambino crime family and was even indicted in 2003 on charges of a telemarketing scandal. However, by this time John had long vanished. In 1998 he had left his wife Filamena a note reading "Fil, went fishing, got call, swordfish are biting. Love, J. I'll call you later." Rather he disappeared and his car, cellphone and keys were found at the Fort Lauderdale airport.

The simplest theory, however, seems preferable. Since Porcaro had been arrested the day before for DUI, one theory offered that he had gone to sea without having fully recovered and simply fell overboard. In response to this, Maureen Porcaro, Dominic's younger brother's wife, declared that Dominic was an avid boater. "He's had many, many boats and has never had any problems."

When accident seems improbable, intentional disappearance always seems a safe theory to fall back on, despite the fact there is no evidence for it as well. Disappearances of this character not only happen frequently, they happen in circumstances that would seem to preclude any intentionality.

For instance, off West Palm Beach on June 18, 2003, Frank and Romina Leone had vanished after leaving in their 16-foot boat from the Lantana Boat Ramp for day sailing. A search as large as the State of Georgia failed to uncover a trace.

On December 20, this time in 2009, it was announced that another boat had vanished, a 17-foot Key Largo with 2 Miami men aboard en route to Bimini from Haulover Inlet, Miami. Richard Alicea and Edwin Pritchard had been missing a week (since December 13) by the time the announcement had been made. A 6 day search turned up no sign of them.

A controversial disappearance is that of James Trindade on January 13, 2006. He left Memory Rock, Bahamas, in his tri-engine Donzi. In company of 2 other boats, a 35-foot and a 22-foot vessel, all three headed southwest across the Gulf Stream to Boynton Beach, Florida, and home. According to the other boaters Trindade, with his powerful Donzi, was ahead of them when their 35-foot boat began to experience trouble. Both vessels attempted to reach Trindade by VHF radio. Although he was in sight ahead, he did not answer. Until they lost sight of him, they continued to try to alert Trindade they were intentionally falling behind. The two vessels diverted to the Boca Yacht Club in Palm Beach, Florida. Arriving hours later, there they were surprised to hear Trindade had never arrived at Boynton Beach. A search quickly ensued. A falcon jet found

Trindade's Donzi aimlessly speeding in circles about 38 miles off Port St. Lucie, having drifted considerably north in the fast Gulf Stream current. A Dolphin helicopter lowered a swimmer at 3:20 a.m. No one was aboard. Everything was shipshape.

Sailor John Batchelor apparently met his fate near Memory Rock as well. Popular and well-known amidst the sailing circuit, he was at 72 described as similar looking to Earnest Hemingway. Friends also knew he had an unpublished manuscript aboard— "The Drunken Monkey." He was considered "a crusty old curmudgeon" and purely a man of the sea. He had been born in England, lived in Nigeria and then Australia where he had left his wife. He didn't own a house but preferred to live on his boat *Joy B*. Always aboard with him on his sailboat was his pet dog Dingo.

When sighted deserted on January 19, 2012, off Memory Rock the *Joy B* was riding at anchor. Rescuers boarded and found Dingo alone and nearly starved to death. Rotten oranges hung in their mesh bag from the pilot house ceiling. The dinghy was still on its davits. The side door was open, the swim ladder down. Had Batchelor gone over the side for a routine reason and simply drowned? Dingo, however, had a deep gash on a hind leg but somehow had survived for about 3 weeks alone, an estimation based on Batchelor's last routine entry in his log.

Salvage specialist Gary Simmons came to the *Joy B* the day after discovery in order to tow the boat back. He found a Kevlar rope hanging from the boat when he arrived. According to the *Globe and Mail*:

> Divers set them up to anchor to the seabed, but they float freely when not in use. Friends believe Batchelor ran over the rope, which slowed his progress significantly. They speculate he anchored and dove into the water. Then he cut the rope, tossed it on the boat, but couldn't, for whatever reason, get back on board. The current was strong and the area is also known for sharks.

An interesting theory, but for one factor: it does not explain the wound on Dingo. Like Rydberg, he also would have

Memory Rock

attached a lifeline to himself, and this should have been found trailing over the side. Moreover, why throw a cut line back on board when it is easier to get back on board and pull it up?

Some of those who had known Batchelor for years were suspicious of the circumstances, especially those in the Ontario, Canada, sailing community from which he had come. According to Robin Morrish: "He was healthy. He was alert. He was competent and, most of all, John Batchelor was not a wuss. If somebody came aboard, he would have tried to take them on himself, which makes me quite nervous."

Robin Morrish's wife echoed the opinion that there was foul play. "Mr. Batchelor had been living on his boat for decades, and it was his 18th sailing trip south, so it's unlikely he made a mistake and fell." Another friend, Ruth Allen, knew he wouldn't go swimming in that water. "The whole thing is just wrong."

More than any of them, Mrs. Morrish captured the spirit of the vast ocean and that unforgiving horizon, expressing a sentiment that can apply not just to John Batchelor's case but to all those who have vanished. "A man disappeared in the middle of the ocean. Nobody's ever going to know. This is what happens when you cruise, it happens in international waters, out of sight of land and there's nobody to rescue you."

On May 26, 2008, the Coast Guard finally suspended the

long search for Peer Steenburg, who was sailing the 36-foot sailboat *Holo Ki Ki*. The vessel was first sighted abandoned by another boat drifting lifeless 20 miles north of West End, Grand Bahama, near Memory Rock. The vessel could not have been abandoned very long, as Steenburg had recently left nearby Fort Lauderdale to take the *Holo Ki Ki* to Holland.

Multifactorial causes no doubt apply to the wide array of vessels found derelict. However, the most interesting remain those that indicate they were abandoned in fair weather before foul weather damaged them, or those with indications they hit something below.

Deserted boats of this nature happen even far from land and potential pirates, and yet curiously the derelicts show signs they were ripped from their anchorage, with cut or frayed lines, or they had hit something.

On January 15, 2014, veteran Dutch sailor Sietse Hagen had left Tenerife for Barbados in the West Indies in his sailboat *Poker Face*. Months later (on April 8) a freighter en route from Savannah, Georgia, to Agadir in Morocco, sighted *Poker Face* drifting aimlessly in the Sargasso Sea. No sign of Hagen was found aboard the vessel. However, when the rescue crew boarded the sailboat (a 27 foot Gib), it was heavily damaged. The captain could only liken it to the boat having been beached, though this was naturally impossible in mid-Atlantic. The weather had also been good, so that the damage was not caused by storm. The paperwork was taken and the sailboat was sunk as a hazard to navigation.

In March 2001, a large sailboat was sighted 300 miles south of Bermuda by the crew of the yacht *Tintinara*. The boat was a wreck, dismasted, the sails tattered and hanging over the side. Carolyn Grant, who was one of those aboard the *Tintinara*, describes it:

> The name on the transom was *Sophia* and the hailing port Nantes, France. It appeared to be about 45 feet with a center cockpit and an aft cabin. I'm not sure what make it was, but since the hailing port was French, I figured the boat was one of those weird-looking French designs. Regardless, the mast was com-

pletely gone. The only thing at the mast step was mangled stainless, which I assumed was a mast pulpit. The starboard life-lines were gone, which gave evidence that it lost the rig to starboard and the scratches on the starboard freeboard added to the theory that it rolled or the rig went down on the starboard side. Shredded sails were daggling in the water from the broken forestay on the bow, and half the boom was hanging off the stern. The waterline had brown stains on it. At the time we thought they were diesel or oil stains from a possible leak or malfunction. There was no sign of life on board from what we could see. We circled a number of times blasting the air-horn and hailing for anyone on board.

Despite not knowing the cause of what befell *Sophia,* Grant still expressed the anxiety that comes with finding a derelict. "Pat and I looked at each other disconcertingly. 'I don't like this,' I said quietly. 'Neither do I,' he replied."

Tintinara was 550 miles north of Antigua, literally in the middle of the Triangle, and equally far from any help for themselves if something should now happen. However, due to calm weather *Tintinara*'s captain, Pat, was able to board the vessel. He was an experienced captain and his eyes noticed much. The cabin was a shambles, but the boat was dry. There was water in the bilge, but not up to the floor. The boat had clearly rolled around. Everything was strewn on the floor. The vessel must have been derelict a long time. The paper products had all disintegrated, and he could find no logbook. He decided to scuttle the *Sophia* as a navigational hazard.

Pat Grant had been right. The *Sophia* had been derelict a long time. A check with the Coast Guard confirmed that the vessel was reported missing a year before. They were thanked, Grant recalls, for scuttling the hazard.

Pondering the mystery, Grant recalled that they continued to wonder what had happened to *Sophia*'s crew. She had noted that the "primary winch still had three wraps from the jib sheet, and the handle was still in the winch. Whoever was on board had been sailing her to the end and most likely in good weather because both companionway hatches were open. The deflated dinghy was lashed to the stern. The dinghy outboard was still mounted to the transom."

Grant admitted that the crew considered many scenarios as to what might have happened. Anxious to know if the people aboard had been rescued, the Grants asked but the Coast Guard never replied. However, Pat had remembered that alerts had been set up the year before for "Sophia" in St. Lucia. This appeared to be the same boat. She had departed France for the West Indies and vanished. The crew of the *Tintinara* had finally discovered her fate. Like so many other vessels, *Sophia* must have been near the Triangle when whatever happened happened. Like so many others the sailboat probably had drifted around the entire Sargasso Sea and came back yet again to reside in the heart of the Triangle.

On July 14, 1997, another yacht had drifted in the currents north of the Sargasso Sea to the Azores and was found abandoned. The *Atlantic Runner* (a 25-foot sailboat) had a broken mainmast but was otherwise shipshape. No evidence was found aboard to indicate what happened to its skipper, John McMurrer, who had been sailing from Massachusetts.

Heart attacks and strokes can overtake the single-handed sailor. In the case of the *Marigold*, a Tayana 37, the vessel grounded on February 6, 2009, on Trinidad, far off course from Barbados where Terry Green, the skipper, had been headed from the Canaries. His body was found aboard. He had last been in touch with the weatherman a month before (January 15) complaining of what he thought was a mild heart attack. His boat was then seen drifting off the Blanchisseuse coast.

Unlike with Hagen and Green, it is more common that derelicts are found with no evidence aboard to suggest what happened to their occupant(s). The disappearance of 69 year old Ulysses Didier is the exception. His 37-foot *Tranquility* was found drifting 65 miles off St. Johns Pass, Florida, October 2007. The first inkling of danger came at 3:15 p.m. when a Sundancer circled the vessel and noticed it had a broken railing. Upon boarding, the log was consulted and it revealed the vessel had not been abandoned long. The last entry on October 15 indicated that Didier was going to anchor for the day, but apparently upon going topside he fell or was pulled over.

Age is a factor quickly raised in any discussion of the large number of 60 plus year old boaters who have disappeared from their vessels, often valuable ones deservedly earned by retirement that no one would willfully abandon. These lost boaters grew up in the 1960s when to be the adventurous sea navigator and surfer was popular sport for the young. Now aging and stubborn they continue to sail the seas alone, either sure of their skill and health or indifferent to the consequences of death at sea. For some indeed this is preferable to the prospects of a slow death in assisted living.

On February 6, 2009, the 24-foot sailboat *Blue Star* had drifted into the inlet at St. Augustine. The skipper, John Franklin, was 69 years old. The last time he was seen was at 9 a.m. the morning before when he left Vilano Beach near the Comanche Cove marina. *Blue Star* must not have been abandoned that long, for the motor was still running when it was found. Still, no trace of the body was found, though this was close to shore.

Age may also be factor in the disappearance of Marcos Arguelles from his boat. He was 67 years old and went on a fishing jaunt off the coast of Florida on June 18, 2008. A search found nothing but did locate his empty 22-foot pleasure craft near Soldier Key.

Among the examples of elderly sailors vanishing from their sailboats is the case of Mark Myhre, 62. Outside Miami Harbor on the ocean side of Elliot Key his sailboat the *Galilean* was found beached on January 2, 2013. Myhre had last been heard from on Christmas Day by family members.

It was simply assumed that Arend Van Der Hoven fell off his 23-foot boat on July 8, 2012. He had left the marina at 8 a.m. but did not return as scheduled by 2 p.m. A huge search finally found his boat drifting aimlessly south of Marathon in the Florida Keys.

Regardless of the age of the individual missing, derelicts have long continued to turn up in similar locations. Decades ago the missing occupants were often much younger than today's victims. Since age is becoming an obvious factor today, one has to dutifully note that older sailors are far more common now than younger ones. The sport is not as popular with the young, and those still in business cannot afford the time.

So called "straw man" arguments are asserted in an attempt to minimize the phenomenon of derelict vessels. These include falling over (most common) from a variety of causes—heart attacks, strokes—going over the side for a reason, such as to unfoul a line or inspect the hull, and, curiously, even from panic. Some of these causes can explain derelicts in the Triangle, but taken as a whole the Triangle's drifters are not so easily explained. Proponents who believe that the disappearances can only be the result of intelligence note that although it may be true that only individuals had been aboard most of these derelicts, it is nevertheless true that in no other section of the world's oceans do individuals fall over so frequently and vanish, despite the fact the Mediterranean and parts of the oceans off Australia are heavily trafficked.

It is interesting to note that in the case of derelicts where the sole operator was older none of them except Green, the skipper of the *Marigold*, if they did suffer a stroke or heart attack did so in a position where they might simply die aboard the vessel. In each case it must have been where they would then fall over.

A general pattern also seems apparent in the Bermuda Triangle disappearances. Once a close-to-shore disappearance was rare and now it is largely the rule. Proponents of the theory that crews are being intentionally removed note that deep water sailing is not so common anymore and hasn't been since Florida's economic decline for the last 15 years, precisely the time in which disappearances have come closer to shore, as if whatever had been causing the disappearances no longer had the ample opportunities far out at sea and had, as a necessity, to move in closer to shore. Noting that a natural phenomenon cannot follow such a pattern, proponents of the "abduction theory" propose the only alternative is an intelligent, directed purpose. Believers in UFO abductions will raise a number of points, as we shall see, to not only assert a motive but also the ability for how UFOs could do this.

Another age-old pattern that plays into these theories is, however, an established fact. Pets, whether dogs, cats, birds, or even monkeys, never go missing. They remain aboard the ship. On the other hand, talking parrots are either found dead or missing with their owners. Ivan Sanderson and Charles Berlitz made a case for this phenomenon suggesting UFO abduction, noting that speech indicated intelligent life to "aliens" and therefore the parrot was also seized. However, it should be noted that parrots have actually been arrested and questioned by police in regards to possible pirate connections. Such was the case of Percy. Rented for a British teleplay based on the tales of Long John Silver, Percy let out with a string of filth just before show time, including telling the director to bloody well "bugger off." Although the actors considered this a normal response to any director, this did not reflect the fine Amazonian background the pet store had pitched to rent the parrot to the production company. It indicated a far more lurid background that brought the parrot in for questioning. Pirates, who are rank throughout the Triangle, would not likely leave a talking parrot behind to somehow divulge something later to the authorities that it might have picked up during the deadly encounter.

Locations for derelicts nevertheless seem to follow the pattern of UFO reports. Anibal Rodriquez is another victim of mystery off Mayaguez, Puerto Rico, a location noted for decades for its high activity of UFO reports. His fishing vessel was found anchored only half a mile off shore, with nets still deployed. He had last been seen on Sunday, December 19, 2004, and intended to return Monday early. If he had fallen off his boat, why did he not get back on? It was riding at anchor.

On June 19, 2009, three more fishermen had vanished near San Juan, this time in a 21-foot Grady White. They had left Piñones on Friday. They went to cast line at a nearby reef and were never seen again. They were due back by 3 a.m. Saturday, giving rise to the possibility they had rammed the reef in the darkness. Without having found a trace, the Coast Guard sector commander, Captain Eduardo Pino, nevertheless said: "This case is a regrettable tragedy and another reminder of the dangers and respect that we must have for the sea."

The disappearance of *Don Chepo* is another case in point in the Triangle's southern corner. She had left the US Virgin Islands (St. John's) bound for Viequez Island on the eastern coast of Puerto Rico and due to arrive there on May 15, 2008. It was not a long voyage for Phil Fredericks, and the 27-foot *Don Chepo* carried enough safety gear and was powered by two 200 horsepower Evinrude outboards. Despite aggressively searching the area for 5 days, the Coast Guard located nothing.

One motive UFO theorists do not raise, however, merits interjecting here— destruction and not abduction. There is only one truly confirmed type of UFO/USO, but it is too small to be involved in abduction. It is an ovoid disc 10 by 12 feet and only a few feet thick. Yet its sightings and observed behavior actually fit the pattern required by the theory. Originally, it was seen far out in the Atlantic, but it has in the decades since first seen come so close into shore that it has been struck at by fishermen and even Coast Guardsmen, the latter incident inspiring a sobering report which was later released through FOIA request initiated by CAUS (Citizens Against UFO Secrecy). This case is the Pascagoula USO incident (not to be confused with the supposed UFO abduction).

On the night of November 6, 1973, this ovoid disc crept silently into the shallows near Petit Bois Island where 4 groups of fishermen—the Ryans and the Rices— were mullet fishing in skiffs. It had some form of light source on top from which it illuminated the water over it. After recovering from his surprise, Rayme Ryan struck at it with his oar. The object was metallic. The group finally concentrated around it and struck at it more. Rayme Ryan then struck at it with "intent to kill." It finally dimmed its light and left. About 30 minutes later he went to check on his fish buoy. The disc had actually been sitting beneath it waiting. It re-illuminated. The group called the Coast Guard. Guardsmen Chuck Crews and Larry Nations came in a 16 foot boat. They too soon found the USO and struck at it. Crews was also sure it was metallic. The USO eventually moved on to the southwest before it finally disappeared.

This encounter was so startling that it was also reported in the local newspaper. Two officers, E.A. Wilbanks and Lt.

Commander C.E. Dorman, were dispatched from the Naval Ship Research and Development Lab at Panama City, Florida, to investigate. After interviewing all witnesses, they report:

> Light from object was directed toward surface; it appeared to come from a coherent source approximately 3" diameter, with a surface intersection circular or elliptical in shape and approximately 10' x 12' in size. Color was generally described as yellowish/amber, or with a light red tint. Intensity varied from "almost too bright to look at" to zero, depending on amount of disturbance (brightest when first approached). When seen from the side, it was described as looking like a parachute underwater.
>
> Object felt metallic when struck, but could not be consistently struck. Portion of oar underwater was not visible from surface when in light beam from object. Object "turned off" when struck with beam from flashlight; when light removed, object reilluminated to previous intensity in about 1 minute.
>
> In its generalized SW travel, object appeared to stop when it encountered an anchored boat. . . It would then remain in area until disturbed for 15 to 30 minutes.

The first time such an object was seen and described it was in the air skimming about 70 feet over the Atlantic. The date was August 4, 1950. The report came from the captain and two crew o f a freighter off the Jersey coast heading toward the Gulf Stream. It is contained in CIA files released under FOIA request. It was silver metallic, an "ovular" or ellipsoidal disc, and the captain marveled that it was only about 10 feet in diameter and a few feet thick. One of the other crew described it as an egg cut in half lengthwise— basically the Pascagoula USO, parachute shape on top but with an essentially flat bottom. It sped off toward Nova Scotia, following a path out of the Triangle.

Acknowledging the existence of these discs does not mean endorsing the "UFO theory," but one can well imagine that the unexpected appearance of such an object off the beam of a boat, especially for a lone sailor, could result in them panicking and falling overboard. There seems no question the Pascagoula USO showed no fear and repeatedly wanted to find a fisherman while he was alone.

The thin bottom sands of the Great Bahama Bank have been host to a strange phenomenon. Lines are found etched on the bottom appearing very much like a furrow made by dragging an anchor or from the wake of something very speedy. However, the problem is that these lines have been observed to cross over small islands, as though whatever caused them could simply fly out and over the sandbar or island and continue on.

Groups of such underwater lights have been known to "haunt" such places as Moselle Reef (Shoals) near Bimini and, to be introduced later, larger versions up to 60 feet diameter have been seen below the waters of the Triangle.

Undersea unidentified objects have been reported in ship losses in the Triangle. Reports of encounters with these objects tend to come from larger vessels since they more frequently survive the impact. While northeast of Bermuda in March 2000 the 770-foot *Leader L.* was hit so hard by a "metallic object" that it knocked a loose hull plate off, sinking the vessel in under a minute. Had 12 crewmen not been able to scramble off, the vessel would in effect have vanished.

Off Tobago on April 11, 2000, the 228-foot freighter *Gran Rio 'R'* sent a weak message saying they had been holed. The captain requested a pump standing by at Crown Point, their destination. Though only 2 hours away, the vessel vanished. No GPS system triggered indicating the vessel had sunk, and the captain had not indicated there was an emergency.

Two years later in September 2002 the *Fiona 'R,'* also owned by the Rambarran shipping clan, and with one of the owners aboard as captain, vanished somewhere near St. Vincent, with nothing more hazardous than a cargo of sand. Its GPS also had not triggered.

On October 7, 2010, the s.s. *Mystic*, from Miami to Haiti, hit an underwater object over Cay Sal Bank and sank into the shallows. The 10 crew were able to get off and be rescued.

There is a particularly disturbing and lightning-like disappearance that remains a curious example of unexplained causes in the Triangle. The *Extra Labor* was en route to St. Petersburg, Florida, from Texas on September 29, 2007. Michael Swindle, the new owner, was an inexperienced seaman so he had hired veteran sailor Lindsay Forde to pilot the 45-foot luxury yacht. Somewhere off Bayport, Florida, north of the Anclote Key area, Swindle went below for some reason. When he came back up, Forde was no longer at the helm. He had disappeared. Swindle had heard no cry for help, nor could he see anybody in the water. The Coast Guard concluded, with a certain ambiguity: "We have suspended our active search pending further developments, meaning if new information comes to light we would consider resuming our search. But at this time, we are confident that if Forde was in the area we searched, we would have found him."

Coast Guard cutter *Kodiak Island* rushed to the scene of another incident on September 18, 2006. A passing boat 9 miles off Clearwater, Florida, south of Anclote Key, reported that an 18-pleasure craft was found partially waterlogged. The fishing poles were still aboard, plus the food cooler and life jackets. The Coast Guard had not received any reports of overdue boaters that correlate with this case.

On June 28, 2011, Randall Ward rented a 24-foot hurricane sundeck from Bahia Mar Marina at Fort Lauderdale for a cruise off shore. He was expected back at 7 p.m. As the Coast Guard summarized: "A Coast Guard Station Lake Worth Inlet. Fla., boat crew was immediately launched and located Ward's rented boat floating adrift with no signs of Ward."

Far from the pirate sea lanes, Andy Richmond entered the Triangle by this same unlikely means on July 1, 2010. He was traveling between home (Ocean Isle Beach, North Carolina) south past South Carolina when his 28-foot *Heads or Tails* was found beached on Myrtle Beach that night at 11:20 p.m., engine still running and no sign of Richmond.

Piracy played some kind of hand (it is assumed anyway) in the deserted *Offshore Pergola*, a derelict and ransacked catamaran that eventually washed ashore in Guyana on April 17, 2015, but probably had been abandoned in the Windward Islands. Axel Verlohr had set sail from the Cape Verdes across the Atlantic in mid-March intending to set in along the tropical islands and then coast down to Trinidad. At some point, probably after he had mysteriously vanished from the boat, "salvagers" came along and ransacked it.

Perhaps more should be made of the case of the *Offshore Pergola* considering its condition was similar to that of Hagan's *Poker Face* of the year before. Both were considered wrecked but not by storm. Perhaps there is even more. Off these same Leeward Islands retired US Navy captain Tom Olchefske was cruising in his 38-foot sailboat *Tropic Bird*. On June 8, 2000, something happened while he was writing the noon log below by his radar set. The interrupted entry in the log read: "12:56 p.m. Off Grenada, making good time" without a finished longitude and latitude notation. He came topside, apparently to check out a radar return, and vanished. On June 22 his sailboat was found beach hundreds of miles north on an Antiguan reef, engine out of gas.

Investigation of single-handed derelicts often does not take place due to the assumption the skipper merely had fallen over. Boat ownership or transference is processed at shore or sometimes the boat is just sunk at sea. The case of the *Pelengina II* is typical. The sailboat was posted missing on January 5, 2015, being then long overdue at Martinique. On January 21, the International Boat Watch Net received the following information from Eelco de Wal, Sr. Operator, JRCC Curaçao, Dutch Caribbean Coast Guard.

> On January 18th 2015, S/V Pelengina II found (Derelict) within territorial waters of Honduras. Vessel has been towed towards port. Person on board still unaccounted for. Assumption is he fell overboard, between 17th and 21st December 2014, North of ABC-Islands.

Abandoned boats are not the only mysteries in the Triangle in the last decade. Disappearances continue to occur, both of boats with individuals aboard and those with multiple passengers or crew.

Although to the preferences of the present observer the Yucatan Channel would seem too far from the strict Triangle, it is actually much closer than those areas far up the Florida west coast and certainly closer than the location of such famous

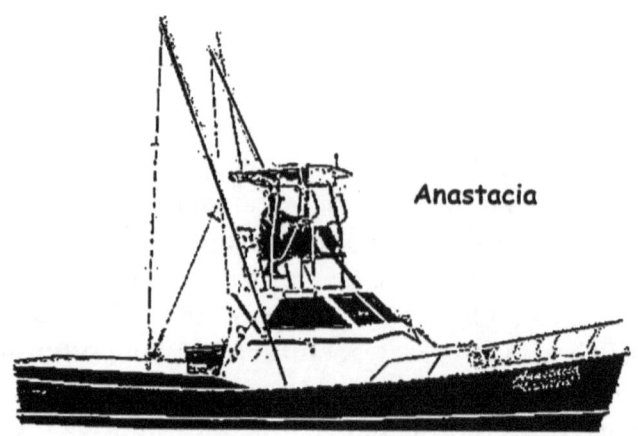
Anastacia

mysteries often included in the Triangle's litany as the *Southern Cities* off Texas. A particularly sensational disappearance here is one of the most recent. The 40-foot sportsfisher *Anastacia* left Isla Mujeres on March 30, 2016, to shark overnight off Punta Molas, Cozumel, with 5 seasoned captains and divers aboard. The distinctive blue vessel has completely vanished, with no trace. There was no SOS.

Long journeys make uncovering disappearances more tenuous. BOLOs (Be on the Lookout) for a vessel are about as much information as there is. Such is the case with the yacht *Lilly-Oh-La-Lah*, a 40 foot ketch. "All yachts in the Bahamas, T&C, Dominican Republic, Virgins":

> Description: the Lilly-oh-la-lah, 40' Gaff Ketch, wooden spars, white hull with green stripe along the hull shearline, possibly New Jersey Reg. Number painted in white on the green stripe, could be under American or British flag, crew/owner Kenny Jackson of Guernsey, Channel Islands and with black cat answering to the name "Buddy." Yacht is equipped with VHF.

Jackson had left Charleston, South Carolina, March 23, 2009, bound for Nassau, Bahamas, with Buddy. After he "uncharacteristically" did not update family and friends, calls to the Bahamian authorities could not confirm he had even made a landfall. Third hand rumor had said that two other yachts *Banderio* and *Windstar IV* had seen the vessel, but this too remained unconfirmed. Without finding anything more, friends finally posted queries.

The same mystery rings true in the case of *Know Patience* and the disappearance aboard of Michael Britt. Aboard his 36-foot Benteau he was headed to Jacksonville, Florida, and last seen by members of the Coast Guard cutter *Kingfisher* on September 15, 2011, only one mile off Port Canaveral, Florida.

Since many boaters do not file boat plans, and day sailors don't intend to go far enough to do so, it is almost impossible to uncover just when a boat goes missing. Sometimes only flares are a clue to trouble, as in a case off New Smyrna Beach, Florida, in January 2009. At 8 p.m. a vessel sighted "multiple flares, being fired off in the distance." The Coast Guard was quickly at the scene, but only encountered more red flares (9 in all), which they could not trace. Other passing vessels also reported the flares. The Coast Guard covered a huge section of ocean but the result was not only negative, there was no one missing. No vessel had been reported overdue.

Captain Andrew Blomme, Sector Jacksonville, commented on the discontinuance of the search: "Every case is different and we look at all the factors involved. We have saturated the area with air and surface assets and we have had no reports of distress and our search units haven't seen any sign of debris."

Yet another tenuous disappearance is that of the *Delilah*. All that is known about the vessel is that its operators were using an essentially obsolete frequency that was soon to be officially discontinued (121.5 MHZ). A Mayday from the vessel had said they were about 140 miles off Savannah, Georgia, with 6 people aboard, and they were taking on water. The person sending the Mayday even got so specific as to describe the vessel's hull scheme (blue). The Coast Guard responded en mass, with several aircraft and 2 fast cutters (*Yellowfin* and *Spence*). But no trace was found. The call came out of nowhere on July 8, 2008, and then receded away.

It should be noted that similar calls have been received over the years by Florida base stations, to the effect that a boat, which can never be traced, is taking on water and people are presently abandoning. In each case, the Coast Guard rushes to the scene, never to find a trace. It is as if the same event keeps replaying, at least over the radio waves.

Either one accepts some distortion of time and space or hoaxers are cruelly at work, not only endangering the Coast Guard by sending them on pointless missions but wasting millions of dollars in funds that are better spent elsewhere in real rescue operations. The possibility of a hoax cannot be ruled out in this case, since the 121.5 frequency does not have that far a range as the one that has now replaced it, the 406 MHZ.

The most sudden cause of destruction at sea is a boat catching fire or even suddenly exploding. In the busy waters of the Triangle, however, it is hard for such a tragic event to go unnoticed. For instance, on August 6, 2013, 26 miles east of Bimini in the Bahamas a 35-foot fishing vessel suddenly exploded, sending not only a loud and disturbing boom over the tranquil waters but also a tall plume of black smoke over the horizon. Other boats were soon at hand, but only found debris and no survivors.

In the case of the disappearance of Glen Brandt there was no search, only alerts. He had left Nassau on May 9, 2010, in his large 46-foot charter yacht *Genesis*. He had reported that he would refuel at Marathon Key, Florida, on May 15, but never arrived. Urgent Marine Information Broadcasts went out, plus alerts for boaters to be on the lookout. Brandt is simply another example of a boater who silently vanishes.

The disappearance of William Brown is hard to explain. It was October 5, 2010. The weather was good; it was daytime. He left his houseboat to row to shore at Geiger Key Marina to pay a court fine. When he was reported missing police boarded his boat. They found his dog Nadine and his cellphone. Brown was never seen again, nor was his dinghy.

In these same waters on March 4, 1996, 26 year old Thomas Crocker was moving a 22-foot sailboat from Garrison Bight Marina on Key West to only a few miles away to Peninsula Marina on neighboring Stock Island. Yet he never arrived. The weather began to blow a bit, but Crocker was an experienced sailor. The water is shallow. If the boat went down, where is it? The course says it must lie in these aquamarine, shallow waters. In fact, it does not.

For many boats their disappearances are summarized only in alerts. Overdue notices were placed for the sailing vessel *Sinbad*, a 50-foot yacht bound from Bermuda to the Azores, June 8, 2013. *Kailua*, a 40-foot sailing vessel left Miami for Brazil and found its way on the same list. She had left in February 2013. Both vessels had three people aboard.

The case of the 36-foot sailboat *Blondie* is a different matter. Bill Smith and his friend, Tom Brewer, had left Marathon in the Florida Keys on January 19, 2013, in order to sail the Caribbean. Both had labored extensively to get *Blondie* ready for a 3 to 4 week cruise. There were rumors in the Boot Key Harbor cruisers' net (a gossip pipeline for boaters) that a life ring had been found in the Gulf, though this was not confirmed and even more so soundly doubted because it was up current from the direction *Blondie* had taken. "We have sort of come to terms with the fact that something terrible happened to the boat and he is not coming back," declared one friend.

Boat Watches were also placed in effect for the sailing yacht *Lady Domina*. On March 31, 2013, the 75-foot motor sailor had left St. Martin bound for the Azores. Aside from her Norwegian captain, there were 4 others aboard. The *Lady Domina* had no real workable sails anymore except an old foresail, but the boat had a 220hp diesel engine. She was capable of 5 to 6 knots.

Working backward in dates reveals alerts issued for the following. No definite word ever came back about S/V *Two Captains*, overdue in September 2009, though an EPIRB was supposedly picked up briefly; *Banana Split* was posted overdue at the Bahamas in May 2007; Sailboat *Johannes* overdue with no word, April 2007; *Cloe*, overdue from Havana to Isla Mujeres, February 2006; Overdue from Trinidad to St. Marten was the sailboat *Marsal*, January 2005. At the end of the month the boat washed up on the beach in Venezuela completely deserted. *Welsh Dragon* left Florida for Holland and vanished November 2003. The *Hudson* disappeared for some time at sea until finally found 900 miles NE of French Guyana abandoned, July 21 2003.

On September 23, 2015, a "Pan Pan" was issued for the 52-foot ketch *Maratango*. She had left Norfolk, Virginia, on July 13, for the Azores, with 3 crew. In this case modern technology helped pinpoint a location. A SPOT GPS stopped transmitting on July 26 at 39.5839 N, 61.33664 W, hundreds of miles north of Bermuda, with nothing heard from the vessel thereafter.

Usually, the location would be considered far too north of the Triangle. However, because of GPS this is a curious example of how a vessel simply vanishes. No SOS or EPIRB signal was heard. Presumably everything went dead at the same time.

Any number of events may have been responsible for the many missing vessels or the boats found abandoned in the Bermuda Triangle in the last decade, but the problem *is* the mystery. Because each totally disappeared, or their crews, we are left with nothing but theory, most of which are nothing but ideas expressed during a gut reaction. Discussions over theories can become so heated that those arguing can lose sight of the fact no one theory can technically account for all of the losses. Even more insidious to serving the subject, isolating each case and simply reacting to it thwarts linking the similarities that exist in many of the cases. Opting to believe a favorite theory does not magically make it into a fact. Falling overboard is a favorite option to endorse in the case of derelicts, except that any serious theory must take into account the broader picture painted by the unsettling studies of the 19th century that show more deserted ships are found in the Bermuda Triangle than anywhere else in the North Atlantic, a phenomenon which continues to this day, only with the addition now that it is more prevalent closer to shore than in the past.

Aircraft disappearances present different challenges, often more puzzling ones because of the limited factors that could contribute to their vanishing. Pirates cannot board them in midair. Pilots don't fall out or intentionally go over the side to repair anything while in flight. Flight plans are mandatory so that all aircraft can be tracked and identified. Travel between long spans is much shorter timewise. Radar covers most of the airways. If a plane vanishes, it should be a dead weight that plummets to the ocean, and if ELTs don't transmit, as is usual, there is now the assistance of GPS. Though it was designed to keep pilots from getting lost, the sudden lack of its transmission signal has turned GPS into an opposite of an ELT— automatic silence rather than an automatic signal now telling the searchers where to rush. Searches are immediate and yet find no trace. This makes aircraft disappearances more unsettling. Fewer in number have vanished in the last decade, but the locations remain the same as those in the decades before.

On November 13, 2003, a Piper PA-32-300, N8224C went missing after leaving Staniel Cay, Exumas; only pilot on board.

On June 20, 2005, a Piper Apache N6886Y vanished between Treasure Cay, Bahamas, while en route to Fort Pierce, Florida, with 3 persons aboard.

On April 10, 2007, Piper PA-46-310P N444JH vanished near the Berry Islands in the Bahamas; only pilot aboard.

After 9/11 several security measures went into effect that retroactively and incongruously applied more censorship to historic accidents, in doing so often humorously living up to the metaphor "locking the barn after the horse has gotten loose." Despite US Air Force accidents from WWII to the present being itemized online on various independent website databases, complete with locations where the accident or disappearance occurred, formal reports cleared through the appropriate agency now come remarkably redacted, even of the information already available online. For incidents after 2002, however, the censorship is excessive and affects all cases. As a result it is almost impossible to discover the disappearance of Air Force aircraft since that time.

Considerable mystery and controversy surrounds the disappearance on December 15, 2008, near the Turks and Caicos Islands, of a three engine Britten Norman Tri-Islander (MK III N650LP) with pilot and 11 persons aboard. At 5:28 p.m. the pilot had sent a garbled or incoherent Mayday to Providenciales Airport, Caicos Islands, and then vanished. However, Coast Guard Petty Officer Barry Bena stated that the plane had "dropped off radar" shortly after departing the Dominican Republic, a disparity of hundreds of miles from the Caicos. An

AP story confirmed that the "plane took off from Santiago, DR, at approximately 3:30 pm Monday...and fell off radar about 35 minutes later, shortly after controllers received an emergency signal"—yet another contradiction with the time of the Mayday picked up by Providenciales at 5:28 p.m.

Because the investigation was in the hands of British air authorities, the National Transportation Safety Board had to blandly conclude: "The pilot and the reported 11 passengers have not been located. The airplane was not found and presumed to have ditched in the ocean about 12 nautical miles south of West Caicos, Turk and Caicos Islands."

It is interesting to note that this is the general location where Dickson sent an SOS in 1960 and Carolyn Coscio in 1969, and in both instances it was not entirely understood exactly what the problem was or where they were by those picking up the distress, exactly as in the case of the Tri-Islander, which apparently did not exist on radar for an hour and a half before its Mayday was heard.

On December 15, 2009, a Cirrus SR22 (N723LJ), took off from St. Petersburg, Florida, and headed west into the Gulf of Mexico, with only its pilot aboard. The NTSB summarized:

> After takeoff from the coastal airport, the airplane made a left turn to the west, and the pilot was approved for a frequency change by air traffic control. There were no further known communications with the pilot. A radar target consistent with the airplane's departure was observed flying westbound over gulf waters. The target climbed to an altitude of 9,900 feet mean sea level (msl), where it remained until radar contact was lost. The last radar target was observed about 1 hour after takeoff, about 150 miles west-southwest of the departure airport, traveling at a ground speed of 167 knots. The pilot's spouse was not aware that he had been flying and reported the airplane missing 2 days later. Search and Rescue personnel conducted three sorties which covered 1,890 square miles with negative results. At the time of this writing, the location of the airplane, and the condition of the pilot, are not known...The National Transportation Safety Board determines the probable cause(s) of this accident to be:
> Undetermined (airplane and pilot missing).

Several changes have occurred in the last decade altogether making it more difficult to extract not only the details of missing aircraft but their actual occurrence. Being listed as stolen is one such hindrance, as already noted. In this case there is no NTSB investigation. There would be an insurance or police report, both quite brief.

Coast Guard searches for missing boaters or pilots do not mean there will be a Coast Guard investigative report. Often the crew or passengers are listed as missing people, and this places the case in the hands of local law enforcement. Often no report is generated outside of a typical officer generated log. Sometimes the only clue to a disappearance at sea is that one of the passengers aboard appears on the Doe Network as a "missing person" and the summary explains the circumstances of their disappearance.

It is in this area where changes have come about as to be advantageous for the investigator. The Doe Network database is searchable. However, the large number of missing person reports still makes it difficult. Each circumstance for a missing person listed therein is subject to much interpretation. In the long run, all that can be definitely ascertained is that the people who are missing at sea have indeed vanished. Whether a crime was involved, an intentional disappearance, or whether the cause was some phenomenon we attribute to the Bermuda Triangle, can only be implied by analysis of those facts listed there, and these facts are admittedly few and far between.

Examples of disappearances contained within the network include the discovery of Gregory Wallin's 19-foot pleasure craft found abandoned at sea 53 miles southwest of Sanibel Island, Florida— the same location where the 21st century Gulf mysteries would occur. He was last seen in Fort Myers on December 31, 1998, and possibly had a woman on board with him.

Yet another derelict uncovered via this way is the 30-foot fishing boat of David Field. He was last seen at the Summits Landing marina in Micco, near Melbourne, Florida, on March 27, 1993, and then later called one of his employees at his car dealership to tell him he was fishing 30 miles off shore. When found, his lifeless boat was then towed to shore. There had been no sign of a struggle.

Charles Dillon and Arthur Sassone vanished whereas the bodies of the other two aboard Dillon's *Double O* were found, along with an ice chest and some life jackets, on January 16, 1994. The 26-foot boat presumably sank somewhere in the Gulf about 25 miles west of where many others would be found derelict— Anclote Key.

Records extend back decades. For one disappearance much must be deduced. There is only the following summary:

> Jesse Markham, a West Palm Beach resident, ex-Navy pilot, daredevil flier who worked missions for the U.S. government, flew out of Palm Beach International Airport July 21, 1982. He hasn't been seen since.

A phone call is all that alerted the Coast Guard and law enforcement there had been another disappearance. On April 27, 1987, James O'Conner called a friend and told him he was in Cozumel. He asked him to pick him up at Boca Raton airport at 12:30 p.m. Accompanying him was Dennis Behr of Dania Beach. They never arrived. There was no record they had ever left the United States for Cozumel, and no evidence they left Cozumel except for the fact their aircraft, a Cessna 337 N25195, with blue and white livery, was never found.

Departing from Dinner Key marina on December 6, 1983, Art Carver and Kevin Wadsworth headed to Bimini in a 21-foot Enterprise. They were never seen again.

Again, this incident and several others just mentioned call our attention to the "Christmastime Hex," a surprising coincidence if these disappearances are just the result of statistically acceptable accidents of unknown origin.

Details must be provocative in the case of the 46-foot Richardson yacht *Sea Fever*, with 4 persons aboard— two men and two women—including Angela Westberry, to warrant the final conclusion: "Foul play is suspected." The vessel left Jacksonville, Florida, on December 1, 1984, so the four could vacation on the boat in a cruise of the Bahamas. However, the yacht was recorded by US Customs at Grand Cayman Island (west of Jamaica) on December 14, 1984. "It is not known if Westberry was still on board the boat at that time. Neither *Sea Fever* nor Westberry have been seen since. Her sister reported her as a missing person to authorities."

For the vessel to appear in Grand Cayman when the cruise was to the Bahamas may have been enough to make the Coast Guard suspicious. The island appears to be a link in a drug smuggling or white slavery chain from Florida, the Bahamas, and into central and South America.

Weeks after the 185-foot freighter *Freedon* disappeared in January 1989, a diver claimed to have seen the coastal freighter at Grand Cayman. When the ship had left Florida, it was supposed to be going to Haiti— definitely in another direction from Grand Cayman. To compound official suspicions the vessel carried a ne'er-do-well German named Florian Bourch who had, for whatever reason, invited 23 year old journalist student Linda Bishop to accompany him so she could see the conditions in Haiti. They were never seen again.

Doe Network records are, of course, dependent on whether the missing person was ever reported therein. But though they are spotty at the best of times, they go back many decades and include hard to explain cases like the simultaneous disappearance on April 16, 1973, of William Forshee, his son William Jr, and their two friends aboard Forshee's boat near Marco Island, Florida. Sheriffs found Forshee's truck and then the boat, but the four men were never found.

Stanley Borofsky was last seen in Fort Lauderdale. He called home a couple of days before Thanksgiving, November 24, 1977, telling his family he would be there the following day. He then vanished. He owned 3 aircraft. The family was able to trace two of them, but the third could not be found. No flight plan had been filed in his name. Just what happened to Borofsky, and where?

On January 13, 1998, John Perez and Raul Diaz left Miami in their boat. Their summary only reads that they "left to go fishing to the Bahamas and never returned."

The cases above, spanning only a few decades, constitute the mere tip of the iceberg for so many others that once resided in police files or in Coast Guard SAR reports but which have long been destroyed because of file keeping rules and regulations. Those cases that did get cross filed into the Doe Network barely give us a clue to the extent of missing persons at sea.

Many of the disappearances are outside of US jurisdiction. Only investigations of air accidents undertaken by Bahamas Air Authority merit listing in their databank whereas the other incidents in their territory (and disappearing constitutes being an "incident") are only given a docket number, without any elaborating details. Almost all investigations undertaken by them in the 21st century have been of aircraft accidents near an airport, of those that were either arriving or after having just recently taken off. Disappearances in mid-flight between far flung destinations, which with few exceptions constitutes most cases in the Bermuda Triangle, are not something for which one will readily find an entry in their databank.

The Bahamas are a national Venice, in their way. Rather than a city with streets of water, the Bahamas is a nation where cities and islands are connected by a highway of water and air, neither of which make it easy for investigators to venture far from island airports. And if there is nothing tangible to investigate, such as is obviously the case in a disappearance, there is simply no investigation. On the other hand, the NTSB will at least investigate the circumstances of a disappearance, including weather data, family information, medical certificates, any clue that might shed light on suicide, pilot experience, or structural defects.

Information in the Bahamas must be gleaned from other sources if one wishes to establish some details about disappearances. These sources would be police reports of missing people, which will then give some circumstances about being in transit either via boat or aircraft when they vanished.

Some facts from accident reports prove interesting reading, especially as some seem to support very unofficial theories that there must be some as-yet-unknown force at work in the disappearances in the Bermuda Triangle. For instance, on May 16, 2005, the pilot of a Flamingo Air Charter Britten-Normal Islander noticed his airspeed dramatically slow over the Tongue of the Ocean while on route to Great Exuma. As a result he was barely able to make land and had to crash in the wooded area 3 miles short of the runway at Moss Town. On December 17, 2009, a Falcon jet slowed suddenly, as if encountering some unknown restricting veil, and without any word from both pilot or co-pilot, plunged from its cruising altitude of 28,000 feet and impacted on Great Inagua, its explosion rattling house windows and doors at Matthew Town miles away and its dark plume of smoke attracting a Coast Guard chopper on routine maneuvers. It is interesting to note that this is the same area where others have gotten lost but could not otherwise explain how to the local radio control towers.

Multifactorial causes for the disappearances in the Bermuda Triangle seem evident from the circumstances that have been compiled over the decades, the most disturbing coming from those cases which suggest "electronic fog," a sudden "winking out" from radar, sudden disappearance even while near shore, unexplained loss of navigation and electronic equipment, and from the reports of UFOs. Instead of approaching a solution along the lines of a single factor, theorists propose a variety of causes to explain the many missing planes and ships in the Triangle, while the most pertinacious have gone beyond this to link the most inexplicable phenomena as having one very disquieting source.

These traditional categories of theories are generally well known in the topic's narrative, but in the last decade more data has come forth to help winnow down just what theories should really be entertained seriously. Some previously sketchy theories are strengthened by the data. Others do not need to be seriously considered anymore. First and foremost of all theories for today is that of "electronic fog."

Chapter 6

Electronic Fog:
The Answer or a Symptom?

Over the last half of the 20th century and into the 21st century, with better documentation of each disappearance in the Bermuda Triangle and the details surrounding their losses, it is readily apparent that many prosaic explanations cannot even approach what is required to explain the most perplexing cases.

Piracy most certainly has taken many boats, especially the power boats, but not those at a harbor's entrance or those rounding a peninsula. Also, piracy does not take the individual and leave the valuable and useful boat behind.

Air piracy is now vogue, but the circumstances are fairly easy to determine. The aircraft is stolen from an airfield, used to pick up and ferry the drugs, and then many times the plane ends up ditched at Rum Cay in the Bahamas. In the shallow waters nearby, compatriots are waiting in their boat for the pilot to swim over. Together they then make their escape. The politer pirates return the airplane to the tarmac at the home airfield. Evidence that an owner's plane was temporarily stolen is seen only on the odometer, which has logged a 10 hour flight, the usual round trip time to some small airfield in the Bahamas or Cuba or, for the faster jets, into South America.

Blood found in empty boats, especially those found in the shallows, may have a less otherworldly motive than alien abduction. Barracudas use the shallow bottom to leap out and assail a boater, biting their neck or chest, as one kayaker found out in October 2010 when a barracuda leapt out of the water and bit her with such force it punctured one of her lungs before it dived back into the water. Fortunately, she was in tandem with another kayaker who called Medivac. This cause must be born in mind, especially for the many small inshore derelict vessels that have been found in this century and found, moreover, after April 10, 2010, when the BP oil spill commenced in the Gulf, resulting in much marine life migrating closer to shore to find its prey.

Minicanes, CATS (Clear Air Turbulence), suicide, pilot error, have all no doubt played their hand considering how deep is the list of missing vessels and aircraft. But none of these can account for the lack of debris, especially from aircraft such as those two that vanished on approach to Harry S. Truman Airport; nor can they explain the terse reports of electronic malfunction, haywire compasses, and repeated reports of "electronic fog" hitherto confided between pilots but a phenomenon which is now finding allusion in official accident reports based on the last words of pilots.

A curious fact underscores the existence of certain phenomena reported by pilots and shipmasters in that types of phenomena seem limited to certain areas, and embellishment has no borders. In the case of electronic fog, for instance, it is reported only in the area of the strict triangle. UFOs, on the other hand, are seen throughout the world but grouped in certain areas of the Triangle. Sections of the Triangle also seem prone to specific types of mysteries. Deserted vessels in the Bahamas and off Florida are shipshape whereas in the heart of the Triangle or eastward of the Windwards and Leewards, approaching the strict triangle, the derelicts are a shambles. This may suggest the area is prone to waterspouts. Waterspouts are suggested in such cases as the *Sophia*, *Poker Face*, and perhaps even the *Offshore Pergola*, though Tom Olchefske vanishing after coming topside on his *Tropic Bird* in response to a radar sighting adds a chilling touch. His vessel was also undisturbed. A waterspout might even explain the *What's Left?*—the cyclone picking it up and twirling it around being the cause of Lisk's transected spine.

But of all the theories none is so quintessentially associated with the Bermuda Triangle as "electronic fog."

Although he is not the first pilot to report the "electronic fog," Bruce Gernon has had the most celebrated encounter with it and is the pilot who has coined the term. Along with his father and friend Chuck Lafayette, he was en route to Miami Beach on December 4, 1970, in his Beechcraft Bonanza. Just after passing Andros Island, they noticed a huge lenticular cloud ahead. It soon morphed with incredible speed, extending upward and then encircling them— to draw an analogy, like hugging arms reaching out to grasp them. Now almost all around them, this fomenting storm cloud sparkled with bursts of light (though these were not lightning bolts). Unable to get above it, Gernon found himself essentially locked in the inside circle of a deadly storm donut. Seeing a space was still open in the cloud, before it completely interlocked into an encircling ring, he sped for the area, increasing his RPMs into the danger zone. Upon entering this narrow area it constricted around him, the walls of the cloud now swirling counterclockwise until the tunnel constricted from 200 feet diameter to touching his wingtips.

Inside the swirling tunnel distance also seemed to change. As he entered the tunnel, he estimated it was 10 miles long but within it, as the walls swirled around him, he now saw it appeared only 1 mile long. It took only about 20 seconds to reach what he thought was the other end and what should then be clear weather. But . . .

> When I looked back, I gasped to see the tunnel walls collapse and form a slit that slowly rotated clockwise. All of our electronic and magnetic navigational instruments were malfunctioning. The compass was slowly spinning even as the airplane flew straight. . . Instead of the blue sky we expected, everything was a

dull, grayish white haze. Visibility seemed like more than two miles, yet we could not see the ocean, the horizon, or the sky. The air was very stable and there was no lightning or rain. I like to refer to this as an "electronic fog" because it seemed to be what was interfering with our instruments. . .We were in the electronic fog for three minutes when the controller radioed that he had identified an airplane directly over Miami Beach, flying due west. I looked at my watch and saw that we had been flying for less than 34 minutes. We could not have reached Miami Beach— we should have been approaching the Bimini Islands.

At this point the "fog" around dissipated in streaks and there Gernon could see Miami Beach ahead. He realized that given the minimal amount of time that had elapsed in his flight from Andros something truly phenomenal had happened. Taken by the ramifications, Gernon checked fuel receipts against the amount remaining in his tank, discovering he had not used the amount of fuel he normally would have consumed on such a flight. Checking time estimates, he discovered he had gained 30 minutes. Taken together it seemed he had been propelled 30 minutes and 100 miles forward into what can only be said was Time and Space.

The storm formation into which the lenticular cloud had morphed could not have extended to Miami Beach, a fact proved by the clear weather when the "fog" dissipated. It had not been a fog bank. Rather Gernon believes he conducted the fog as he exited the storm tunnel north of Andros and somehow it stayed with him until it dissipated over Miami Beach.

Possibly because the walls of the tunnel had been swirling around him in vortex motion some form of field was generated, he has speculated, that allowed for the conduction of the "fog." It was at this point that he felt zero gravity and a forward thrust. Free of the vortex, the "electronic fog" must nevertheless have remained.

Any electric charge remaining on an aircraft is unexplainable. Aircraft come with leach lines designed to drain off a buildup of static electricity. Yet in Gernon's encounter the effects can only be explained by a powerful electromagnetic *field*, one that produced a clutching, visible fog.

Bruce Gernon began a lifelong (and still continuing) search for the answer to the phenomenon he experienced. He believed whatever it was he encountered it is crucial to the answer of the many mysteries in the Bermuda Triangle. His observations about the "electronic fog" not being a fog bank are especially pertinent for other flyers. "I believe the airplane was flying in clear weather but it appeared to be IMC because the Fog was attached to the airplane. In other words, I wasn't flying through the fog, I was flying with the fog. It takes a different perspective of the mind for a pilot to realize this, and this could be the reason for a pilot to become immediately spatially disoriented."

Over the decades since, he has attracted a number of scientists serious to pursue some of the ramifications of his experience. It is not so much the storm cloud that is hard to explain. Nor is it the fact that the electric power in it seems to have acted like the catalyst for the vortex tunnel, in a sense forming a horizontal tornado. It is the fact that Gernon and his companions seem to have survived traveling along the *inside* of a tornado and are therefore first person eyewitnesses to the potential of the interior of an electromagnetic vortex.

Gernon is far from believing he experienced just one of those rare moments when all the elements came together to form a phenomenon of nature. Reports from other pilots who have had experiences in the Triangle, plus some of the details contained in the official reports on missing aircraft, suggest others have had encounters with the "electronic fog." Some survived, whereas some misjudging the situation may have become spatially disoriented and crashed.

Such may be the case of Gary Purvis on February 1, 2001, when he was playing tag with a Coast Guard interceptor for drug interception training. Flying in the Keys near Marathon in his Piper Cherokee Six, he was about 10 miles ahead of the Coast Guard aircraft. Weather was excellent, with visibility up to 12 miles. Everything appeared normal, but then suddenly Purvis radioed the Coast Guard interceptor that he was "IMC;" easily translated, "instrument meteorological conditions" means that visibility was gone and he was flying on instruments. He had not encountered clouds, however, but said a "haze" had just developed. He then vanished. In this case some debris was later sighted, indicating Purvis crashed. The NTSB concluded that he was not experienced enough to fly on instruments yet, a rating he had only recently acquired.

Gernon has considered this case. Everything suggests the "electronic fog." But it obviously was not created by a complex storm cloud. However, Gernon feels "electronic fog" has other origins. While flying over the Keys in the same general area, in 1996, Gernon had his second encounter with the mysterious fog and this helped him to understand some elements of it. He noted that it conducts around an aircraft as a vortex, forming a donut shape that will constrict close enough to touch the wingtips. This was confirmed by looking straight down. He could see the ocean, and if looking straight up he could see the sky, confirming the donut or vortex shape to it. He speculated that if over water it would be wise for a pilot to recall where land was and fly in that direction, as a change in terrain seems to help vanquish the phenomenon. But the most important conclusion he came to is that obviously the "electronic fog" does not require the power of that strangely building cloud formation or lenticular cloud. It seems to manifest on its own. Although what is causing it remains mysterious, logically we must concede it must play along the lines of a completely invisible energy vortex and yet have near the power of a visible storm cell.

While Gernon is not the first pilot to encounter the phenomenon, he is the first to analyze it and realize it is not a sudden appearing fog bank although it gives that illusion from within the aircraft. Reports of the electronic fog are not far more common, most likely, because many pilots who encounter it thought it was a fog bank or, quite frankly, they vanished. This seems the scenario in the strange disappearance of Peter Jensen in 1980, in which a time and space distortion also is suggested, in that there was no real evidence where Jensen was when he made his Mayday. The last radio message also placed him alive and still in the air 6 hours after fuel starvation.

Despite only a few cases being publically reported Gernon estimates that about 100 pilots have told him they too have encountered the sudden strange haze and malfunctioning equipment.

On record, the first pilot to report a "fog bank" that caused electromagnetic havoc with his navigation equipment was no less than Charles Lindbergh. He had taken off from Havana in *Spirit of St. Louis* to head across the Gulf of Mexico. He records what happened in his *Autobiography of Values* (1976):

> The last flight of my around-the-Gulf-and-Caribbean tour should also have been routine. I took off from Havana airport about 1:35 in the morning on February 13, 1928, intending to fly nonstop to St. Louis. It should have been an easy flight— about a third the distance from New York to Paris. My take-off was quick, my cruising speed high. I felt no need to be miserly with fuel. I climbed to an altitude of four thousand and settled back to enjoy the night and piloting. But halfway across the Straits of Florida my magnetic compass started rotating, and the earth-inductor-compass needle jumped back and forth erratically. By that time a haze had formed, screening off the horizon.
>
> At first I thought the *Spirit of St. Louis* had dropped a wing and was banking; but the turn indicator needle held its center, and a push with my foot on the rudder showed the gyroscope to be working properly. I had only once before seen two compasses malfunction at the same time. That was over the storm I encountered crossing the Atlantic en route to Paris. But then the magnetic compass only oscillated. Although it was through an arc of close to one hundred eighty degrees, I could get an approximate idea of direction by taking the midpoint of the card's swing, and I could hold it by the stars. Over the Straits of Florida my magnetic compass rotated without stopping, and my earth inductor was completely useless. I had no notion whether I was flying north, south, east, or west.
>
> A few stars directly overhead were dimly visible through haze, but they formed no constellation I could recognize. I started climbing toward the clear sky that had to exist somewhere above. If I could see Polaris, that northern point of light, I could navigate by it with reasonable accuracy. But haze thickened as my altitude increased. High thin clouds crept in to make the stars blink. Surely a storm area lay not far away— very likely above the southern states I had to pass. Should I spiral until daybreak,

when I could get a general direction from the sun? That would prevent flying in the wrong direction and possibly finding myself hundreds of miles over the Atlantic or gulf.

Clouds thickened, formed a layer, lowered. I descended to less than a thousand feet to keep contact with the sea. Even then I could barely distinguish water from the haze it joined. Turbulence increased. The compass card rotated too erratically to give an indication of direction. Dawn came slowly. Its diffused light seemed to originate in every azimuth, helping my navigation not at all. But while waves below were still half merged with night, a darker shade drew in toward me like a curtain— land, vague in early twilight, only a narrow strip with more water beyond. . .

Charles Lindbergh had discovered he was over the Bahamas. "That would mean I had flown at almost a right angle to my proper heading, and it would put me close to three hundred miles off course!"

A fairly good indication that this was the "electronic fog" comes from the fact that Lindbergh could see both directly above him and directly below him. Yet when he climbed altitude to break out of what he felt was only a fog bank he could never make it. The fog, which seemed to have a limit, then seemed limitless as he kept trying to get above it, a possible indication the fog was flying with him and he was not flying through a fog bank.

Volcanoes and igneous flows are places over which compasses will constantly deflect or spin. In the Triangle, however, this phenomenon comes and goes and is not limited to specific locations, indicating it is not caused by some wreck or anything static below the surface.

"Dead spots" are known in the area and remain fairly constant though unexplained. These locations earned their ominous name due to the fact that radio communication is nonexistent during transit through these places. Officially they are not charted, though old hands in the area pretty much know the main locations.

Advised of one of these spots by a jet pilot at the Navy Flying Club, Cary Trantham took it in stride. He had cautioned, she recalled, that there was no need to panic if she lost radio communication because it would only be for a brief time. For her proposed course he had said one was south of Everglades City near the Bay of Florida, a location that was far from eerie to her. "Everyone should see the Florida Keys from an altitude of five hundred feet. The water is so clear below that you can see sharks, stingrays, dolphins, turtles, and an abundance of other sea life. The different hues of blue are awe inspiring. Turquoise water, mangrove islands, sand flats and sea grass meadows intertwine in a swirling display of color."

She took off from Ormond Beach, and headed south on her return trip to Key West, beginning what she did not realize would be her most harrowing trip in the Bermuda Triangle. Over southern Florida she encountered unusual turbulence, and it took all her strength to control the stick. A front was moving in behind her. Believing she was experiencing the front's advancing wind shear, she reported it to Miami, which the operator acknowledged only as a matter of form. By dusk, the wind shear had long passed. She was now coming to the coastline of the Bay of Florida. Her radio and all equipment had been working fine through the wind shear because she had reached Miami instantly. When she approached the Triangle, things changed.

> I was now ahead of the front, but there was high cloud cover, which obscured the moon and the stars. Passing Naples I glanced out of the cockpit to the east and, to my amazement, I could see the lights of Miami on the horizon. It was a beautiful sight that made me catch my breath. I felt alone in the cockpit and adjusted the interior lights. . .
>
> Flying over the everglades, a surface haze began to develop. Land and water began to merge. Gradually, as the sun set, the lights on the instrument panel intensified and an eerie feeling began to creep through me. Then it happened! Suddenly, it was as if someone threw a blanket over the airplane. . . The horizon was gone. Panic set in. I wasn't sure if I was right side up, or upside down. Death was looking me in the face, and I said to myself, 'Cary, get control of this airplane, or you will end up in the Gulf, and they will never find you,'

Electronic Fog: Answer or Symptom? 159

In a "situation like this" she admitted many thoughts went through her head, from silly and inconsequential ones like "Will my house be clean when they come to clear out my personal belongings?" to more serious ones like considering this was the mysterious "dead space" she had been told about to, finally, what comes to most every pilot's mind in the area: "Is this the Bermuda Triangle?" This question especially seemed pertinent when she looked at her dash panel.

...When I looked at the instruments, nothing seemed to make sense. The compass was erratic. The illumination in the cockpit began to fluctuate from dim to bright and back again. The altitude indicator began to roll and there was a high pitched buzzing in my headset. I finally got the airplane level and glanced at the altimeter, but I had no idea what the altitude was.
...I tried to keep my wings level, but I was so shaky that I was over controlling the airplane. I couldn't tell if I was over land or water. It was totally black outside the cockpit— no city lights, no horizon, nothing!

Now near panic, Cary Trantham discovered another problem: she had no radio communication. She had no idea if Miami's lack of response was because she was in that odd area of dead air space or if there was some other problem. But she finally got another channel punched in and then raised Miami and what she felt was an indifferent operator. "He said that he had just turned me over to another frequency, and couldn't talk to me. My response was: 'Yes, but I am up here all by myself, and I don't know where I am.' He suggested that I 'climb to a higher altitude.' This should have put me over the edge. I was in a total state of shock, trying to fly an airplane that seemed to have a mind of its own and nobody would talk to me."

Eventually things returned to normal and Cary discovered herself near Marathon in the Florida Keys, far off course. From there she followed the intercoastal highway and finally identified Key West below. She admits that she had to pry her fingers off the stick after she had landed. She later wrote of her account for an article in the *AOPA*, and ended up musing at how they changed her title from "Surviving the Bermuda Triangle" to "Surviving Get-Home-itis."

This isn't the first time pilots have been edited from making any reference to the Bermuda Triangle, but it is a reflection of how the topic is not discussed in some aviation quarters except with levity or ridicule. As one might imagine, weekend winging is an expensive hobby and there are many people who are afraid of any side effects on their lucrative business or political positions. Considering this factor caused one ambassador to shy away from coming public about his encounter with electronic fog, though he confided it to Bruce Gernon.

One exception, and a very notable exception, was the boisterous Martin Caidin, test pilot, author and screenwriter. He went so far as to publish the account in his *Ghosts of the Air* (1986). This concerned his flight of a restored vintage PBY Catalina from Bermuda to Jacksonville, Florida, through the Triangle. On board were his wife, Didi, Connie Edwards, and a few other aviation luminaries. The day was bright and the visibility was unlimited. Suddenly, however, they couldn't see the nose of their airplane because of a fog that quickly formed. Looking out along the wings they saw the wingtips disappear into a bottle of "eggnog," Caiden's description of the fog because it was slightly yellowish. Then they were directed to their instruments.

> . . . the magnetic compass began to rotate. It picked up speed and went whirling around as if it were a whirligig. We checked the photo printout from the weather satellite. . . The metsat picture showed us in absolutely clear air. The nearest clouds were two hundred miles south of us. Just about that time the metsat print machine died. . . The electronic innards of the Catalina, all two million clams worth, shriveled up inside. The LORAN went out. The electronic fuel gauges sogged to fuzzy markings. The long-numbered navigation gear [digital] read 888888888. The radios died. Everything still had power, but nothing worked.

Changing altitudes made no difference. It was impossible to get on top of it. This "electronic eggnog" lasted for 4 hours. Then about an hour out of Jacksonville the eggnog fog suddenly dissipated. "We could see for ever and ever. The mag. compass settled down. The directional gyro quit its foolishness and steadied. The electronics emerged from their funk, and everything worked perfectly."

Due to the LORAN resetting and then freezing, Caiden felt they were completely engulfed in whatever it was that had formed around them. However, Cary Trantham felt that GPS was not affected, forming the theory that the phenomenon is dependent on something below the sea, perhaps because she felt she was near the mysterious "dead space" of which she had been forewarned.

Varying intensities of electromagnetic effects may be directly proportional to the strength of the "electronic fog." In some instances pilots can communicate over the radio for a while. In others there is no "donut" shape to the vortex of fog (or the pilot may be so stunned they are unaware they can look straight down or straight up). What the combined experiences amount to is that no one can explain what causes the electronic fog let alone its vagaries. They do agree, albeit for some reluctantly, that it exists and so far defies our own attempts to disperse electric-static charges in aircraft.

Since there are degrees to everything, the occurrence of unexplained moments of spinning compasses, tumbling gyros, and erratic electronic panel readouts in clear weather, may indicate that the conditions were beginning to form but nevertheless did not come to full fruition to form the fog around the aircraft or boat before the effects then passed away.

For the most intense and potentially alarming effects of time and space displacement—those experienced in Bruce Gernon's flight—a fast forming storm cell was required. Spontaneous manifestations of "electronic fog" in clear weather, however, present only a fraction of the power. Bruce Gernon's encounter does, in fact, seem one of those rare moments in which all the elements came together to create phenomenal effects and yet still the ability to survive them.

Naturally, this raises the question as to just how serious is "electronic fog," that is, how relevant is it to explain the many missing ships and planes in the Bermuda Triangle? Its generation without the storm cloud seems capable of causing spatial disorientation in pilots unaware (or in denial) of its existence, but still debris was located in the Purvis case in 2001.

From the confusing radio messages of Charles Dickson in 1960 and Carolyn Coscio in 1969, who apparently could not see clearly below her despite being near safety, the "electronic fog" could have been a crucial factor. Dickson's compass was thought to be nonoperational though he had two compasses and one of them was independent of the electronic gear.

Both aircraft may have vanished as a result of getting lost because of the "electronic fog" rather than something as dynamic as implied in Gernon's encounter— devolving into time and space. Both occurred in deep and open waters near the Caicos Islands where many others have vanished (though without sending any Mayday first perhaps because they were unable). Since the exact location of both aircraft could not be determined the sea may merely have had time to disperse and hide any traces of their respective crashes.

Mike Roxby's death on December 16, 1974, on Great Inagua, an island near the Caicos, may be a deadly example of the potential of "electronic fog." He was flying from Miami with two others, Don Parris and Kelly Hanson, in his Cessna 177 N2128Q. Both survived to tell what happened. While passing over Bimini, instrument malfunction began. The radio ceased to operate, the gauges were erratic. At times the radio and equipment returned, allowing Roxby to reorient himself and continue the flight. When they reached Great Inagua, they thought they were finally safe. Now at 6:45 p.m. they were coming in for a landing. Hanson recalls: "One second everything was clear and we could see the airstrip perfectly. Then suddenly we were in the middle of a swirling cloud that came from nowhere." As a result, Roxby crashed and was killed. Hanson and Don Parris not only walked away, but Parris walked away a believer in the Triangle. "You have heard about the Devil's Triangle—you see movies about it—but you can't believe it, really. Well, I believe it now."

A similar encounter could be posited for one or both of the KC-135 Stratotankers. If one or both had conducted the "electronic fog" this may explain why they seemed to collide in midair or suddenly explode, and one is tempted to wonder what caused the C-133 and Sting 27 to vanish after their electronic SIFs faded from the radarscope.

Although far rarer, ships have also encountered the "electronic fog." One case is that of the tug *Good News* in 1966. It is famous largely because her boisterous captain, Don Henry, didn't shy away from talking about it. Don Henry was a big man, hardhat, diver, salver, and he looked like he could come out the winner in a fight with a Great White shark. His account was also matter-of-fact, and the event was witnessed by his crew. They were along the Tongue of the Ocean en route from Puerto Rico to Miami, with a barge on a 600 foot towline. The tug was 160-feet overall, with 2,000 horsepower, and the barge was about 2,500 tons. It had carried petroleum nitrate, but it was empty now. It was while he was below in his cabin that it happened. The chief officer called down and asked Henry to come look at the compass. Due to the alarm in his voice and the men hollering about the bridge, Henry admits he burst through the doors and yelled: "What the hell is going on here?!" The first mate pointed to the compass.

> I walked over and looked. The gyro was tumbling, and the magnetic compass was going completely bananas. It was simply going around and around. I had never seen anything like that before. We had no communications of any kind over the radios. There were no lights. We lost the generators— they were running but produced no energy. There was just some kind of electronic drain at this time. There was just nothing. A case of fifty batteries I had picked up in San Juan had to be thrown away. They were completely shot. This we found out later. We didn't know this at the time.

Instinctively Henry rushed back to the stern to check on the barge. But "the sky caught my attention first. There was no horizon now; you couldn't see where the sky ended and the water began. I looked down on the ocean. All I saw was foam; it was like milk. The sky was the same color. There was just no definition between the two as there always is, so that's why I say there was no horizon."

When Henry looked back to the barge he was shocked to see it was not there. "The towline was leading back, the way it was supposed to be, but there was simply no barge. Pulling on the line revealed it was still taught. The barge still seemed to be attached, but it was completely lost to sight. There was a fog or something around it, like clouds, and the towline was running aft into that. It's hard to explain. I've likened it to the old Indian rope trick. The towline was just sticking out of a fog . . . but the fog was nowhere else. It was just around where the barge should be. The water was also more choppy immediately around where the barge should be."

Don Henry admitted that he had had enough. He plowed into the bridge and kicked the throttles forward. However, there simply was no response. He felt like the *Good News* was in a tug o' war with something holding them back.

This frightening incident lasted between 7 to 10 minutes and then as suddenly as it had arrived it dissipated. Not like a fog bank that fades away behind one, but it just parted and was completely gone. "We could see the horizon again. We got everything back: the radios, the lights, the gyros, the generators. We got the damn barge back! The line was leading back to it. That fog was gone."

After some distance, when the feeling of safety returned, he stopped the *Good News* and took a boat back to the barge to make sure it was all right. Henry considered it much warmer than it should have been. "It wasn't hot. You could touch it. But it was much warmer than would have been normal."

A former agnostic about the Bermuda Triangle, the incident finally made a believer out of him.

What is particularly interesting about Don Henry's encounter is the twofold nature of the "electronic fog." It seemed, at least to those on the *Good News*, that it was all around them, but from their vantage a cloud had seized the tug. This may be the case, but it may have been that Henry's tug would have looked the same to someone outside of the "haze" around them. From his perspective, however, it seemed they were in a milky white bottle pulling a tug obscured by a cloud.

This observation bears a striking similarity to that which Bruce Gernon encountered. He believed he picked up the "electronic fog" upon exiting the swirling cloud tunnel. In the *Good News*' encounter, they seemed to be in the "electronic fog" which surrounded the more powerful cloud over the barge— in other words, the "electronic fog" existed outside of the cloud which could therefore have been the intense epicenter of the phenomenon.

One wonders if more heat had been generated by the cloud what the effects would have been. If such a fog condensed around a yacht or even a large tug like Henry's, could an explosion result that would effectively make the ship or yacht look like it had vanished?

It really comes back to the source of "electronic fog" as to whether it can play a much more dynamic factor in aircraft and ship disappearances than briefly causing alarm in seamen or panic and sometimes vertigo in pilots. In no case but Bruce Gernon's has "electronic fog" caused such alarming effects. The disappearances in the Bermuda Triangle, of course, could represent those pilots who did not safely skirt what seems to be a window in time and space but may have been propelled far beyond the mere 100 miles that Gernon and his companions experienced.

Arguments over a source for "electronic fog" other than a strong, electrically charged storm cloud must accept that in Gernon's case at least its formation was the result of an obvious electromagnetic vortex formed as the cloud closed in. Short of such a storm cloud there must be some other genesis for electronic fog, still unknown, and in each case it seems safe to presume it is electromagnetic in origin and the aircraft or ship may be *necessary* for its materialization.

Further developing the theory of "electronic fog" in the next chapter, we will see where ships have been in proximity to fogs that registered on their radarscopes while at the same time experiencing a wide and disturbing array of electronic effects. In effect, the circumstances are identical to those that befell the *Good News*— a cloud on the surface of the sea forming an intense epicenter with outlying electromagnetic effects. Only in these cases, the ships weren't near the epicenter of it but skirting the periphery.

Still, the origins for spinning compasses and sudden radio blackouts are elusive in other cases, though no less alarming. British film producer and director Simon Ludgate was filming a documentary on the Bermuda Triangle for National Geographic in 2004 (*Named Science* series), a principle part of which was to retrace Flight 19's flight path (before they got lost, of course) in the Bahamas. For this flight he had secured an immaculately restored TBM Avenger similar to the planes of Flight 19. Sparing no part of his budget he had asked the Danish Meteorological Office to analyze "their satellite data on electromagnetic anomalies around the earth" and made no secret of the fact to them that they were "investigating what scientific basis or otherwise there might be for the high incidence of disappearances in one of the most patrolled, busy and tracked areas of sea in the world." They began running their tests. Meanwhile:

> . . . we set off from Fort Lauderdale Airport in Florida in a beautifully-reconditioned Avenger bomber. Flown by a contemporary of the pilots who disappeared in the legendary Flight 19 Squadron, we took off at the same time 2:10 p.m. and set the same course to Chicken Island and Grand Bahama Island as Flight 19. I was being filmed by a chase plane and we had five cameras running on the Avenger. It was a beautiful day—better weather than Flight 19 had, and middle of the summer. We used old school compasses and a stopwatch to navigate with a modern GPS standing by. . .just in case.
>
> Almost immediately, I was struck by two things. The ocean and the sky are so similar in colour in that area that you could quite easily invert especially in a cloudless sky like that day and not realise it as the horizon had almost disappeared. There was hardly any difference in the sky and the sea. It was like flying inside a goldfish bowl. The second thing was how similar all the

little formations of islands looked. We could have been anywhere in a 200 mile radius.

We flew on for two hours and then something very odd happened. Our turn and slip indicators in both planes froze at exactly the same time. These are simple little devices like a carpenter's spirit level which tell you whether or not you are skidding sideways in a turn. Even stranger, both our compasses started to behave weirdly. They were spinning and wavering as if magnetic north was moving round and round. I spoke to both pilots and suggested we fly on for a while, estimate our position then switch on the GPS and see if our satellite position was the same as our calculation.

The next 20 minutes were really unsettling. You can see me checking the time on my dive watch at the moment the problem first starts. Then we played a dramatic reconstruction of what was heard by air traffic control from the leader of Flight 19 at the exact same moment—two hours into the flight as us. They reported their compasses looked wrong and the sky looked all funny. That was the last thing ever heard from them [sic]. I already knew this as my producer James Buchanan and I had been studying the transcripts as the basis for our reconstruction.

Do you know— the next 20 minutes were very uncomfortable. What if the GPS didn't work? What if we found ourselves 200 miles from our calculated position like another contributor to the programme had experienced in his Cessna between Grand Bahama and Fort Lauderdale? Twenty minutes passed and we fired up the GPS. We were 80 miles away from where the pilot thought we were. I think we experienced exactly the same anomaly as Flight 19. Despite the hot summer sun beating through the Plexiglass cockpit, I felt a chill run through me where I sat in the navigator's seat behind the pilot.

The sting in the tail was as we flew back towards Fort Lauderdale after a five hour flight— low on fuel— I looked up directly above me for some reason. We were at about five thousand feet and way, way up in the blue of the sky above me were five silver objects. I thought at first they were military jets practicing dog fights or an array of weather balloons. But these objects, which looked shiny and spherical, were darting around in big circles like the rings of the Olympic logo. They were so high I could only just make them out. And they were not leaving contrails like a jet. At that height they would almost certainly have been if they were jets. I estimated their speed, assuming my guess at their height was also roughly correct at 50,000 feet, was between 1,000 and 5,000 mph.

When we landed we were all wrung out from the heat, stress and complexity of what just happened. And the Danish Meteorological Office satellite data analysis? They handed me a piece of paper when I got back to London with a printout of a map of the world. There was a blue triangular shape over the area stretching between Bermuda, Miami and Costa Rica as well as a similar shape over the South China Sea. The chief officer who gave me the printout said the blue area represented a drop of 6 % in the electromagnetic field in both areas. Not gravity. EMF. He couldn't explain it but said that sort of anomaly was unprecedented. 0.6 % would be more what he'd expect. He went on to say that sort of inequality between two regions would act like two levels of water finding the same level. Which would store millions of amperes of electricity in the upper atmosphere. And as Nikola Tesla and latterly the much maligned John Hutchison in Vancouver discovered, Tesla coil type fields can change the molecular structure of metal and make it granular and brittle. It can also spin a compass like a Ferris Wheel. You can't beat a bit of good science to bring a little clarity to a crazy story.

QUESTION: How big would you estimate the objects to have been?

SIMON: Hard to say as it was hard to judge the distance. I really couldn't say accurately but maybe 20 feet wide apiece.

QUESTION: When did the compass begin to spin and when did it finally return to normal?

SIMON: After we passed over Grand Bahama and it returned to normal after we turned back over Grand Bahama so it was for about an hour.

While independently arrived at, Simon Ludgate's magnetic field discoveries nevertheless compliment some old and esoteric theories of other researchers and yet at the same time provide a far more rational basis off which to theorize. For instance, the late Dr. J. Manson Valentine believed that strong magnetic

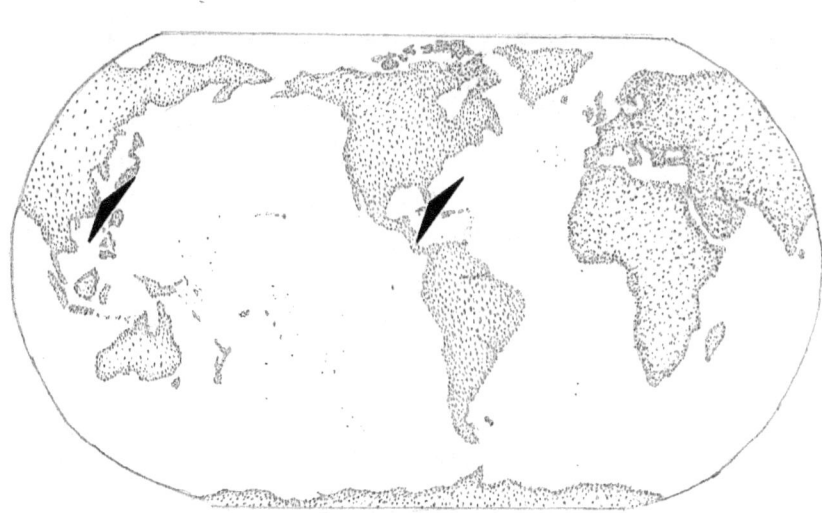

The charted areas of magnetic anomalies based on the readouts given Simon Ludgate by the Danish Meteorological Office. The triangle in the Pacific is on the exact opposite side of the Earth as the triangle in the Atlantic/Caribbean. It corresponds with the area known as the "Devil's Sea," a section of sea known for mysterious disappearances and often considered the Bermuda Triangle of the Pacific.

fields could open up doors to other dimensions. However, without any catalyst for the creation of anomalies, he opted to propose that the areas of magnetic anomalies encountered in the Triangle had been created in the wake of UFOs, which his studies had indicated visited the Bermuda Triangle more than any other place on Earth. Somehow the UFOs could create these anomalies through their own still-unfathomable (to us) type of propulsion, in order to come and go from other places on this planet or into outer space or even into and out of other dimensions. In doing so they ionized pockets of air— and these were the locations in which planes and ships conducted the "electronic fog." Or they created intense magnetic fields through which the craft slipped into other dimensions. As Simon's flight experiences convey, these two phenomena—UFOs and electromagnetic anomalies— are the most frequently encountered enigmas in the Triangle.

While the verified existence of an overall magnetic field

fluctuation in the Triangle does not bolster Dr. Valentine's personal theory regarding UFOs, modern magnetic field readouts, such as those provided to Simon Ludgate, outline for us an entire area that is anomalous. In and of itself the overall anomaly does not affect travel. We should, however, appreciate that it may turn the area into the medium in which more intense and localized electromagnetic phenomena can be created or it may even play a role in intensifying periods of electromagnetic anomalies from other sources.

Among the scientific tests done in the region (for other reasons) some have provided tantalizing clues pointing to the existence of local magnetic anomalies. The most provocative are readouts indicating the Triangle is prone to natural magnetic vortices. In essence, they were vertical but invisible tunnels similar to the horizontal tunnel Bruce Gernon had experienced in the power of the electric storm cloud. We must recall that it was within that vortex tunnel that Gernon had conducted the "electronic fog."

Valentine and Gernon are not alone in positing that there must be more than one source for the generation of electronic fog and, perhaps, for even more astounding effects than experienced by Gernon. In their theory's favor are the repeated encounters by pilots and shipmasters of electronic fog on clear days. Valentine believed that these could indicate the locations used by UFOs to materialize in our planet or dimension while Gernon is more conservative, believing that if invisible vortices have the same or more power than the tunnel he experienced they may be a door to Time-Space.

Esoteric theories notwithstanding, the purpose of Project Magnet and a study of its results reveal the disquieting potential of what can only be called unexplained vortices and their significance to the phenomenon of the Bermuda Triangle.

Chapter 7

Vortices, Space-Time Continua and Electromagnetic Anomalies

There is perhaps no greater mystery facing collective science than the forces around and within us that though they are invisible they leave effects in the physical world to confirm their existence. The Earth's magnetic field is largely still a mystery and along with this the origins of gravity. Gravity is evident whereas magnetism is reproducible. Gravity exists in varying strength on all planets, the product or partner of its collective mass. But not all planets have magnetic fields. Either they are considered too small (dwarf planets) for the theory of convection of the molten iron core to conduct an electric current (dynamo) or, for the Moon, possibly because it does not rotate on its axis like the Earth (and other major planets) and therefore enough constant fluid motion of its conducting liquid iron core does not take place to generate the current.

To an extent magnetism seems less mysterious to us than gravity because we know how to generate a magnetic field. Gravity, on the other hand, isn't a field per se, apparently, but a force or, more acceptable to say today, a "natural phenomenon," which means it is a byproduct; and phenomena are the byproduct of several factors or conditions. And our inability to harness these factors and create gravity has kept us from conquering the Universe. Its blueprint is all around us. Yet we have not been able to read it properly.

In a sense all creation is the result of vortex kinesis— the swirling motion of energy. It is inherent and perpetual in the atom by the tremendous speeds of the electrons in orbit around the protons and neutrons in the core. Since atoms are the building blocks of all matter everything therefore is energy. When the planets formed, it could not have been the power of gravity or their mass revolving around the Sun that made them coalesce. Centrifugal force was involved, but like a forming tornado the mass and energy turned in on itself and intensified the cycle. As the planets condensed, gravity came with the mass, and with mass came the bending of space around the planets. Compacted together in all this mass was the sum of the planets' EMR (electromagnetic radiation), and from within the molten cores electric currents put out magnetic fields that cocooned the planets.

This fairly simple sounding origin has, however, created complex and intricate tiers of phenomena— gravity, magnetic fields, EMR, and the planets themselves distorting space.

This is the blueprint. Albert Einstein was the first to try and read it, believing the doorway to Time itself lay within it. He famously postulated in his Theory of Relativity that Time and Space are intertwined. He also proposed that gravity is related to the bending or curvature of space which occurs around a planet by its mass and as it hurls around the Sun. Proof of Einstein's theory came from studies of stars and quasars passing behind the Sun during an eclipse. In each case the light of a star or quasar deflected in accordance with the computations predicted by Einstein's theory. Space was undeniably curved around the Sun. Electromagnetic wavelengths (like light) bend though it. Further proof of Einstein's theory was revealed by the comparison of atomic clocks at orbital heights with those at sea level; those closer to the center of gravity (at sea level) record the passing of Time just infinitesimally slower than those at orbital heights. Atomic clocks have therefore revealed that Time Continua are set by the tempo of energy— the stronger the gravity, the slower the continuum. Simply put, the intensification of gravity can slow the Time Continuum because it is affecting the tempo of our own atomic structure, out of which we and our entire continuum are comprised and intricately interwoven.

Because of this harmony we are completely unaware that we are in a distinct (though minor) continuum that is nanoseconds slower than the solar system's. Equally we are completely unaware of the planet's speed and shape because we are oriented toward the center of gravity here, and all things within this planet's gravitational field move together in sync, with the same load, in the same continuum. Without this "force" or "phenomenon" *no* world is possible. Gravity is required to form any habitable pocket of life.

Unlimited progress therefore comes with the power to be able to artificially create gravity. Long distance space flight would require spaceships to be the center of their own gravity. Shuttling back and forth from a planet to the orbiting spaceship would require some propulsion force other than weighty and volatile jet fuel. Anti-gravity propulsion is not only practical for travel in an atmosphere, it is essential for speed in space travel. It is impossible for us to propel a spaceship at the speed of light (186,000 miles per second), and even if we could the nearest star, Alpha Centauri, would be a trek of 4.3 years, with a round trip being almost 9 years. Moreover, at those speeds the mass of a spaceship would increase and with this the curvature of space around it. The result is that a time continuum would be created, one so slow for those in the spaceship that they would perceive a round trip to Alpha Centauri to take about a day. They would, however, return to an Earth that is 8.6 years in the future.

As the reader can appreciate now, Time is no longer a concept. It is accepted to be the extension or progression of any continuum, and adjusting (warping) a continuum is the natural byproduct of the strength of gravity and mass curving space around it. The problem with trying to harness gravity is that as a byproduct we have not been able to bring together all the components to create zero gravity around the aircraft (or spaceship) so that it is the center of its own gravity and free of the Earth's pull; so that, more importantly, a spaceship can speed through space in excess of light speed and maintain the Earth's Time Continuum and prevent the disastrous warping of Time by the extreme bending of space around it.

However, failure at nullifying the Earth's gravity in a restricted area, with the purpose of assisting in avionics and rocketry liftoff, has been the constant result of several skunkworks type projects. Nevertheless, theorists believe it is possible to create aircraft (or spacecraft) that are capable of creating their own center of gravity. They speculate that even if gravity is created or assisted by the curvature of space around a planet, an enormous effect impossible to replicate, it does not necessarily mean that gravitational fields cannot be created in other ways. The bending of space means the bending of wavelengths in space. And this would mean, naturally, the bending of electromagnetic wavelengths.

Other than a planet, what indeed could bend space or those wavelengths within it enough to turn them onto each other into a vortex? And what would be the effect on space, gravity, time, and even dimensions?

The closest mankind has come to seeing electromagnetism and matter together create a swirling vortex of energy is a tornado, one of the most visible earthly vortices. They are not just a funnel of air currents swirled into a violent maelstrom. Observers close enough by chance or design to see a tornado pass over or at a slight angle have been able to see up inside the funnel. Although the event has obviously not been frequent, in each instance the observer has noted two vortices in action, an outer or shear vortex, and an inner, more organized or lazy vortex and a center void that is highly charged. From one particularly rare vantage point, the central core was seen to be glowing like a phosphorescent cloud, almost as if, to the observer, it was an electric filament.

One fortunate observer, Roy Hall, in Texas on May 3, 1943, survived to describe the central core inside one tornado with mesmerizing detail. While the bottom rim was still 20 feet off the ground and about to destroy his house, he looked up.

The interior of the funnel was hollow; the rim itself appearing to be not over 10 feet in thickness and, owing possibly to the light within the funnel, appeared perfectly opaque. Its inside was so slick and even that it resembled the interior of a glazed standpipe. The rim had another motion which I was, for a moment, too dazzled to grasp. Presently I did. The whole thing was rotating, shooting past from right to left with incredible velocity.

. . .I was looking far up the interior of a great tornado funnel! It extended upward for over a thousand feet, and was swaying gently, and bending slowly toward the southeast. Down at the bottom, judging from the circle in front of me, the funnel was about 150 yards across. Higher up it was larger, and seemed to be partly filled with a bright cloud, which shimmered like a fluorescent light. This brilliant cloud was in the middle of the funnel, not touching the sides, as I recall having seen the walls extending on up outside the cloud. . . As the upper portion of the huge pipe swayed over, another phenomenon took place. It looked as if the whole column were composed of rings or layers, and when a higher ring moved on toward the southeast, the ring immediately below slipped over to get back under it. This rippling motion continued on down toward the lower tip.

There is a particularly intriguing observation within Hall's statement as it pertains to the subject at hand. The bright or charged cloud hovering in the center was created by the vortex around it. There is a potential corollary here with explaining electronic fog. In itself it may not embody an energy vortex. Rather it may be at the center of an invisible vortex of energy around it.

It is in the light of these real and visible vortices, and the electromagnetic component to or side effects from them, that the work of Canadian electrical engineer Wilbert B. Smith is particularly relevant as it applies to trying to explain some of the mysteries of the Bermuda Triangle. In 1950 he set out to find areas of anomalies in the magnetic field in the hope of harnessing these areas as a source of energy. Anomalies were necessary, to use an analogy, much in the same way one can more easily exacerbate an eddy at the side of a river into a stronger whirlpool; in Smith's goal, to eventually learn how to manipulate power from the magnetic field.

Project Magnet, the official name of Smith's endeavor, was sanctioned under his directorship and first set out to test the magnetic field. Numerous test flights revealed fluctuations existed, sometimes up to 1,000 feet in diameter. Compared to the normal readings around them, a marked lack of attraction to the Earth was noticed in these circular areas, which Smith termed "areas of reduced binding." Essentially the circular shape of these invisible areas suggested magnetic vortices, though he was cautious about their origins.

"Areas of reduced binding" were not static. When returning to look for them months later, Smith's project could not find them. He believed they either moved on or had dissipated. Thus unlike ore deposits there was nothing static below the sea that created the magnetic variations. Although they were not chartable, relevant to the study here they did predominate in tropic waters like the Triangle.

During Wilbert Smith's tenure with Project Magnet (1950-1954) he had proposed that some of these "areas of reduce binding" could be dangerous to aircraft. Potentially each could produce powerful wind shear around it, apparently like a visible tornado vortex. Remaining purely invisible, however, a pilot could never see them in order to avoid them.

Destruction by invisible vortex is not unknown, the vortices in these cases being the invisible swirling and deadly horizontal funnels created in the wake of a large airliner. Obviously, they are unnoticeable except in those rare cases where a smaller aircraft was seen to be sucked into an airliner's wake and twisted around and thrown to the ground.

For example, on September 23, 1958, witnesses saw a small plane so close to the stern of a large Air Force C-124 that they thought the larger aircraft was towing the smaller aircraft. Others then heard a loud boom, and 5 witnesses saw a small plane drop "straight down," its wings folded around it and pieces falling off. This turned out to be a small Piper Cub en route to Virginia from Amityville, New York. After a careful consideration, the accident report concluded that the wing vortex of the C-124 ripped apart the Cub, "the nature of the failure— its remarkable similarity on right and left side— can only be explained by violent downloads to both wings applied simultaneously, causing simultaneous failures. . .Evidence strongly indicates that the overload was caused by the destructively energetic vortex in the wake of a large aircraft."

Decades after Smith's discovery, another curious discovery helped to place an intriguing interpretation upon his "areas of reduced binding." Quite by accident by Dr. Evgeny Plodkletnov seems to have created a magnetic vortex in a laboratory. Experimenting at Tampere University, Finland, with a superconductor he noticed that smoke from a pipe immediately floated straight up to the ceiling after it had wafted over the superconductor. At present his staff was spinning the superconductor at such high speeds it had to be encased in an outer shell of liquid nitrogen. What can only be assumed is that an invisible magnetic vortex had been created, to which all in the lab were oblivious until it became visible through its astonishing effect on the pipe smoke. And this effect was obviously on the strength of gravity over the superconductor.

In a very real way, Smith's "areas of reduced binding" seem like a much larger and natural example of what Plodkletnov discovered. However, Dr. Plodkletnov nor his staff ever noted any form of atmospheric disturbance in the lab. In comparing his example with Smith's theory, one wonders if a sudden rise and then plunge of the aircraft would rather not be the result of flying through such an "area of reduced binding;" in some instances the plane breaking apart.

Radar has never captured a midair breakup in the Bermuda Triangle that would test this hypothesis. Telltale clues would be the scope recording debris remaining in a fairly confined area in the air (within the vortex), unlike in more common cases of midair explosion or implosion where large pieces, including wings, can be hurled thousands of feet and picked up on the scope as a separate target (for at least one sweep).

Horrific booms overhead, however, have been heard by witnesses, often with dramatic results. Storm clouds obscured from one fisherman's view off West End, Grand Bahama Is. on

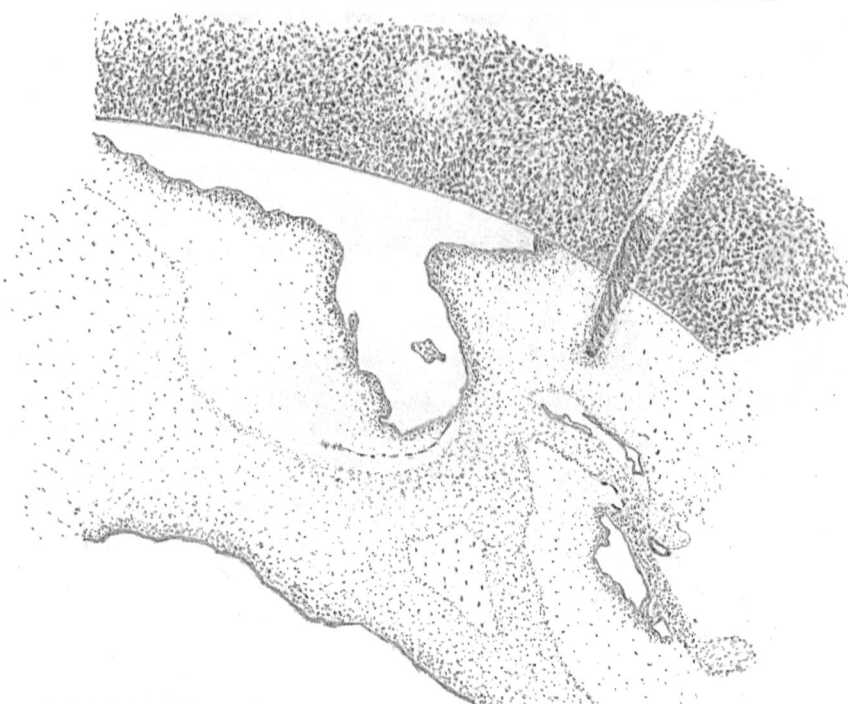

Artistic concept of an "area of reduced binding" leading upward into space.

March 24, 2008, a light Mooney SR22 overhead with two persons on board headed to the nearby airport. Although turbulence and heavy rain were prevalent at sea level, the weather should not have been enough to cause the level of destruction that happened. In any case, after a loud boom, almost to the level of thunder, the fisherman saw "what appeared to be an airplane engine falling from the sky. The engine blew up upon hitting the water." A moment later "several other pieces of what was thought to be an aircraft wing and other pieces fell from the sky." Although he didn't retrieve any of the pieces, the fisherman caught glimpses of airplane wreckage and what appeared to be a shirtless body.

It should be underlined that the engine was actually separated from the fuselage, testifying to dynamic destructive forces at work. There was no evidence suggesting fire or explosion. Convective activity in the storm could be to blame, but considering the unusual extent of the destruction the investigators only tentatively assumed the weather might have been a factor.

This is not the only example of unusual destruction in the Triangle that would result in zero recognizable debris on the ocean bottom, no matter how shallow. A sudden "winking out" on radar, as if the airplane vanished through a "hole in the sky," however, is far more common.

There is more reason to believe today that Wilbert Smith's discoveries of these transient areas of "reduced binding," if they are magnetic vortices, would not make their presence known by atmospheric disturbances such as wind shear, but rather make their presence known on the electronic equipment on the airplane or boat passing near them or through them, causing the compass to spin and the gauges to jump about and act erratic. No physical disturbance was noted over Podkletnov's vortex, only the obvious elevation of any matter when placed over it.

It has always been a fact that those aircraft and boats that have experienced the "electronic fog" have never experienced turbulence. They have power but "nothing works," the effects perhaps of passing through the vortex and perhaps of even conducting "electronic fog" as a result. Again, as in Gernon's experience, the presence of the plane or ship may be necessary to give centrifugal direction to the energy which may lead to the forming of the vortex and fog around the craft.

Large ships do not encounter "electronic fog" perhaps because they are too big for a vortex to use them and form around them. Instead when hypothetically passing through one of these vortices they experience unexplained and spontaneous electronic effects and the spinning of their compasses.

On a case by case basis in the Bermuda Triangle there is great varying in the intensity of electromagnetic phenomenon as experienced by pilots and shipmasters. Sometimes it is sufficient to send the compass spinning but little more. Other times it is more intense, affecting gauges and power output. Still other times it becomes so intense that the "electronic fog" appears or, apparent only at night, even blue-green glowing auras around the vessel similar to St. Elmo's Fire. Most interesting of all, some general locales seem prone to the reoccurrence of the phenomenon and yet not exactly at the same specific spots within these locales. A link must exist that is not the obvious one of a wreck or some other stable magnetic source.

Locations for such unexplained magnetic deviations seem to follow the continental shelves, of which there are many in the southwest corner of the Triangle if we include the Bahama banks and their steep and sudden drop off from shallow depths to abyssal voids. The phenomenon is particularly noteworthy along the Tongue of the Ocean's rim. On the same shoot in 2004 as when he flew in the Avenger, Simon Ludgate was out in a boat with his crew off Nassau when their compass went berserk. "It was the area on the sea charts which indicates no magnetic north, and sure enough the compass began to spin 'round uselessly until we left the area; then it reverted."

Below the sea here there is evidence for the existence of transient magnetic fields. Areas of once-charged material have been found. Testing the dipoles in the rocks of these flows or "oozings" has revealed a different alignment with the Earth's magnetic field. Since some of these flows are recent, their rocks' skewed dipoles indicate that there had been a local distortion of the magnetic field since no global fluctuation had occurred at that time.

The potential of Wilbert Smith "areas of reduced binding" interacting or even bending or deflecting in response to one of these nearby concurrent magnetic flows is intriguing to consider. Potentially it gives us a warped rather than a purely vertical vortex.

Accepting that Smith's "areas of reduced binding" are magnetic vortices, then Smith's funnels come up from the core of the Earth, where they are created as eddies in the molten fringes of the dynamo's current. Then they continue upward into space. On the other hand, the charged material seeping up from the continental shelves is an event happening relatively close to the surface of the planet. If these two unrelated events occurred in proximity to each other, one can imagine a redirection or bending of these invisible magnetic funnels. Perhaps one of these magnetic vortices could even deflect into a horizontal plane and thus be an invisible yet similar tunnel through which flew Bruce Gernon. Encountering these tunnels at an angle or even horizontally rather than vertically, the aircraft or ship would travel inside the invisible vortex and not simply and quickly pass through it.

Given that tornados produce charged clouds in the center of their vortex, one wonders if some of these invisible vortices could produce large masses of "electronic fog" at sea level. These would become temporarily visible on radar if they were intense enough, in addition to being visible to the eye if they lasted long enough. False land echoes on radar have been reported frequently enough so that the source for some can be categorized as visible but "electronic" fog.

During a voyage in the summer of 1980, while cruising along the Andros Island drop-off of the odd and deep Tongue of the Ocean on the northeast of Andros Island, Curt Rowlett and the other bridge crew of their Coast Guard cutter had an encounter with unexplained forces which may suggest the power of these interactions. He recalls:

> What this amounted to was a radar return that suddenly showed what appeared to be a land mass three miles dead ahead of our ship where no "land" actually existed. At the same moment that the "land" appeared on the radar, our ship's compass began swinging wildly for about three minutes until, without explanation, the radar return simply disappeared from the screen as suddenly as it had appeared.
>
> This incident was taken seriously enough that the Captain was woken up by the officer of the watch and the details were recorded in the ship's log. We never did hear any explanation as to what might have caused the false radar return (it was determined that our radar was not malfunctioning), but at the time it happened, I remembered having read about how other sailors had experienced similar phenomena in the same area. (I was on helm watch when this incident occurred and was steering the ship when the compass went haywire. I also saw the radar return and watched as it slowly disappeared from the screen when we were approximately a mile and a half away from the object. I should also point out that our ship's lookout on duty that night never reported a visual sighting on any "land mass" and that the sky was clear with no rain or clouds present).

What Rowlett and his bridge mates may have seen on radar

was "electronic fog," captured for minutes just after it was visible and before it faded away.

In 1956 Guardsman Frank Flynn experienced a visible fog while serving in the Coast Guard. It had registered so densely on the radarscope they too thought it was a landmass. In this case, however, they approached the radar target and energized their search light. It bounced off a solid vapor. Although they did not experience problems with their compasses, the vessel began to lose power as they entered the fog, at which point they put the helm over and broke free again. Coincidently, or not, it was then that the power returned.

In Rowlett's experience it seems there was the spontaneous formation of some energy field powerful enough to affect the ship's compass from a distance and dense enough to register on radar. The difference between the two cases is that Flynn encountered the visible fog in deep water whereas Rowlett's cutter was along the shelf of the Tongue, the area where it seems more than one factor could intertwine to create more intense electromagnetic phenomena and even, perhaps, in this case the distorting of a transient magnetic vortex into a horizontal electronic fog tunnel that soon disappeared again, leaving only the relatively harmless effect on the compass and considerable bewilderment in those who experienced it.

It is precisely along the "drop offs" where the most inexplicable disappearances occur, where aircraft disappear while coming in for a landing, yachts cruising over and then suddenly gone, and where many had to cross in order to sail over the Bahama banks' shallow waters but never left a trace in the transparent waters indicating they had reached them.

With the advent of the worldwide web an old crewman of the USS *New* could recount his ship's encounter in the Triangle on the ship's website and brave collective ridicule if he was not accurate. Joe Hurd admits that it meant little to them that they were in the Bermuda Triangle, as they had traveled it many times on their route from Norfolk to the Caribbean. Until this cruise in 1973 they had never experienced anything. He recounts the following:

Vortices, Space-Time Continua and EM Anomalies

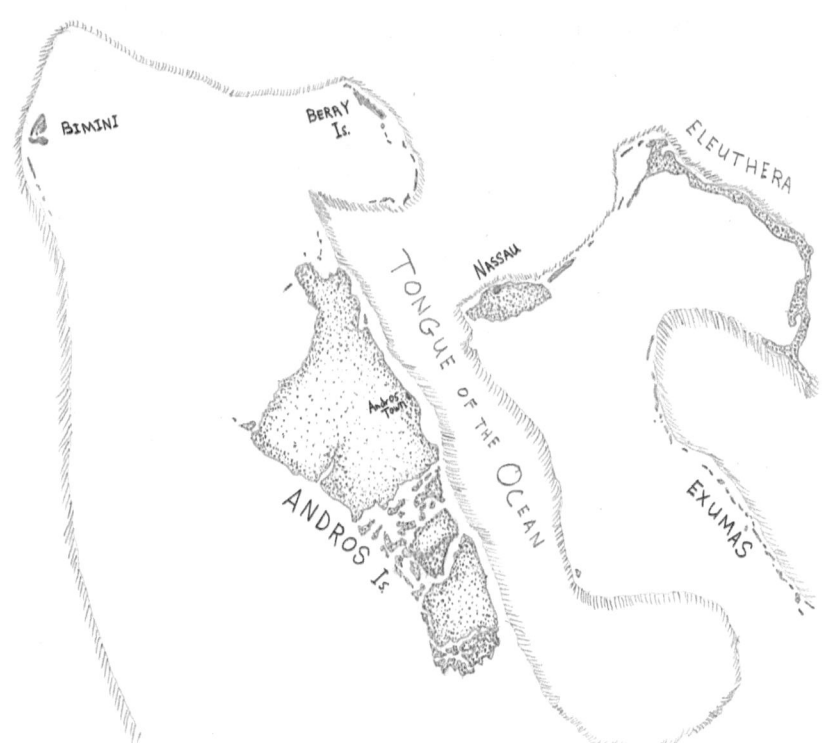

A geologic oddity unique in all the world, the deep Tongue of the Ocean is the center of unusual encounters with electronic fog and other electromagnetic anomalies, especially along its perimeter, the precipitous "drop off."

This particular incident took place on the mid-watch while I was at the helm... I had been steering a steady course for maybe 20 or 30 minutes. It was a calm, clear night and the mood on the bridge was relaxed. The Skipper was in his quarters. I had looked away from the gyro-compass readout that the helmsman steered by for several seconds, and when I looked back down at it I was horrified to see that the readout was spinning as though we were in a hard turn to starboard.

Hurd immediately checked to make sure the rudder was 'midships and then he admits he called to the Boatswain with more urgency in his voice than he intended. The Boatswain, the Officer of the Deck, and the Junior Officer of the Deck, all responded. "The OOD immediately checked the gyro-compass itself which was mounted at the starboard end of the bridge. The readout on the gyro-compass was also spinning. As after-steering was being contacted to ascertain whether there may have been a problem with the rudder, I glanced at the magnetic compass which was mounted just forward of the helm. The magnetic compass was also spinning! . . . As the OOD stared blankly at the magnetic compass I knew that he was thinking what we were all thinking. There was no earthly reason for both the gyro and the magnetic compasses to be malfunctioning in the same way, because each operated completely independently of the other." The *New* survived its one odd experience in the Triangle, but Hurd conceded "that the Triangle gave us a small taste of why it has such a mysterious reputation."

Transient electromagnetic anomalies are the backbone of the enigma of the Bermuda Triangle. The varying degrees they present may be explained by the intensity of the source, the most severe generating an "electronic fog" that develops around a plane or in a cluster on the surface of the sea whereas lesser intensity only causes compasses to spin and other electronic equipment to become erratic.

Small to medium size aircraft, however, may still vanish, though not because of turbulence. Combining the results of artificial vortices (Plodkletnov's) with the potential of a much larger and infinitely more powerful natural one ("areas of reduced binding") it would not be farfetched to consider that an airplane can disappear by being thrust upward beyond its ceiling, the result being breaking up and the final resting place is the ocean far from where it was flying.

Several theorists believe something less destructive but equally sensational could be the result— to cut to the chase, the aircraft or boat could disappear by being sent into another space-time continuum. This last theory is predicated on the belief that the vortex intensifies as the plane enters it, focuses on it, becoming strong enough in a fraction of time to bend space and therewith create, at least according to the parameters of this theory, a space-time warp.

Once consigned to the "fringe," even "idiot fringe," the theory of time warps is no longer dismissed as fantasy or the fodder of science fiction. In a very real way the essence of time warping now commands a healthy respect within theoretical physics and modern philosophy, and after this the next step is applied physics. In fact, time warping is so understood that a lot of research in physics has gone to figuring how to prevent time warping in spaceflight to make intergalactic travel feasible. A spaceship hurling through space just under light speed, as it has already been pointed out, would experience such an increase in mass it would be bending space around it. The result would be far more intense than what the Earth does. Instead of a couple of nanoseconds difference in the time continuum the effect would be years.

It is postulated by those who seek to conquer Time, at least intellectually, that if space could be bent enough Time within the center of that space could be sufficiently slowed so that in essence a person could travel into the future, or to use a more accurate but not so often employed phrase, let the future travel around them.

The problem with using time warps to explain disappearances on Earth is that time warps represent a *different* continuum and not a *different* dimension. It can hardly be said that the Earth is in a separate dimension from the other planets in our solar system despite the fact there is a micro difference in the space-time continuum at the surface of the Earth compared to orbital heights. In trying to apply this theoretically to the phenomenon of missing aircraft in the Triangle, the rub is, to use the analogy of Wilbert Smith's vortices, that a plane traveling into one of these magnetic vortices, even if the vortex was strong enough to bend space and slow Time, the plane really does not physically pass into another dimension. Nor would it be impervious to impact from another aircraft as it is still ultimately a part of our greater space continuum.

For a magnetic vortex to be able to cause a disappearance, theoretically, it would have to be able to do more than bend space. It would have to open a pathway to somewhere else. Or it would have to completely change the wavelength of the atom, perhaps to a wavelength upon which atoms of an entirely parallel universe function. Precisely just such a clue that this manipulation is possible comes from the fusion of dissimilar material seen in the wake of tornado vortices— though, naturally, this does not mean that a vortex in the Triangle could do this.

The seas off eastern Australia have a similar reputation as the Bermuda Triangle. UFOs are frequently reported and strange maritime disappearances and other mysteries have been recorded throughout history, including the sudden appearance of unnatural looking lenticular clouds, recorded in one vivid case by no less than Sir Francis Chichester. He was flying his *Gypsy Moth* from Lord Howe Island to the coast on June 10, 1931. His encounter draws a disturbing parallel with the above reports while at the same time adds chilling elements pointing to instantaneous disappearance. As he reports on page 165 in his autobiography *The Lonely Sea and Sky*:

> Suddenly, ahead and thirty degrees to the left, there were bright flashes in several places, like the dazzle of a heliograph. I saw a dull grey-white airship coming towards me. It seemed impossible, but I could have sworn that it *was* an airship, nosing toward me like an oblong pearl. Except for a cloud or two, there was nothing else in the sky. I looked around, sometimes catching a flash or a glint, and turning again to look at the airship I found that it had disappeared. I screwed up my eyes, unable to believe them, and twisted the seaplane this way and that, thinking that the airship must be hidden by a blind spot. Dazzling flashes continued in four or five places, but I still could not pick out any planes. Then, out of some clouds to my right front, I saw another, or the same, airship advancing. I watched it intently, determined not to look away for a fraction of a second: I'd see what happen to this one, if I had to chase it. I drew steadily closer, until perhaps a mile away, when suddenly it vanished. Then it reappeared, close to where it had vanished: I watched with angry intentness. It drew closer, and I could see the dull gleam of light on its nose and back. It came on, but instead of increasing in size, it diminished as it approached. When quite near, it suddenly became its own ghost—one second I could see through it, and the next it had vanished. I decided it could only be a diminutive cloud, perfectly shaped like an airship and then dissolving, but it was uncanny that it should exactly resume the same shape after it had once vanished. I turned toward the flashes, but these too had vanished. All this was many years before anybody spoke of flying saucers. Whatever it was I saw, it seemed to have been very much like what people have since claimed to be flying saucers.

It does not seem that Sir Francis was seeing flying saucers at all, but an odd joining of theories is unavoidable to contemplate here. Flashes of light were independent of the appearance of the "airship," as if to suggest the unnatural cloud was the product of massive electromagnetic energy. Unlike those experienced by both the *Mohican* and Bruce Gernon, it did not move on or morph into a powerful storm cell. Just as suddenly as it had appeared it instantaneously vanished. Presumably, it would have destroyed or taken with it any craft had it been present. This pearlescent form seems identical to those experienced in the Triangle, only here this was sudden appearance and sudden disappearance as if doorways were electromagnetically opened.

Superstring and Wormhole theories have tried to explain not only the existence or other universes but the pathways by which these dimensions can be reached. Each, of course, is within its own curvature of space, within its own continuum of Time, whether it is equivalent to our own, slower or faster.

From there it expands to cause us to more than wistfully contemplate the Universe. To believe that the Universe is linear, that is, follows straight lines, is equivalent to insisting the Earth is flat because visually we can see no curves. It is increasingly possible that we live not in a Universe but in a Multiverse, our particular Universe being only one massive bubble of curved space abutted and pushed upon by the curvature of other adjoining universes. Our eyes see along the path of light, and we simply cannot see beyond the curvature of our own Universe to even get a glimpse at other possible universes. An example of how our vision works on Earth seems apropos. If light was so bent, and we had the vision, we could look around the Earth and see the back of our own head. The same may be true of the Universe in which we live. What universes lie beyond the curve of our universe that we cannot see or detect?

It could be that such theorizing represents wasted time and energy, if the pursuit of truth could ever or should ever be gauged that way. Explanations or theories of this nature would strike the humbug as trying to explain a lack of evidence, an attitude which overlooks the fact that the very nature of "to disappear" implies a lack of evidence. There is a vast difference between clues and evidence. Certainly collectively the circumstances of those missing in the Bermuda Triangle constitute a powerful clue that warrants our attention to at least consider what potentially could explain incidents that defy our current strictures of physics.

It is the nature of anti-thesis to be reactionary and not progressive, the purpose to render sterile the thesis, often because of an uncomfortable proposition, a habit that leads nowhere but to the stifling of progress, particularly tragic at a philosophic level since discoveries often only follow the expression of the idea or the desire to prove an attractive mystery. Scientifically put, the process properly applied is called testing an hypothesis— which naturally implies that the hypothesis had to come first. If the losses of so many aircraft, ships, and the people they carried can help us to understand and even unravel Time, Dimensions, and Space, we cannot hesitate to take the chance, even if it is just intellectually, else their deaths (presumably) have been in vain.

All those not satisfied with the esoteric ramifications of time-warps and vortices, however, do not recoil into the realm of banal suggestions. On the contrary, they note that no natural explanations can account for the circumstances of the disappearances, asserting that attempts to take natural phenomena to a more esoteric level is merely willful avoidance of the evidence that points to intelligence behind the disappearances. This idea of UFO abductions has always been a popular theory, but it has achieved chilling confirmation in more recent years, both in startling developments in the Triangle and in the sum total of disappearances of aircraft over the whole world, and yet these disappearances are confined to locations only over the oceans, where pilots' last words before they vanished identified what our science today insists is purely unidentified and it continually reassures us that these unidentified flying objects are by no means manned spacecraft from another world.

Jose Santos disappeared in his father's Ercoupe with Jose Torres in 1980. (Evelyn Rivera)

Cary Trantham's aircraft, in which she had her unusual encounter in 1995.

The Mystic *sinks on Cay Sal Bank, 2010. Below, the* What's Left? *beached at Cape Canaveral, 2003. (Coast Guard Photos).*

Flying in a restored Avenger in 2004 Simon Ludgate and his chase plane experienced a phenomenon that may bear on how Flight 19 got lost. (Simon Ludgate)
Below, the Healing Well on East Bimini flanked by a strange mound. (Bruce Gernon)

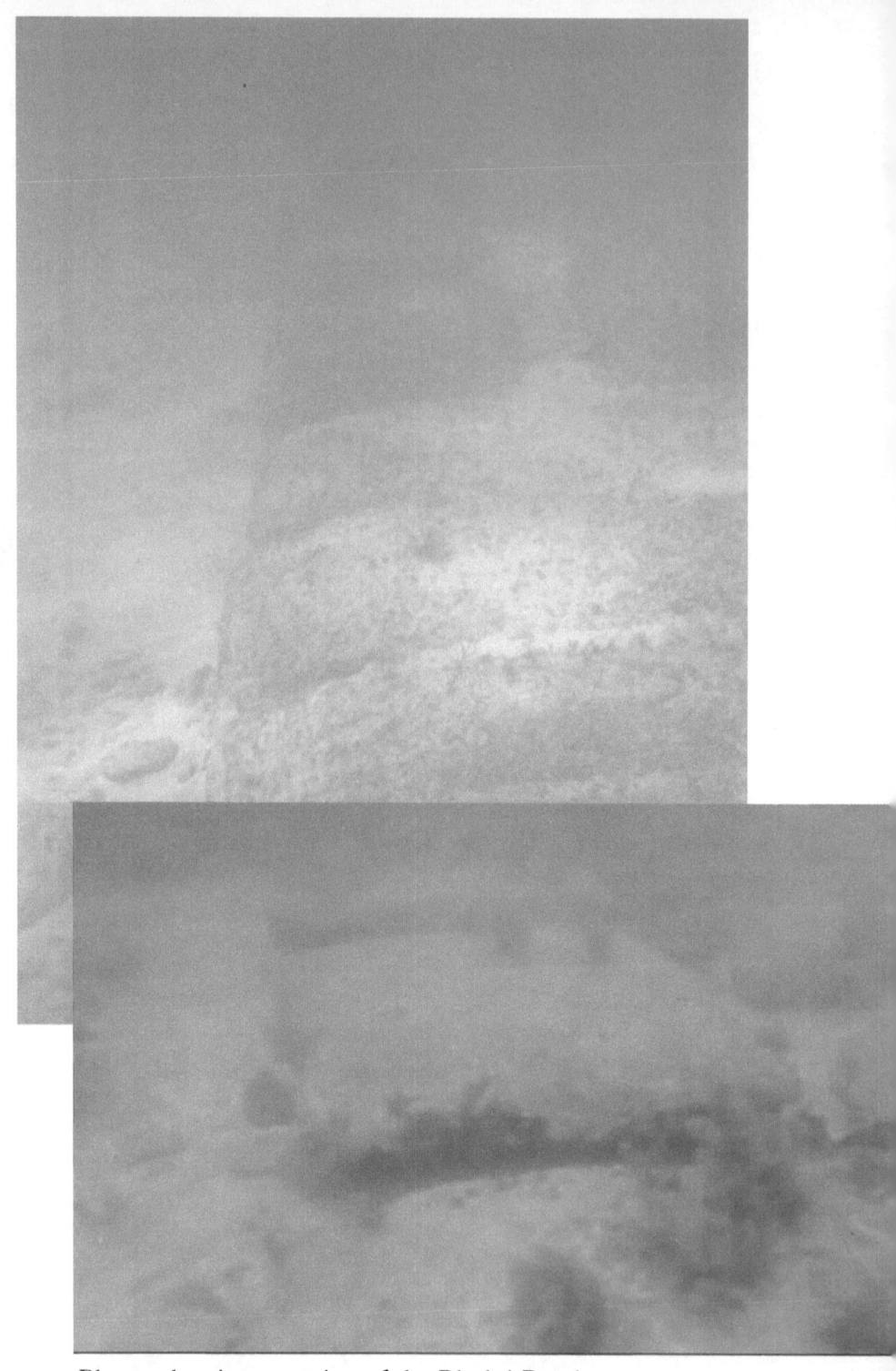

Photos showing a section of the Bimini Road.

Chapter 8

Worlds Above; Worlds Beneath

For the last 70 years the existence of UFOs in the atmosphere of the Earth is undisputed, though the origin of these UFOs remains hotly debated and the debate itself often ridiculed as applying only to the realm of dreamers and fantasists despite astronauts, generals, admirals, even heads of state, participating lively in the discussions and even declaring their firm belief in the existence of UFOs as more than just unidentified flying objects, the literal meaning of the acronym, but specifically endorsing UFOs as that which many have either worried or alternatively hoped— spaceships from another planet. Conspiracy theories and the occult aside, if the pro-ET theorists are right that the UFOs are from another planet then their decided lack of communicating with the inhabitants of Earth over the last 70 years or perhaps longer gives rise to some disturbing theories about the extraterrestrial occupants' regard for mankind.

Occult adherents would have us believe that they have been in communication with the ET entities, either physically or, more often, telepathically— the favored and unverifiable method of communication in the occult.

Outside of the fringe, there still resides in believers a deep certainty that UFOs are solid spacecraft, some unmanned probes, but most with inhabitants, relatively small in stature and likely insectoid in makeup. Believers include scientists, often air force pilots of almost every nation on Earth, politicians, and members of almost every national security defense program, NASA engineers, and astronauts. It is a remarkable tribute to the more disciplined nature of these vocations that UFOs are referred to within their discussions by the more outdated term "flying saucer"— a term that is simply accurate no matter what cartoon image it eventually came to conjure.

Witnesses to UFO sightings invariably describe them as saucer shaped. Over time a pattern has even emerged. Small discs of about 2 feet diameter, silvery chrome in appearance, have stalked and paced aircraft and rocket launches. Larger ones of about 30 to 60 feet in diameter are the most frequently seen, and may contain crewmen. Then there are those that are at least 100 feet in diameter and possibly ovoid in shape. Rocket shaped UFOs of the same length have also been seen. However, these too are most likely ovoid and when seen from the side they have a flattened rocket look, the observer having assumed an overall cylindrical shape to the craft, an optical mistake easy to make especially considering the state of shock the observer is immediately in after seeing one unexpectedly. And according to some there are those that are huge "cigar shaped" UFOs, so large they are dubbed "motherships" because they are proposed to be intergalactic super carriers.

Reports of flying saucers were so concise and numerous beginning on June 24, 1947, with Idaho pilot Ken Arnold reporting 9 disc-like objects flying along Mt. Rainer in Washington State, that they were unequivocally accepted by the US Air Force as real. Released Air Force documents contemporary to this period reveal an unhesitant certainty while at the same time reflecting a healthy skepticism that they were Russian experimental craft built by captured Nazi technology. Some holders of impressive rank expressed their suspicion they were a US secret project but one carried out by a compartmentalized branch of aeronautics so that they were unknown to the various

Air Force field commands, those who were most frequently fielding the reports and questions about sightings. Such a reserve ranked No. 1 on the list of General Nathan Twining, head of Air Materiel Command, when he assessed their origins to Intelligence.

Soon, however, it became apparent UFOs were not only *not* a US black project it became apparent UFOs were also not Soviet in origin. It is perhaps a humorous and forgivable quirk of human nature that the Air Force, some of whose highest ranking members endorsed the existence of flying saucers based on the clarity and multiplicity of sightings, now insisted they didn't exist. Obviously, the evidence had not changed. What had changed were the options for UFO origins. The options now excluded everything *but* extraterrestrial entities. Because of the prohibitive distance of intergalactic space, with flight times longer than a lifetime to get to Earth from the closest solar system, an origin from outer space was considered impossible. In short, the only alternative origin was not considered possible, so the reports of flying saucers that were once so clear were no longer considered to have been that clear and irrefutable. The new Air Force attitude was innocent enough, but the early documents wherein officers expressed a pro attitude (after their release to the public decades later) have only served to foster the notion that conspiracies and cover-ups brought about the change in attitude. To conspiracy theorists the new goal of the Air Force was to keep silent the truth about extraterrestrials visiting Earth but decidedly not deigning to communicate openly with its inhabitants— a haughty and sinister implication.

Some of the released documents from 1947 contain a frank exchange between Brigadier General George Schulgen of Intelligence and General Nathan Twining, in which Twining tells him plainly that the "phenomenon is real." The context, however, between the two is clearly that flying saucers exist in the vein of Russian secret weapons, which General Schulgen had suspected from the beginning. Since no plot is too farfetched for Intelligence personnel, Schulgen's theory included that perhaps a rogue group of Nazi scientists, who included some of those taken by the US at the close of WWII, were plying their knowledge to the German group of scientist taken by the USSR after conquering Germany.

A number of claims were circulating both in the popular press and within more restrictive channels that pieces of these "flying discs" or small versions of flying saucers had dropped to earth or had been discovered abandoned and out of power and, naturally, had been collected by those who had found them. Schulgen wanted every piece that had been retrieved, and even wanted the FBI to step in and investigate. Tracing the origins of the metals of these discs and the method of manufacture would obviously be something the FBI could do, an organization that otherwise has no edge in anything avionic or aerospace in nature.

A memo with J. Edgar Hoover's handwritten response was later released into the public domain. On the memo one assistant advised him to acquiesce to Schulgen's request and another wrote to refrain, forewarning that most of these cases of recovered discs had been "pranks." Hoover, however, wrote he was disposed to do it, adding the codicil that the FBI must have access to "all discs recovered," complaining that one had been grabbed by the Army and they wouldn't even let the FBI have a cursory examination of it. It seems nothing came of the FBI's involvement because soon enough the Air Force dispensed with Schulgen's theory that flying saucers were Russian in origin, essentially therewith dropping the idea of the FBI needing to investigate what must be material left by pranksters and a phenomena that was largely a misidentification of known objects. For those within the military who still believed flying saucers were real they believed them to be interstellar spacecraft, and the FBI was obviously of no use in proving this point.

Admirals and Generals joined Ret. Major Donald Keyhoe's civilian UFO organization NICAP, which developed into a credible reporting and investigating body to follow up on flying saucer reports independent of and in a more open manner than which its members felt the Air Force was doing in its own various projects (which eventually coalesced into Project Blue Book). Based on the continuing reports of sightings by credible observers, each member of NICAP was spurred on to believe that flying saucers were from outer space. These observers included pilots, scientists and qualified individuals who understood azimuth, distance, and the various degrees of light, etc., all which made it easier for the investigator with the same knowledge to assess the observed actions of the UFO in the sky.

Many of these observed UFO actions continued to defy any explanation from an Earthly standpoint. No conventional craft could make the maneuvers that the flying saucers were seen to do, such as right angle turns at a high rate of speed, sometimes in excess of thousands of miles per hour; hover, ascend with incredible but silent liftoff, and as it became repeatedly clear no Earthly government had any saucer-shaped aircraft. Some were observed so high up by Air Force pilots as to be traveling in low orbit.

Flocks or squadrons of flying saucers were observed more than once by Air Force pilots, including astronaut Gordon Cooper while flying with his squadron over Germany. What can only be called a "flock" was captured on the "Utah Film" taken on July 2, 1952, by Delbert Newhouse of the US Navy. Two glowing saucers move smoothly against the wind in the "Montana Film," taken on August 15, 1950, by Nick Mariana in Great Falls, Montana. Both films were examined by the military and said to contain genuine flying objects.

In the chronology of the phenomenon, the most disturbing reports are those that continued to not only show flying saucers to be real but to be following a disquieting pattern of checking our defense and aerospace installations. Flying saucers were seen most frequently by staff at key air bases and by those at missile defense and testing bases.

In a rare moment of transparency this fact was published in a national magazine. US Navy Commander Robert McLaughlin was the first military officer from the development side of research to have an article cleared, perhaps by accident, which appeared in *True* magazine in March 1950. In the article he describes the actions of saucers over White Sands Missile Proving Grounds in New Mexico, where he worked on top secret projects. Not only were these flying saucers observed by sight but also tracked by theodolite, ruling out illusions and hallucinations or auto-kinesis on the part of the observers.

Noting that they observed two 20-inch diameter discs follow a rocket from launch and through its course, McLaughlin is perhaps the first to inadvertently (or intentionally) suggest that the inhabitants of such craft could only be insects in order to fit in something that small. However, in a more serious way he suggested that only insectoids were designed to man *any* of the saucers, including the huge ones. Theodolite picked up and tracked one saucer which he and his companions then visually observed. They estimated it to be a 105 foot diameter ovoid disc. Unlike the smaller saucers, the big ones remained high up in the atmosphere. The saucer was traveling quickly and then ascended after sudden stops, maneuvers that required any living thing inside to be able to absorb terrific G force. McLaughlin noted that a bee can pull 20 Gs, the amount of pull which anything inside the saucer would have experienced from its observed maneuvers.

So predominant was the idea that only insects could man the saucers that Gerald Heard proposed the alien inhabitants were "super bees" from Mars in his book *Is Another World Watching?* (Bantam 1953). But there is a great difference between "super insect" and insectoid.

As a "dollar a year man" Dr. Robert Sarbacher worked in conjunction with many government projects in the early 1950s. Whether he picked up the "watercooler" Pentagon chat about theoretical insectoid origins of the flying saucer inhabitants or had direct statements from those in the "need to know," he later asserted that a flying saucer had actually crashed and the occupants were retrieved and were, in fact, insectoid in makeup. His recollections have been used to foster the legend of a UFO crash at Roswell, New Mexico, but if true, always *if,* then it could explain why the "UFOnauts" have never made contact— insects and humans cannot communicate with each other.

Thanks to the work of the late Dr. Karl von Frisch the language of the bees is the most understood and to an extant translated language mankind has of any species other than of himself. However, it does not change the fact that bees cannot communicate with mankind or mankind with the bees. To draw a Biblical analogy, we are like God sitting upon the dome of the Earth and watching mankind move about like grasshoppers. Scientists have observed the bees as far more dispassionate entities than anything godlike and watched them communicate with each other but they cannot intellectually bridge the gulf between them or any insect species.

Despite the impressive collective intelligence of the bees and many other insects there most likely is no real individual intelligence with which to communicate. Like all insects, each bee is an individual cell in a body. There are no philosophers or independent thinkers. All insects follow a stifling behavioral pattern which they cannot break. They act in tandem to bring about the benefits of the hive or nest.

There is little reason to consider that a highly developed insectoid species would be significantly different and free of its behavioral pattern. In fact, considering the intelligence level of insects on Earth it would be likely that the next most intelligent species in the universe to mankind would be insectoid, but this intelligence would be a conglomerate intelligence like thousands of cells forming an organ, not an intelligence that is ever directed outward except for scouting, hunting, offense and defense.

Praise is heaped upon the chimp and dolphin, but it is nevertheless true that they are practically morons compared with the collective intelligence of ants and bees. The most intelligent creatures do not blindly follow a master and "ape" what they are shown; and yet it is this behavior in both chimps and dolphins that make us classify them as intelligent. Insects cannot be manipulated, either individually or collectively. It is it equally true that the intelligence of insects is a collective one and no individual breaks free of it to act on its own. A large, highly developed species could represent a threat to mankind. They would operate according to behavioral programming, but be a developed, cohesive culture like humankind.

Despite the metaphysical nature of the UFO debate, flying saucer behavior can best be explained only through the lenses that have watched and studied insects. Flying saucers display an insect's complete lack of interest in mankind and a behavioral pattern which may have a very disquieting goal— that the Earth is more or less like a flower to them, to be gleaned in springtime and in harvest.

Until modern times records were not so meticulous regarding human travel and census. Therefore it is not possible to assess whether the alarming rate of human disappearance each ear is out of proportion with the past. It is, however, a given that humans are better documented from birth to death in the world today and yet tens of thousands still disappear each year without trace— a veritable major city population just taking into account the last 20 years.

Accepting merely for the sake of argument that "aliens" could be visiting this planet but have no ability or inclination to communicate with its inhabitants, a highly developed insectoid species would still have interest in its own self-preservation and would therefore take a keen interest in the aggressive capability of Earth's inhabitants. After seeing there was little threat to them, they would then go about gathering the pollen, so to speak, that they desire, which some fear could be us.

Such a thought is anathema to the entire modern "UFO experience" which has preferred to paint a rather rosy picture of UFO inhabitants as angelic in nature and having a very benign or even altruistic purpose for mankind, conditioning us and preparing us for greater galactic love. However, the observed behavior of flying saucers has ranged only from indifference to reconnaissance, and on some occasions to what appears to be outright aggression, nothing beyond the pattern of highly developed but still conditioned insects.

While all this resides only in theory, there appears to be no doubt about the existence of flying saucers— the instigating factor of all UFO theories. Their behavior must have some consistent interpretation that fits their observed pattern for the last 70 years. They have been seen, tracked on radar, and even observed to have landed, even at official bases and yet without any attempted contact.

One of the most alarming examples of the latter happened at Edwards Air Force Base in 1957 when a 20-foot diameter saucer landed on the far edge of the desert testing area and was filmed by a crew that was there already to film some other experimental work. This film was developed and given to their commander, future astronaut Gordon Cooper, who looked at the negatives and later admitted it was clear film of a "double saucer, lenticular" craft that had put down a tripod landing gear and briefly landed. The film was immediately sent to Washington DC and its whereabouts thereafter have been lost.

Over the last 70 years a narrative has developed and within its strict parameters the discussion remains, with emphasis coming and going from various "new" chapters as the marketing of "UFOlogy" has evolved, each chapter advancing from sightings, to contactees, to abductions, to pseudo-religious cults and popular mythology, each becoming viable from a sales point of view only after the other chapter had become oversold and no longer of interest to the public. This is counterbalanced by prosaic, often humbug debunkers who seem less sincere than "believers" and far more interested in profiting off naysaying for attention or gain as much if not more so than those believers they accuse of creating their own cottage industries.

To the observer it seems the believers are quite sincere, and this represents a more frightening proposal considering the vast cult they have forged out of nothing more empiric to the rest of us than indifference on the part of silver discs in our atmosphere, that is, their indifference with human culture. UFOs have a preoccupation with the oceans or any remote location, a pattern that should really be viewed as confirming their overall indifference with us.

Skeptics appear even more dangerous for another reason. They will not only deny the pattern seen in genuine UFO reports, but try to intimidate others from considering the possibility UFOs exist outside of the oppressive formula laid down by marketing rather than encouraging a serious look at whether the phenomenon is real. After facing skeptics, one comes away with the same characterization as presented by the late French General Lionel Max Chassin when he penned in the forward of *Flying Saucers and the Straight-Line Mystery* by Aimé Michel:

Obsessed with the notion of his own omniscience, it enrages him to be confronted with phenomena that do not agree with this conviction. Finding in his limited armory no explanation that satisfies him, he chooses to doubt rather than himself, and rejects the most obvious facts in order to avoid putting his faith to the test. The mistaken pride and anthropocentrism that supposedly went out with Copernicus and Galileo make him a peril to science, as history abundantly proves... That strange things have been seen is now beyond question, and the "psychological" explanations seem to have misfired. The number of thoughtful, intelligent, educated, people in full possession of their faculties who have "seen something" and described it grows every day. Doubting Thomases among astronomers, engineers, and officials who used to laugh at "saucers" have seen and repented. To reject out of hand testimony such as theirs becomes more and more presumptuous.

It is a fact that in its attempts to overcome the space distance barrier theoretical physics has been advanced by a culture that allowed itself to be immersed in at least the discussion of UFOs and their possible existence despite the concept violating our current understanding of the limitations of space travel. Flying saucers, in essence, have become like portents of old, directing us, even in our disbelief, to consider the shape of a saucer in aerodynamics, and any number of quantum theories on bending space and the use of wormholes. Perhaps just the ideas UFOs have inspired will make it possible that we can travel to other planets in a quick and efficient way on a regular basis, progress that no naysayer is capable of inspiring.

Despite the personal unbelief for many in aerospace, there are many who believe, either from their own personal encounter or after having assessed the total and reliable data available.

University of Nebraska's Dr. David Pares is an example of the former. Because of his encounter as a teenager (to be discussed later), he accepted that some other form than conventional rocketry must explain the presence of flying saucers. Eventually many factors led him to believe it was based on the bending of space. In putting it in simple terms, he observes: "Originally proposed by Miguel Alcubierre in 1994, a concept of Space Warp which is a method of stretching space in a wave which would in theory cause the fabric of space ahead of a spacecraft to contract and the space behind it to expand. The ship would ride this wave inside a region known as a local warp bubble of flat space."

The result would be that impressive distances could be achieved, some proposing 10 times the speed of light. Light speed would no longer be the limit of speed. Sirius, 9 light years away, would no longer be an 18 year round trip. There would be no bending of space around the spacecraft and hence no time-warping. The crew aboard would not experience only a day's transit as compared to 18 years elapsing on Earth. Hearty salts and settlers braved the Atlantic for over a month to gain America, and such spans in time now await future travelers to distant planets.

Somehow the current growing conviction that flying saucers are real and from outer space reminds us of the certainty the Air Force upper echelons expressed in the early days of the UFO phenomenon. Flying saucers were here because they were Russians and therefore they *could* be here, this underpinning their acceptance of the reports because in this framework they were believable. Since Alcubierre's theory was considered proved in 2012, even NASA prepares its design of spaceships that will create such warp tunnels. For UFO believers this is considerable justification for their ardor over the last 70 years. In essence, flying saucers can be here and therefore perhaps more serious consideration should be taken to assessing the pattern that discs in the sky have followed, which remains a disturbing one of spectator, indifferent interloper, or even predator when necessary.

The first pattern flying saucers displayed was an interest in military bases, indicating a sophisticated intelligence and precaution on the part of those operating them. Then, should it not be reasoned, might not these same inhabitants have an interest in our aircraft and ships? If they follow rockets, would they not follow ships and aircraft to determine, if nothing else, the capabilities of these craft?

It is precisely with this interpretation that the most credible UFO encounters can be understood, some with very, to say the least, very alarming results. Namely, the result is the total disappearance of the aircraft. This always occurs over the ocean as if the UFO, to personalize it, doesn't wish to cause the undisputed alarm that would result in our society if an aircraft vanished over land, a pattern which gives a rather insidious and ongoing motive to "aliens."

The most documented and as a result the most famous case is the disappearance of Fred Valentich in Bass Straits south of Australia, an area like the Bermuda Triangle noted for many unusual UFO and USO sightings and disappearances at sea, though the Valentich case is the first time such UFOs were overtly associated with a disappearance. It is the most documented case not because it was investigated (when actually it was not), but because before Valentich disappeared he plainly declared to the radio controller that the strange aircraft pestering him was "not an aircraft."

Valentich had taken off in his light Cessna 180 from Melbourne at 6:19 p.m. the evening of October 21, 1978, and headed to King Island. After proceeding out into the straits past Cape Otway he contacted Melbourne Flight Service. It was now 7:06 p.m. He asked if there was any known aircraft in the vicinity around his altitude (4,500 feet). Melbourne confirmed there was not. Over the next harrowing few minutes Valentich continued to relay to Melbourne that some type of large aircraft seemed to be stalking him. "It seems to me that he's playing some sort of a game. He's flying over me two, three times at a time at speeds I could not identify." When Melbourne tried to get a description in detail, Valentich could only say it was so bright it was like a landing light. Then, when it approached again, and hovered over him, he was able to say: "It's got a green light and sort of metallic (like) it's all shiny (on) the outside."

More than once he had no choice but to declare "it is not an aircraft," though he would not call it a UFO. Nevertheless he described it as silvery, large but of a size difficult to estimate because of its fast speed as it passed. Because of the craft's game of approaching from different directions and then retreating, Valentich had stopped and circled. This is when it too hovered over him. Straining at an angle upward to see it, he was unable to put what he saw any more clearly than "the thing is just orbiting on top of me." It then vanished again, or so he thought. It would seem the "thing" was simply capable of such fast speeds so that when Valentich had turned to look another way or at his instruments or to speak to Melbourne the craft could dart off and effectively seemed to have vanished, one reason why Valentich continued to circle, trying to find it coming and going from any direction. His final words bear quoting. After it had disappeared for the last time, he reported it was coming back at him on a straight line course from the southwest. As it grew nearer, his engine began to cough and lose power. "Ah Melbourne that strange aircraft is hovering on top of me again. . ." He paused, leaving the microphone open. Then: "It's hovering and it's not an aircraft." His microphone remained open for 17 seconds. Then there was nothing. No trace of Valentich or of his Cessna 180 was ever found.

In a strange way the scenario this incident presents is an incarnation of the theories much earlier proposed about missing aircraft and UFO abduction in the Bermuda Triangle. It is so evident as to almost make the theory seem more of a prophecy. "Prediction" is a key step in scientific method, made powerful when there is fulfillment. Years before this incident, without any real proof, merely based on the circumstantial evidence, theorists had proposed that only alien abduction could explain the missing aircraft and ships in the Triangle, though none of them predicted it as vividly as it was displayed in the Valentich disappearance a world away.

More to the point, however, this very disquieting incident is not proof from afar. Until 1992 it was not known that a nearly identical disappearance had occurred in the Bermuda Triangle, off the west coast of Puerto Rico, until this represent writer discovered it in the files of the National Transportation Safety Board. The flight had taken place on June 28, 1980.

Jose Maldonado Torres was flying the light Ercoupe N3808H from Santo Domingo, Dominican Republic, to San Juan, Puerto Rico. His passenger was Jose Pagan Santos, the son of the owner of the aircraft, Jose Pagan Jimenez, an aero police officer of Puerto Rico. Approaching the west coast of

Puerto Rico, Torres' alarmed voice came over the radio frequencies: "Mayday, mayday." The object of his angst: "We can see a strange object in our course. We are lost, Mayday, Mayday [25 seconds later] . . . Mayday, Mayday, We are lost. We found a strange object in our course."

Over the next couple of minutes Iberia Flight 976 and San Juan International tried to understand what was happening. Prompted by the Iberia flight, Torres responded: "Ah, we are going from Santo Domingo to, ah, San Juan International but we found, ah, a weird object in our course that made us change course about three different times. We got it right now in front of us at 1 o'clock. Our heading is zero seven zero degrees . . . our altitude is one thousand six hundred at zero seven zero degrees . . . Our VORs got lost off frequency."

Continuing communication was marked by considerable alarm, even panic, in Torres' voice, and in the background one can hear Santos saying "Look, look!" as he calls his friend's attention to the "very weird object." Several evasive courses were executed by Torres, all to no avail. Simply put, the "weird object" was intentionally keeping Torres from making the coast only 35 miles away. At 1,500 feet altitude now, Torres made yet another course change to avoid it. The result: "We are right again in the same stuff, man."

At 8:07 p.m. the Ercoupe vanished from Atlantic Weapon's radar. At 8:15 p.m. a blip reappeared, tracking 266 degrees, away from Puerto Rico. It then vanished forever.

In unnerving similarity to Valentich's consternation, Torres could only describe what they had encountered as "we have something weird in front of us that make us lose our course all the time." In his personal report, Santos' father, Jose Jimenez, who had flown many search missions in his own police helicopter, summed up the "weird object" as "objeto luminoso" or glowing object, drawing yet another unintentional parallel to Valentich's silvery non-aircraft that had manifested first as a bright landing light until it hovered over him and a green light became apparent.

Based on a 070 course to the Aguadilla VOR and the statement that the flight was about 35 miles from the coast, the position of N3808H is plotted within the circle and the course directions reveal the flight possibly turned around before vanishing.

Similarities between the two incidents can probably be explained by the fact the same type of object was responsible and that human reaction, given the unbelievable circumstances, simply cannot take it all in at first. From the transcripts it would seem that Fred Valentich kept his cool more. However, the Melbourne flight controller, Steve Robey, has stated that the alarm in his voice was very apparent. Neither pilot would call it a flying saucer or UFO. Even if they believed that is what it was, they may have instantly felt that the radio control operator might think this a hoax despite the tenor of their voice and not understand how truly urgent it was to them that the tower understand they're in trouble.

There is a substantial component missing in these cases, at least on the surface, with the theory to explain alien abduction of aircraft in the Bermuda Triangle. Specifically, there is an enormous logistic problem, which any solid entities have to deal with. Aside from the obvious and most disturbing question of all—why?— there is the question of "how?" How to retrieve a large object? In itself it would seem a rather hard thing to pull off even for a sophisticated and advanced civilization.

A disturbing answer to this logistic question, however, suggests itself in the October 18, 1973, encounter had by the entire crew of an Air Force helicopter over Ohio. While in flight near Mansfield at 10:03 p.m. Sgt. Bob Yanacsek was the first of the 4 crew to notice a reddish light bearing down on them from the right. After 30 seconds he notified the others it was converging on them. Speed seemed to be about 600 mph and it was on a collision course. Captain Larry Coyne took the yoke. The helicopter was currently cruising at 2,500 feet. He set the controls for dive. No sooner had he done this when the light became apparent as a flattened cylinder or ovoid, with a dome on top, its silvery nose glowing with red light. It stopped right over the helicopter and hovered. Suddenly a green light came flooding into the chopper. It lasted from only 12 to 15 seconds and then the craft quickly moved on. Afterward, Coyne gathered his wits and noticed that the stick should have taken them down rapidly from their 2,500 feet altitude. Yet he now noticed that they had actually gained close to 1,800 feet altitude before leveling off close to 4,000 feet.

Circumstances, collated by the 4 witnesses aboard, basically credit the UFO as following the pattern of any stalking animal: watching quietly, then zooming in on its prey, seizing it— in this case elevating it with it as it quickly rose— but then for some unknown reason abandoning it almost immediately and taking off on its way.

Larry Coyne's description of it as silvery, big and oblong, with the greenish light, is startlingly similar to those features stated by Fred Valentich in 1978 before he too vanished. Unfortunately, though Jose Jimenez clarified for us that the weird object which his son and his son's friend Jose Torres had seen was in actuality a glowing light, he did not clarify what color this light was. Whatever the source of his additional information was, this crucial point had not been passed on.

In disturbing deference to the theories on UFO sizes and

shapes, some have felt that Valentich could have been describing the large "mothership" type UFO in which apparently the kidnapped Earth craft are taken (according to theorists) but Captain Coyne and his crew—Arrigo Jezzi, Robert Yanacsek, and John Healey— described one of the smaller saucers which, in order to abduct a ship or airplane, would have to raise the craft up rapidly to the mothership hovering high above, which it seemed more than capable of doing considering the elevation the helicopter experienced in only a few seconds.

Another interpretation as to why the UFO abandoned its initial capture of Coyne's helicopter could be that it was over land, and if we are to attribute the most sophisticated intelligence to the supposed UFO occupants, then the disappearance of a craft over land would be something they would avoid, as such an event would have no explanation whatsoever in our frame of reference unless it was over jungle, in which cases we would naturally assume we simply couldn't find the wreckage of an ordinary accident, precisely what we tend to do with disappearances over oceans.

It is interesting to note that in both the Valentich and Torres/Santos cases the "weird objects" assailed them at dusk when human eyesight and depth perception is at its poorest— a very disturbing coincidence if we are to accept a sinister motive behind the disappearances.

We must bear in mind Gordon Creighton's admonition when theorizing on these cases, that these things do not exist and are not capable of doing the things of which we theorize, something that becomes increasingly hard to do as more incidents accrue.

Along with UFO interest over military bases, which has proven itself to be periodic, with the heaviest concentration taking place in the first "flap" in the late 1940s, UFO sightings have been more numerous and consistent over the oceans and especially in the areas of the Bermuda Triangle, the very disquieting pattern which inspired the theory that many of the disappearances, especially those of the most inexplicable kind, are actually the result of UFO destruction of the aircraft or intentional kidnapping of the inhabitants therein. Apparently, now with Coyne's case set forward, this is done by the smaller disc pulling the aircraft up higher in altitude to what is called the mothership where it can then be deposited inside.

There is a particularly confusing disappearance in the Triangle in which a UFO exists only by inference. One of the most qualified pilots to ever vanish was Richard Yerex, with over 16,000 flight hours. He had retired from Ford Motor Company and was now, at 56 years old, part time shuttling people back and forth to the Bahamas in a beefy Cessna twin 402. At 9:15 a.m. May 27, 1987, he had taken off from Palm Beach International for a 50 minute flight to Marsh Harbour, Great Abaco. Radar tracked him up to 12 miles east of the airport. However, another pilot claimed that she heard him reporting what he thought was a large balloon, and this was taken to mean the US Aerostatic balloon at High Rock, Grand Bahama Island, though this is far from only 12 miles east of the Florida coast. The National Transportation Safety Board would only concede that an aircraft resembling Yerex's Cessna had been seen passing over Marsh Harbour around ETA and continuing into the open Atlantic, never to return. This observed behavior is enough to suggest that either Yerex was dead inside or not even in the aircraft any longer. Perhaps the NTSB's reluctance to accept the other pilot's claim is that there was no reason for Yerex to be reporting anything routine to another pilot, and the alternative to a large balloon is a UFO.

Sightings of UFOs in the Bermuda Triangle have described a similar progression to their behavior as the saucer reported by Captain Coyne except with a noteworthy exception— no levitation, indicating that in Coyne's case at least it was intentional and possibly an aborted abduction, a mistake never made in the Triangle.

Shipmaster Jon Carpenter, in his day a tough, red-headed no nonsense skipper, had such an encounter. He is also one of the few to publically speak about it, a trait only the heartiest of salts seem to possess. As with other encounters, the first indication was an electromagnetic effect. He confessed to Richard Winer, a Miami filmmaker (*The Devil's Triangle*, 1974), the following account:

We noticed that the compass begin to act up. It was oscillating just like you had a strong magnet in the proximity of the compass. We happened to notice about this time a strange, greenish light coming in low over the water out of the southeast. And it was coming at a very slow clip. And it came in and hovered right above the water, and the water that night was very calm because there was no clouds, no storms, the moon was almost full and the visibility was excellent. And this object hovered right above the surface of the sea for a few moments and then it just turned up on its edge and descended right out of sight into the depths.

Another encounter was had by diver Bruce Mournier, who can almost be said to have sighted the same object only at a different time and place, after it had entered the ocean. His account also uncannily reflects the shape of the Pascagoula USO, only larger. While in the Bahamas near the Gulf Stream he saw two USOs— underwater submersible objects— but which nevertheless fit the description given by others of aerial UFOs or flying saucers.

There's two underwater UFOs or two things you never seen before. They've been buzzing alongside the boat and now they're off the front kinda heading from south to north. So I looked out. I seen these two things. I guess they're about 60 feet apart. They're buzzing along in formation. They're egg shape, they're round, more or less egg shape/round; I guess 'bout 40 or 50 feet in diameter, and the same distance long, a little bit to the egg shape side [ovoid]. And I follow them [visually] for about, oh, I don't know how long. I just watched and tried to figure out what it was. I couldn't believe my eyes. They looked like they were really moving out faster the further they got away. It looked like they were about 40 feet underwater— maybe 20 feet, 40 feet. It's out in the crystal clear Gulf Stream. They kept on going off. As they faded away, I don't know if they faded off in the distance or whether they made a dive down or what but they were gone.

Repeated sightings of UFOs, both within and without the Triangle, have often gone hand-in-hand with a blue-green glow and, most often, in proximity to the sea. In a curious and disturbing parallel, on July 19, 1965, Australian diplomat Denis

Crowe came upon what he estimated to be a 20-foot diameter flying saucer sitting on the sand at Vaucluse Beach, Australia. He approached it to within 60 feet, his dogs barking all the time, at which time the saucer lifted off the beach, with the sound of gently rushing air, and zoomed away. Because Crowe was also an illustrator he was able to draw a distinct shape to the "flying saucer." This showed two flattened cones, the lower making up the saucer shape which had a rim that glowed blue-green, but which turned to orange-red when it zoomed away at tremendous speeds, an event which left his dogs eerily silent.

An essentially identical flying saucer was photographed near Darmstadt, Germany, in August 1953. The lower cone or disc, as opposed to the central cone or dome, rotated in a clockwise motion in both instances, setting off the glowing blue-green light or pulses from the rim.

Nearly identical saucers were seen to liftoff in Russia, two within a minute of each other. The event must have been detected by the nearby Soviet military base because the witnesses then saw search lights come on and sweep the sky. The event occurred on October 4, 1955, and the three witnesses were no less than Senator Richard Russell (R, Georgia), Lt. Colonel E.U. Hathaway, and Ruben Efron, committee consultant to the Senate Armed Forces Committee. They were traveling by train in the Trans-Caucasus region, between Atjaty and Adzhijabul. The time was 7:10 p.m. when they saw "two round and circular unconventional aircraft resembling flying disks or flying saucers" taking off "almost" vertically. "Disk aircraft ascended near dusk with outer surface revolving slowly to right and two lights stationary on top near middle part." Sparks or flames were seen coming from the craft. The disks ascended fairly slowly until at 6,000 feet where they then zoomed off northward. "Flying attitude of disk remained same during ascent as in cruise, like a discus in flight." From the intelligence report, classified at the time as Top Secret but released decades later, one gathers the impression that the three witnesses thought this could have been a secret Russian experiment. With hindsight now, this was obviously not the case since nothing this dynamic

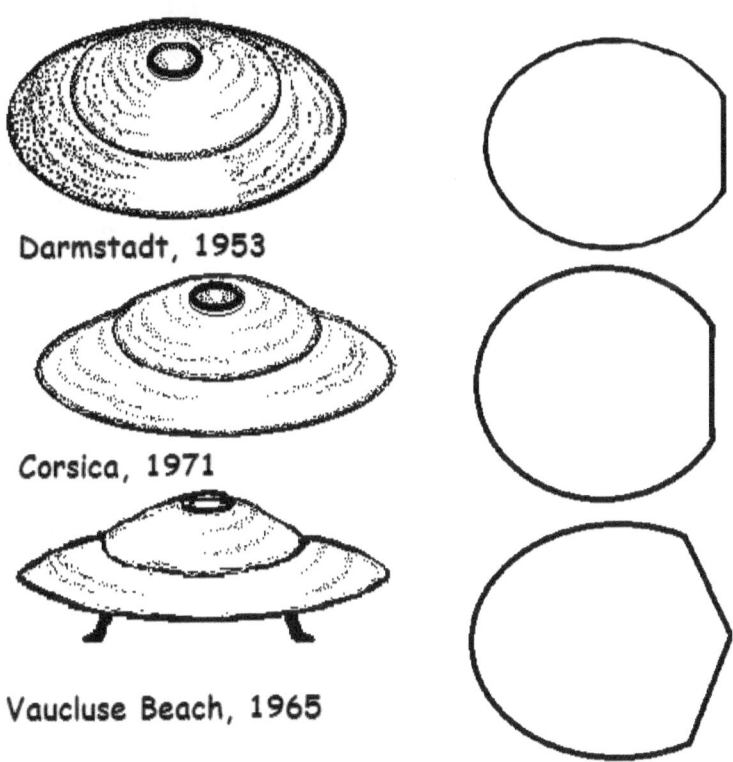

Darmstadt, 1953

Corsica, 1971

Vaucluse Beach, 1965

The most clearly photographed flying saucer has presented itself as two flattened cones. The flatter, outer cone revolves around the central cone or dome. There is a hole in the top of the dome. Contrast this on the right with the earliest described "flying saucers"—ovoid or ellipses. Top is Ward, Colorado, 1929; bottom is Ken Arnold's saucers he saw on June 24, 1947.

has ever become part of mainstream military materiel.

The concept of a flying saucer as a dome or cone within a rotating disc was pervasive in the early years of UFOlogy. In the hands of Donald Keyhoe this description helped to explain their motive power as being based on magnetic energy. With the help of Wilbert Smith, who was keenly interested in the phenomenon, he was able to explain the many shifts in color that UFOs displayed. Smith believed they were caused by the disc's rotation. When it is heating up it is pink, then as it grew hotter the coronal light would be red, then red-orange, yellow, and then white at its fastest speeds. The bluish-green would be at lower altitudes in certain atmospheric conditions.

Smith's interpretation, of course, was based on his theory that the saucers used the Earth's magnetic field for energy, creating a "magnetic sink" in which they funnel the power into their discs. He also believed they would have to be unmanned. However, according to NASA scientist and UFO believer Paul Hill the light seems to come from the saucers because of ionized air around them. He notes that in many of the encounters the saucers appear to be maneuvered by intelligence inside and not by remote control. Ionized air, more than anything, would best explain the phenomenon of the varied colors of light.

One encounter in the Triangle seems to combine the blue-green coronal light of UFOs and the effects of "electronic fog." This was experienced by Chuck Wakeley, who confided in Dr. J. Manson Valentine about his experience. However, in this case, though it happened at night, the pilot was unaware of any fog or saucer possibly because the aircraft was intensely glowing blue-green.

It was November 1964. He was flying a charter for Sunline Aviation, on the near identical course as Bruce Gernon, from Nassau to Miami. He had just passed the northern tip of Andros and was soon expecting to pick up the Bimini VOR en route. He was at 8,000 feet. At this moment: ". . .I began to notice something unusual: a very faint glowing effect on the wings. At first I thought it an illusion created by the cockpit lights shining through the tinted Plexiglas windows because the wings had a translucent appearance, appearing pale blue-green, although they were actually painted bright white." After the glow became so intense he had trouble reading the instruments his "magnetic compass began revolving, slowly but steadily; the fuel gauges, which had read 'half full' at takeoff now read 'full'." Alarmed by his auto pilot taking the airplane into a hard right turn, he flew manually yet totally blind. "I could not trust any of my electrically run instruments, as they were either totally out or behaving erratically." Soon the whole aircraft was glowing: ". . .At this point I could no longer rely on my gyro, horizon, and altitude indicators." Fortunately, after about 5 minutes the glow began to fade. After it dissipated "all instruments began to function normally."

Although Wakeley believed the glow was being generated by his aircraft for some unknown reason, a consideration of his encounter, in connection with other UFO incidents, will give rise to Valentine's theories that UFOs may sometimes unintentionally destroy aircraft while inspecting them. Had Larry Coyne and his men not seen the UFO approach, they would only have been dazzled in a green light of unknown origin, which if it had lasted as long as Wakeley's encounter it could have disrupted all the panel instruments.

Many of the above accounts reflect the most disturbing pattern uncovered in the reports of UFOs. More than their pattern of visiting or surveilling military and defense development bases, they are seen to come and go from the ocean, as though they dwell in the ocean or enter the Earth's atmosphere over the oceans so as not to be detected by radar. They are associated with disappearances only over the ocean. And they frequent particular locations in the oceans more than others.

UFOs almost seem based off the west coast of Puerto Rico. Both large and small UFOs have been seen here, as if to suggest a symbiotic location for the motherships, bearing in mind that motherships and flying saucers do not exist. Long before the Torres/Santos disappearance, and even before the Adjuntas "flap" of 1972 with the attendant disappearances of boats or their occupants off the west coast, the following report was filed.

For 30 minutes on May 14, 1952, five witnesses standing on a bluff near Mayaquez Bay saw two spherical orange glowing lights "bright like the sun" on the dark horizon. Again, it was just at sundown, which had occurred only 4 minutes before. Apparently the intensity of the light was the reflection off the objects of the setting sun over the horizon. Visibility was 20 miles, making for no obstruction. One of the objects was large and stationary and the smaller one moved about near it. The objects were so distant that the movement of the smaller light could only be discerned through binoculars.

The Air Force Intelligence investigator wrote the following (Report #IR-24-52): "There was no regular formation but one object thought to be the larger of the two appeared stationary while the smaller of the two seemed to dart away from the other at a rapid rate of speed and then to reappear in close proximity to the larger. There was no exhaust, sound, or conventional type of propulsion noted."

By far, the most contact with UFOs or, interchangeably, USOs has been claimed by members of the Russian Navy, which in a series of articles beginning with *Russia Today* (published July 21, 2009) specific mention is repeatedly made of encounters in the Bermuda Triangle.

Concerning his own encounters as a sub commander, retired Rear Admiral Yury Beketov has stated that instruments frequently malfunctioned for no apparent reason, adding that since it always went hand-in-hand with sonar tracking unexplained objects it could have been deliberate disruption by the UFO "creatures." Speed of such sonar returns was sometimes clocked as incredibly surpassing any known undersea vehicle built by man, reinforcing Beketov's belief their sonar was picking up alien USOs.

Frequent contact with USOs was normal. Russian Navy intelligence veteran Captain 1st Rank Igor Barklay noted: "Ocean UFOs often show up wherever our or NATO's fleets concentrate— near Bahamas, Bermuda, Puerto Rico. They are most often seen in the deepest part of the Atlantic Ocean, in

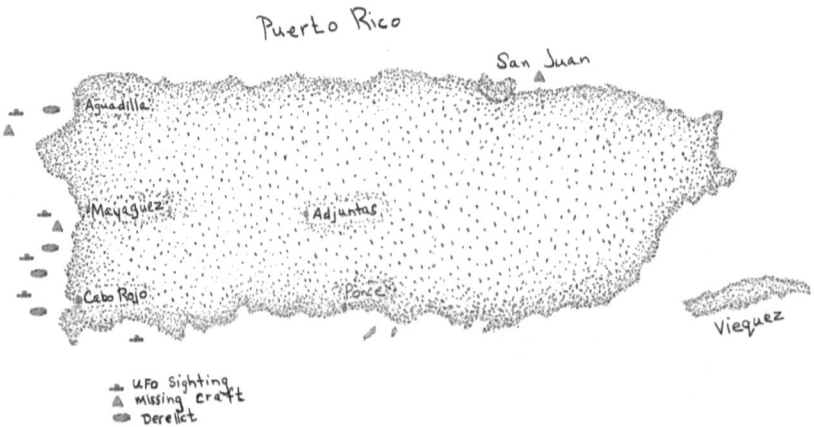

Locations of disappearances, derelicts, and UFOs off Puerto Rico.

the southern part of the Bermuda Triangle, and also in the Caribbean Sea."

Unquestionably, Admiral Vladimir Azhazha is one of the most famous Russian UFOlogists, inspired to become one by his own encounters in the 1960s while commander of the sub *Severyanka*. In an article for *Svobodnaya Pressa* he rendered an apt summation to a lifetime of collating data. "Fifty percent of UFO encounters are connected with oceans— fifteen more with lakes. So UFOs tend to stick to the water." Admiral Vladimir N. Chernavin, former chief commander of the Soviet Navy and deputy minister of defense of the USSR from 1985 to 1992, dryly corroborated Azhazha, specifying that most ocean sightings (44%) were actually in the Atlantic, with 16% in the Pacific, and 10% in the Mediterranean.

Echoing such theorists as the Anglo-American naturalist Ivan Sanderson, Admiral Azhazha speculated on the idea of underwater bases and boldly replied with a "why not?" attitude. "Nothing should be discarded. Skepticism is the easiest way: believe nothing, do nothing. People rarely visit great depths. So it's very important to analyze what they encounter there."

Azhazha has not been put off by the current official Russian Navy dismissals of UFOs, knowing that the officers still hold their official duties and their demeanor must reflect caution. The only officers speaking out are retired from Soviet days and have little worry about their futures being affected by a long dead and discredited regime.

The question remains, however, how many of these reports are from firsthand knowledge in the Triangle by the Russians who, except for well-monitored visits to Cuba, were not welcomed in a Caribbean where the US Navy was essentially the only dominant naval force? It is not always easy to determine the reliability of Russian information, as Russians often tend to speak with dogma as if what they relate is a given, and that the challenger must be quite uninformed to even request verifying information.

According to *Russia Today*, only former rear admiral and nuclear submarine commander Yury Beketov was a direct eyewitness when "describing events that occurred in the Bermuda Triangle." Of underwater UFOs, he declared: "We repeatedly observed that the instruments detected the movements of material objects at unimaginable speed, around 230 knots (400 km. per hour [250 m.p.h.]). It's hard to reach that speed on the surface— . . .The beings that created those material objects significantly exceed us in development."

One reason for such frank admittance of UFO encounters by ranking Russian military is the different attitude the Russians have toward many topics as opposed to their more cautious American counterparts. However, Captain Prikhodko observed it may be more innocent. We simply may be unaware of how much activity goes on undersea or we misinterpret it. "The problem is humankind is rushing upwards with great interest and not too intense downwards," adding, "Maybe this is a big mistake."

During perestroika Dr. Marina Popovich, one of the most celebrated Russian test pilots, sometimes called the Chuck Yeager of the Soviet Union, and wife of cosmonaut Pavel Popovich, who later became head of the Committee on UFOs, became outspoken about Russian Air Force encounters with UFOs. This culminated in a press conference in San Francisco in 1990 in which she showed some of the photographs Russians interpret as proof of flying saucers, including the big cigar shaped "motherships" in space. She said that the photo had been taken by a Russian space probe, which soon after mysteriously stopped working and then vanished. Popovich asserted that the Russian authorities concluded that UFOs have been around as long as the planet, a point of view shared by many western UFO researchers. However, she also declared that she had seen hybrid children, a remark which delights the US intelligence community because it convinces them the Russians are engaged in some PsyOp or just plain crazy.

UFOs, if we are to limit ourselves to the acronym's literal meaning of unidentified flying object, have been seen in the skies of the Earth for a considerable time—even millennia—and variously described as spindles, triangles, kites, and always as luminous blobs or orbs. However, the clearest descriptions have always been of a shiny saucer. Both the armies of Alexander the Great and Roman annalists describe seeing a glowing or flaming shield pass through the sky, such as Julius Obsequens in 216 BC who records that "at Arpinium a thing like a round shield was seen in the sky." It is remarkable that considering 2,000 years has passed that flying saucers have not changed in design by any appreciable amount.

One of the clearest descriptions of a flying saucer before their "official" discovery in June 1947 comes from traveler and visionary Nicholas Roerich while traversing Mongolia in the summer of 1926. He recorded in his diary and later published this account in *Altai-Himalaya: A Travel Diary* in 1929 by Skotes. It is contained on pages 361-62 of the first edition.

> On August 5th— something remarkable! We were in our camp in the Kukunor district not far from the Humbolt Chain. In the morning about half-past nine some of our caravaneers noticed a remarkably big black eagle flying above us. Seven of us began to watch this unusual bird. At this same moment another of our caravaneers remarked "There is something far above the bird." And he shouted in his astonishment. We all saw, in a direction from north to south, something big and shiny reflecting the sun, like a huge oval moving at great speed. Crossing our camp this thing changed in its direction from south to southwest. And we saw how it disappeared in the intense blue sky. We even had time to take our field glasses and saw quite distinctly an oval form with shiny surface, one side of which was brilliant with the sun.

—Again, it remains remarkable that the shape and size, including the speed, has not altered, the above account a mirror of what the ancient Greeks and Romans reported so long before and what so many modern people reported again after 1947, only now far more frequently.

The consistency of these descriptions again underscores how long the phenomenon has occurred and equally how long there remains no contact with earthlings by those inside the craft, if anybody really is. Instead they've entered our folklore, today being the province of the occult and the séance crowd who have forsaken 3,000 year old Egyptian priestesses or winsome Indian chiefs as their mediums for little gray aliens. The entire UFO enigma only flirted with scientific explanations for the first few years after 1947 when UFOs were thought to have a very understandable origin in secret Soviet experiments or as interstellar craft from Venus or Mars.

Many UFOlogists theorize that more than one different type of people or, if insectoid, creatures visit the Earth, noting that many oddly shaped craft among the more ubiquitous saucers have been consistently reported in the skies over time, indicating more than one engineering science and perhaps culture behind the spaceships.

Be that as it may, too many theorists try to include almost every sighting report into their dossier rather than becoming critical and focusing on the quality of the reports and the caliber of the witnesses. Critical analysis repeatedly highlights only the saucer-shaped "UFO," with rare exception to the cigar-shaped "motherships." It is so consistent that the former Chief of Defense Staff of Great Britain, the Lord Hill-Norton, said that "U stands more for unexplained than unidentified" because a disc is invariably the shape of a "UFO."

Analysis also reveals that historical sightings of genuine "flying saucers" were very rare and always distant. However, after 1947 there was an explosive increase in sightings, so many in fact that a pattern could easily be discerned. Saucers were based in the Bermuda Triangle and showed a habit of gathering off the US east coast at the 37th parallel (near Norfolk, Virginia) before dispersing to reconnoiter. The August 4, 1950, report of a flying version of the Pascagoula USO is a case in point. Its reported reciprocal course in the direction of freighter indicated it was coming from the Norfolk area.

The 37th parallel has become so identified with flying saucers it is often dubbed The UFO Highway. A sinister slant was given to this pattern in the 1970s during the great cattle mutilation scare when it was discovered that the most inexplicable mutilations were occurring along the parallel in southern Colorado and northern New Mexico. Although the most obvious mutilations have an easy answer in predators, several of the cattle were found drained of blood, part of their lymphatic system removed, and some were found dropped in trees.

Photographs are always subject to interpretation, but it is curious to note here that one of the earliest photos of a flying saucer is dated April 1929 over Ward, Colorado. It shows an ellipsoid disc identical to the descriptions of the Pascagoula USO and the one contained in the August 4, 1950, report in the CIA files. Another coincidence is found in the description of the object by the photographer, Edward Pline. He said it was as large as a "very large boulder," which fits the description of 10 x 12 foot ovoid disc.

While the ramifications of the cattle mutilation scare are not of direct relevance here, the coming and going of flying saucers from the Bermuda Triangle is. And in addition to the pattern that shows they enter the US over the 37th parallel, the pattern of sightings reveal they return to the Triangle via the Gulf of Mexico, indicating that they had largely concentrated their reconnoitering over the West and Midwest.

By far one of the most astounding encounters confirming this pattern is also one of the most documented concerning the return of saucers to "motherships." This vivid radar encounter happened in the dark early morning hours of December 6, 1952, when a B-29 crew found themselves between 3 groups of UFOs. They were about 200 miles south of Texas in the Gulf of Mexico when each group, at intervals over a period of 6 minutes, sped past them at 5,000 mph in a direct line to the Bermuda Triangle. The three groups amounted to a veritable fleet of 20 radar returns. Visually they were blue-white streaking lights. One group zoomed past the B-29 within only a few miles— a potentially fatal proximity at their incredible speed. After a few minutes the third group reappeared on their radarscopes, this time behind them and approaching them. Although keeping their distance, radar showed that the targets slowed and paced the aircraft for several seconds, as if scouting or considering the B-29. Then a half inch spot appeared on their radarscope indicating a UFO truly incomprehensible in size. The smaller blips rushed to the huge blip and merged with it. The large blip then accelerated and left the radarscope at fantastic speed.

In a very real sense, this encounter was replaying in reverse an earlier rendezvous, this time visually observed and in circumstances that bear on it and the subject at hand. It was the night of July 14, 1952. At 9:12 p.m. a Pan American DC-4 was over Chesapeake Bay and heading south to Miami when the pilot and copilot saw off the left front quarter 6 flying saucers glowing amber-red come in from the Atlantic. They were in echelon formation, with the trailing 5 slightly off to the right and incrementally above the lead saucer. The pilot and copilot, Bill Nash and Bill Fortenberry, estimated each had the diameter of 100 feet. The first one slowed, causing the next two to waffle and almost overtake it. They all slowed and then the lead saucer banked on its side and headed west and the others did likewise and followed. "Immediately after these six lined away," jointly recalled the pilots, "two more objects just like them darted out from behind and under our airplane at the same altitude as the others. The two newcomers seemed to be joining the first group on a closing heading." The 8 flying saucers headed inland and finally vanished.

It is the event above (the first recorded along the 37th parallel) that piqued the interest of NASA aeronautics engineer Paul Hill. He was located nearby and had already been interested in the possibility that saucers were real and from another planet. He had noted the pattern they had already displayed: seeming to come from the oceans, and their propensity to appear at dusk/evening. With a friend he went out to a viewing location near Norfolk at dusk on July 16, 1952, and sighted more saucers. A report was duly made to Project Blue Book, and his encounter was significant enough to be included in Captain Edward J. Ruppelt's 1956 book *Report on Unidentified Flying Objects*. Later, Paul Hill elaborated in his own book *Unconventional Flying Objects: a scientific analysis*.

In like manner as the flying saucers had appeared to Nash and Fortenberry, they came into the coast from offshore at dusk. They were between 15,000 and 18,000 feet altitude, traveling at 500 mph. He reports: "They slowed into a left turn to pass directly over our heads toward the west. They practically came to a stop as they approached. It was then that they started their strange jitter, a surprising phenomenon. First one leaped a little way ahead of the other as fast as or faster than the eye could follow—you couldn't be sure. Then the other seemed to jump ahead. They kept up these odd mincing steps for a few seconds as they passed overhead, while we craned our necks." Now the saucers made what Hill recalled was an "astounding maneuver." "Maintaining their spacing of about 200 feet, they revolved in a horizontal circle, about a common center, at a rate of at least once per second. After a few revolutions, and without a pause, they switched their revolutions into a vertical plane, keeping up the same amazing pace."

Now completely "awestruck," Hill noticed that another saucer was coming in from the Atlantic. It quickly joined them. Then a fourth came along the James River and joined them. They floated along briefly and then accelerated to the west. During his own personal investigation, he discovered that the third saucer had traveled north off shore— even aircraft spotters had noted it— in order to join the others. In other words, he discovered that the flying saucers come in from the ocean at dusk (in this case the Bermuda Triangle) and then at night reconnoiter over land. He deduced that the orbital motion of the two saucers was "a rendezvous signal."

Connecting just a few of these reports from 1952, the year of the "Great Saucer Scare," underscores not only the oceanic origin of the UFOs but their base in the Bermuda Triangle. More than one wave came in from the Atlantic (at the 37th Parallel), and the B-29 later that year encountered 20 returning back out into the Gulf of Mexico, there merging with a huge blip on the B-29's radarscope. The waves coming to the coast did so at dusk. Those returning to the sea did so in the early morning. This pattern is truly disturbing, for it reveals that the UFOs consciously took up a pattern to avoid being detected by prowling over land only at night. This may have been a nightly occurrence, but only on these three occasions (that year) was it witnessed.

Over his lifetime Roy Hill compiled data on observed UFO behavior in flight, always comparing it to the laws of physics and in doing so discovered that flying saucers did not violate physics; rather they conformed to it. It was unquestionable, however, that they used a very novel source of propulsion.

One wonders if this unique electromagnetic or gravitational force does not prevent radio communication between the saucers. This would explain the many insect-like manners the saucers display. They don't seem capable of radio contact between each other, but rather they must communicate through gestures. This was also noted by Nash and Fortenberry. When the lead disc slowed, the next two almost overtook it, as if they weren't ready for the change in maneuvering.

Regardless of the bizarre and sometimes erratic flying gestures of the saucers, it seemed evident from their pattern that they were controlled by intelligence. Their pattern to survey military installations was so obvious that this inspired Hill to choose his viewing location. There were 5 military installations around this area of Virginia and lots of water. The pattern had also shown that they appear off the coast and return the day after, "as though they had not concluded their observations." (Although the actual answer may have been because he was at the 37th parallel.)

In developing his studies, Hill learned that on some occasions a UFO was shot at by an observer (usually in the woods or near a lake) who had a gun handy. The sound indicated they were made of hard metal (even if at the time surrounded by a halo of light). In a case where a supposed landing was examined by French authorities, the weight of the object that had been seen to make the impressions was estimated at 30 tons. Working out the math, he discovered that this indicated the saucer was 96 percent as dense as water, "very close to the density of a submarine." "This density, if representative," he concluded, "could explain the observed underwater operation and the apparent multiphibious nature of the UFO." He observes: "It's particularly important that we take note that an object of this density, equipped with a retractable landing gear, is a very substantial 'flying' machine made to land on land and having properties consistent with operation from water surfaces or even underwater."

Long before the concept of the Triangle's "electronic fog"

Hill noted that "motherships" were sometimes spotted generating a white cloud around them, if they were observed operating lower in the atmosphere.

Due to the fact that some form of flying saucer had long been reported in the Earth's skies, and variously interpreted as portents by the ancients, the flap of the late 1940s has prompted much speculation, even official speculation in the Air Force's early assessment, that visitors from outer space had observed the dropping of the atomic bomb and were now worried about mankind's capabilities, considering our warlike past. The Air Force writer implicitly and perhaps even quaintly leads us to envision Martians or Venusians watching us with telescopes and seeing the horrendous blasts and mushroom clouds.

However, in light of the fact it took until 1947 for the flap to materialize one is more tempted to speculate that some mothership constantly on sentinel duty had to return to a distant planet first and marshal enough interest and then en mass the "aliens" returned in order to assess the situation; they themselves perhaps more perplexed by what mankind had done since they may never have thought along the lines of the atom.

These scouting expeditions would naturally concentrate in the American southwest, where the bombs were developed and then dropped in the first tests. The "aliens" would then need to assess delivery systems— Air Force and missile bases— but more specifically aircraft and ships. It is during this the first UFO flap in history that the most inexplicable disappearances occurred in the Bermuda Triangle.

Scouting or reconnoitering would also follow a pattern dictated by logistics. A finite number of craft can only uncover so many military installations from overflights. After locating one air base the easiest way logistically is to follow an aircraft to its next destination. This pattern seems strangely evident only in these early years, testified by the frequent reports from airliners and military flights of pacing UFOs. Between sightings of UFOs over two military bases, an astonishing disappearance happened over *land*.

Hours before a large 4 engine DC-4 airliner would take off from Elmendorf AFB at Anchorage, Alaska, on January 26,

1950, base personnel reported a glowing object over the base. This was the second time that UFOs had been seen. On one occasion two were seen hovering over a hangar and emitting a green light. The DC-4 carried 44 military personnel headed to Great Falls, Montana. After a routine report over Snag, Yukon, the large airliner vanished, presumably somewhere over the dense Pacific Northwest. Great Falls would next experience UFO sightings, with the most famous film being taken there in August 1950 by Nick Mariana. The film shows two silver discs keeping pace with each other while they overflew the town.

There is no evidence for the involvement of the two UFOs in the disappearance of the military airliner, but the pattern would suggest they discovered one base first and then the other, coming back yet again over a period of months to reconnoiter. While there is no evidence that the UFOs stalked the plane that night, there is evidence that such UFOs would not feel intimidated to "check out" an airliner that large.

Such is the Sanviti Case, an encounter chillingly similar to that experienced by Larry Coyne and his helicopter crew, in which a UFO stalked a large DC-4 over Peru on the night of February 2, 1967, and either could not or eventually would not take on the large airliner. It first appeared as a star but then it grew closer and brighter, so bright that all the passengers saw it and one even exclaimed: "There's a UFO!" Judging it to be about 8 nautical miles off at this point, the captain, Oswaldo Sanviti, described it as "really a spectacle." Due to the controversy created by so many witnesses, Captain Sanviti had to explain on company letterhead. The controversy was not merely over the sighting, but from what the UFO did next. "After a while the UFO passed over my plane and stopped right over us. At this moment we noticed a 15 degree left oscillation on our Radio Compass and later a 20 degree right without stopping, all the lights in the main cabin started to reduce the intensity, the same as our fluorescent lights of the cockpit and all radios (reception) out, almost a bit of static noise." As if the UFO had been feeling the aircraft out, it then moved over the plane to the east. He reports what it did next: "increasing its light about a 50% into a bluish light and disappeared with a fantastic speed (perhaps the speed of light). After 5 minutes the UFO returned with another one and situated itself on a close distance with our tail section and in this formation we flew until 5 minutes before landing at the Lima International Airfield."

Occurring as the UFO hovered closely above, the dead radio becomes a particularly chilling clue. In both the Valentich and Torres/Santos cases, they were able to use the radio right until the end when, apparently, the UFO came in very close. Valentich gave us the same clue in his last words: "Melbourne that strange aircraft is hovering on top of me again. . . it is hovering and it's not an aircraft."

Proponents of UFO abductions in the Triangle have always explained the lack of an SOS from a ship or Mayday from a plane as being caused by the UFO because from all examples the dead radio comes only with *close* contact.

It is beyond the scope of this topic to analyze the UFO phenomenon in detail, but insofar as it is relevant here it is necessary to note that in that momentous July of 1952 for the first time a US Air Force pilot shot at a flying saucer. Thereafter the pattern changed. No more large daytime flights were observed. By day they confined themselves to the oceans or presumably their "motherships." Flying saucers appeared concentrated in the Triangle more than elsewhere. They grouped at the coasts at dusk and headed inland.

In a cautious but definite agenda to debunk flying saucers, in 1966 Walter Cronkite hosted a special show *UFO: Friend, Foe or Fantasy?* on CBS. At one point in the segment we are reassured that the Air Force through NORAD has perfect radar surveillance over the USA, and nothing can remain unidentified for long. Although this radar surveillance system's omniscience and omnipresence was itself later debunked in the 1970s, it is humorous in retrospect to recall that during the show when NORAD's plotting board is shown, the 2 unknowns plotted thereon were both in the Bermuda Triangle, one over the Bahamas and the other moving toward Florida over the Gulf.

There was a reason for CBS to take flying saucers so seriously in 1966. This was the first year of the second great "flap," which was most intense in 1966 and 1967. During this period there occurred some of the most unusual encounters since 1952, namely the Sanviti Case and the disappearance of the *Witchcraft* after striking an underwater object. The difference is that the flap did not entirely fade away as it had after 1953. Cattle mutilations began in 1967 and reached epidemic proportions in the mid-1970s. There would be the first recorded disappearance in relation to a UFO (Valentich, 1978) and then 2 years later the Torres/Santos disappearance after encountering the "weird object."

David Pares, physics professor at the University of Nebraska, is open-minded to the idea of UFOs. He is convinced some are real spaceships and therefore they must be coming here somehow independent of our known understanding of time and space travel. He is sure because of his own experience as a 16 year old young man when, during this second great flap, he too witnessed a UFO and its behavior. He had such a clear view that he could describe details. These details are not those of quack contactees who seem to invent a different spaceships and blond Venusians each time they meet one, complete and replete with all sorts of vivid gadgetry. The "flying saucer" Pares saw was just that. It was a plain lentil, just as the most credible observers have reported, such as Gordon Cooper and many others.

It was a clear August morning 1969, he recalls, at Goodyear Lake, New York, where he and 5 of his friends were waiting for swim class.

> . . . Everyone was laughing and having a good time, when all of a sudden after turning away from the group laughing I noticed something out of the corner of my eye over the mountain. I was stupefied; a sliver metallic disk was just clearing over the top of the mountain on my front left 2 o'clock high. I pointed and shouted out to the group, "Look! look! Holy shit! it's a flying saucer."
>
> . . . The vehicle was platinum in color (a luster that only platinum presents), no windows, greenhouse, no hatch or panel outlines, protrusions, engines, smoke or noises with one exception. A light air buffing sound could be heard as the craft moved through the air, a similar sound when air buffs against the canopy

when flying in a glider. The disk was about 60 feet in diameter with about a 10 to 12 foot girth to the middle of the craft.

Pares and his swim mates soon checked a topographic map, discovering that the mountain was four hundred feet high, giving the saucer an elevation of 500 feet when first seen. It was moving, he estimated, at only 20 mph, which no aircraft could do without stalling. It banked 15 degrees revealing its entire topside showing it was a "symmetrical convex lens shaped object" with "very distinctive edges."

To this day Pares admits that his hair still "bristles when I mentally replay the encounter." The view was so clear that it hit home that he was seeing a craft that no human had made.

The craft never lost an inch of altitude when banking. What was even more intriguing was that when it banked, the sun illuminated very subtle striation patterns in the metal surface, which ran from the front of the leading edge over the center girth to the back of the craft. This observation made it clear that the craft did not rotate and that it appeared to have a front, back and top even though it had a symmetrical disk shape.

After the craft came back level, it accelerated rapidly, across the lake and valley and then disappeared 10 miles away over the next mountain range. Pares expressed the usual frustration that no adult came out until too late. One of their moms made it out in time, but she could not get a visual on it as they pointed to the horizon just before it faded over.

The encounter was to have a profound effect on him. He admitted it changed his life forever. The details he saw continued to haunt him. He dropped all of his extra curricula in his senior year in high school and took a new track. "I keep thinking of the encounter and the possibilities of flight over unity, but also realized that there was a greater probability we are not alone."

Being convinced that flying saucers are here despite the prohibitive arguments of space travel, Pares has been broadminded about considering alternative modes of space flight. He has probed into the theories of bending or warping time and space. This led him to consider and accept Bruce Gernon's encounter in the Triangle and to believe it may be the key to far more than the enigma of lost ships and planes. Rather, perhaps, it is the key to how we can master time and space and travel between galaxies in a relatively short time, the method by which, possibly, the inhabitants of the flying saucers are frequently coming to Earth; too frequent, the believers note, for these to be remote, unmanned probes or the result of side trips between more regular destinations.

While Miguel Alcubierre's warp drive is considered proved, there are still many reasons to consider alternate modes of deep space travel. Principally, there is the problem of a spaceship fitting within the center of Alcubierre's drive. Detractors believe the energy needed to activate the warp drive would decimate any spaceship therein. An illustrative mockup has been commissioned by NASA showing exactly what a huge version of the warp drive would look like housing a spaceship within it. Not so surprisingly, it looks like a long, segregated cylinder with the spaceship bolted by long arms to the inside of the outer cylinder. It is in this way rather like the tunnel through which Gernon flew...and survived. Thus if there is any connection to a natural magnetic vortex and an artificial creation such as Alcubierre's drive Gernon's flight would indicate that a craft could survive within such a device if it were "tweaked" by newer discoveries.

In a very real sense the illustrative mockup of a spaceship inside a giant cylinder reminds us of the "mothership" category of UFOs— long, cylindrical yet far sleeker than imagined by the artist trying to render Alcubierre's warp drive in action.

With our present knowledge of warping space, it seems impossible that flying saucers in shape and design could have the power. But a giant cylinder would be perfect, as essentially the entire outer section of the ship is itself the powerful warp drive. Somehow "mothership" reports of the last 70 years seem too coincidental with our own newly acquired visions of Alcubierre's warp drive to be just that. It seems more that we may have stumbled upon the science necessary for intergalactic travel. For flying saucers of either 20-30 feet diameter or even bigger at 100 feet to be here they would need to come in a carrier that could travel long distances in space in relatively short time spans and it seems only the "motherships," designed like a giant cylinder, conform to the science required as we now understand it.

Reports of giant UFOs both on radar and visually at night (as a light) have confirmed that at times they appear to launch smaller craft, noted by more blips on the scope or visually by lights issuing forth and traveling along with the original light. The larger saucers could be launching the smaller, 20 inch discs (or even the 10 x 12 foot discs), but on occasion, especially high in the atmosphere, one wonders if radar is not picking up the motherships?

A notable sighting was on February 22, 1950. Two huge blips appeared on Boca Chica radar, at Key West. They were estimated to be about 50 miles up. Visually they were only 2 bright lights, and the interceptor sent up could not get near them. They soon streaked out of sight.

If sight and theory ring harmoniously true, it still strikes the observer as hard to imagine that insectoids could develop such modes of travel from planet to planet, display human ingenuity, and yet remain so insectoid in behavioral pattern that they never see any reason to contact mankind, especially considering the many years and perhaps centuries over which they have been observed visiting Earth. It could be, of course, that the language between insects and humans cannot be bridged, and the "aliens" merely remain pragmatic and go about their business. It may mean, however, that there is more than one type of alien lifeform visiting this planet and the insectoids are relative latecomers and because of language or behavioral patterns remain aloof.

Flying saucers' frequent if not predominant association with the seas, in particular the Bermuda Triangle and the seas off the eastern coast of Australia, plus their almost exclusive association with remote locations over land until 1947, have suggested to some that there's a colony on Earth from another planet, that the "aliens" live underwater or need to live underwater, or that they even are native to the Earth and had developed underwater. The last theory seems too impossible to conceive, but it is a curious coincidence with the modern theories of "aliens" having an insectoid makeup that even Biblically we are told that God created the birds and insects out of the oceans as opposed to the heavy, solid and relatively sedentary mammals like mankind and the animals which he created out of dry ground.

If UFOs are to be considered the prime factor in causing airplanes and ships to disappear by removing the airplanes upwards or by actual invasion of a small boat to get at the crew, the explanation for the difference in number between the mysterious events off Australia and those in the Bermuda Triangle is that the geography of the Triangle with its many Caribbean pleasure ports is more conducive to kidnapping (or space-napping) as there is simply so much more opportunity.

The above suggestion for the numerous disappearances in the Triangle has been offered repeatedly, almost to the point it is offhand. Upon consideration, however, it more than ably fulfills the military maxim that "Strategy is easy, but Logistics is difficult." It offers no reason why aliens would need so many examples of aircraft or, if disgorging the plane from its mothership's holding bays and only keeping the human occupants, for whatever sanguine or nefarious reason, why bother when it is so much easier to take people from lonely places, shorelines, and from ships, without needing to dump the cumbersome and bulky aircraft afterward.

It seems obvious there must be a correlation between motive and frequency, and there doesn't appear to be any when it comes to UFO abduction theories. There is only one case of an aircraft disappearance in the Triangle in which the circumstantial evidence supports that a UFO played a factor in it. Admittedly, one is enough to prove the principle. Another disquieting coincidence is that the disappearance was that of a very light aircraft. Given the power of the UFO experienced by Larry Coyne's helicopter, it was more than capable of lifting a small airplane.

But the most often asserted theory, namely that aliens are

checking humankind's technological progress doesn't fit. The taking of a puddle jumper Ercoupe in 1980 was a major step back from the jets and airliners that had vanished earlier in the Triangle. And any technologically sophisticated culture could easily see this from afar. This leaves the only and disturbing alternative— namely, it was relatively easy to interdict such a light craft and the UFO was ultimately only (and always) interested in the occupants.

Even if this last supposition is truly the answer, the disappearance of the Ercoupe remains a relatively isolated case, just as the disappearance of Fred Valentich is quite isolated. Being in the province of civil aviation, the accident reports and summaries for both incidents were not restricted. The small and lightweight nature of both aircraft also suggest that UFOs cannot or do not bother with the larger aircraft, erasing them from being responsible for most of the most sensational and unbelievable disappearances in the Triangle, especially the airliners and those craft close to shore within reach of radar. No UFOs were seen in relation to the two remarkable disappearances of aircraft coming in for a landing at St. Thomas, though the inference of a USO is there in the disappearance of the *Witchcraft* at Miami's harbor mouth.

Equally, it seems UFOs have visited or seen boats and ships and left them alone, although it seems they can interfere when they want, always in some way conveying their superiority, as in the Sanviti Case.

Of course, many planes have vanished so far from shore that their loss is more or less summed up by a Spartan "aircraft damage and injury index presumed" rather than an investigative report. Any number of these may have fallen afoul one of these UFOs and it is impossible that we could ever know. If UFOs are really interstellar spacecraft, and if their inhabitants are fairly intelligent, then they know to refrain from kidnapping close to shore where they can be observed doing so. Most disappearances in the Triangle traditionally have been those far out to sea where little can be guessed as to what happened.

But it can equally be said that too much can be second-guessed for what goes on in the deep sea. Whatever can be definitely said of UFOs, it can be said that there seems the frank and apparent association between them and the oceans, and judging by the two disappearances on record in which a UFO was associated they wait to strike only over the seas.

Aside from frequency of travel, the Triangle offers something else. The unique geography of the shallow banks and deep water gorges may be a prerequisite for or they are even conducive to the needs of UFO inhabitants. Or it may be that in this world beneath there is something they need.

Proponents of the abduction theory have one other factor to support their ominous view. It is something outside the Triangle but directly in line with it. Aside from the shores of the Triangle, UFOs are seen most frequently off Nova Scotia, Newfoundland, and Labrador; again, it is at dusk and, again, they flee back out into the Atlantic, heading south to the Triangle. It is along these flight paths where the most eerie cases of disappearances outside of the Triangle occur. This includes deserted vessels.

There is no room in this present work to detail these, but a recent one is rather curious. It is the case of the deserted *L'Actuel*, a large French sailing vessel with two experienced sailors aboard, regatta racer Gaétan de la Goublaye and his friend Denis Guilmin. They had set sail from Newfoundland in May 2009 for Le Havre, France. However, on June 21 the yacht was found deserted west of the Azores, far south of its course and where it could not have drifted. Presumably, the duo had turned south toward the Sargasso Sea, where they then vanished from the *L'Actuel* and it continued to drift in the current. The sailboat was trailing lines, the mainsail was set but dangling, and the headsail was torn but partly furled. The satellite phone and survival gear had been left behind. De la Goublaye had sent his last call on May 24 from about 1,000 miles to the northwest from where the vessel had been found, a location that confirms the vessel had headed south.

All aspects which may be involved or at least considered are, in the eyes of this observer anyway, interesting to contemplate, for so we do here, but the probability of UFOs contributing significantly to the disappearances seems negligible unless some motive which can be fitted to the location is proposed— such as they are simply protecting their own home or bases here and their acts against our own craft mean little more than when we swat a fly or bee trying to get into our house; a shoe-on-the-other-foot approach to theorizing if we accept that the inhabitants of the UFOs are insectoid.

It may be of little comfort for the isolated traveler, but if the reports of UFOs over the millennia truly represent the same phenomena reported today, and that they are, in fact, extraterrestrial in origin complete with inhabitants, mankind has in these millennia spread over the globe, and though we may have been displacing them in the process in the last hundred years of our air and space-age accomplishments mankind has never seriously been interfered with.

Nevertheless, reports of their existence in the Triangle, and their coming and going from the oceans, draw our attention to this world beneath. The bottom of the Triangle is the most unique in the world. Some of the most exotic geologic formations exist there, more intriguing than the "Domes on the Moon" or the "Face on Mars." Surprisingly, many manmade features are being uncovered as well, some at impossible depths, intricate designs and configurations that indicate at some very ancient time intelligence was at work in the area on land and, unbelievably, perhaps even on the bottom of the sea, long before the dawn of our own civilization when our own Greek and Roman ancestors lived in mud huts like barbarians.

Chapter 9

Beyond Forgotten Tides

It would be so shocking as to render the discoverer incapable of speech if at a newly uncovered ancient archeological site, having excavated through the buried city's successive layers of habitation, from the present dirt level, through the debris layers, through successive layers marking its decline, its golden epoch, the Bronze Age, and through the layers wherein was contained the developing city, testified by artifacts of crude stick idols of burnt clay and ungainly utilitarian pottery, to then dig below this and discover a jet airplane.

Yet in many respects the march of civilization on this planet intimately reflects this same paradox, only that it is contained in such a broad scope it has remained largely invisible until the last century. Even civilizations we assess as being crowning achievements in the march of mankind's progress, like Greece and Rome, seem anemic compared to the mysterious ambition contained in the first monuments of mankind.

Going back into ancient Egyptian history for comparison brings forward the sense that progress was at one point compromised almost in the vein we consider mass production today to have compromised the artistic and philosophic expressions of our own civilization. The Late and even Middle periods of Egypt pale by comparison to the Early Kingdom, some 2,500 years before Christ, when such epic feats of engineering as the great pyramids were dared and accomplished.

Even older than these are the temples or observatories made of blocks of stone fantastic in size. They continue to inspire and dazzle modern man not just by their size and astronomical precision but by the fact they represent a kind of collective ambition we seem to have lost but which seems spiritually to dominate the character of the earliest civilized men, if we are to judge them solely by the stupendous monuments they have left behind. This assessment is not utterly misplaced on our part, for their monuments are so massive as to have earned them the classification of Cyclopean, recalling the giant Cyclops of Greek mythology and reflecting our impression only giants could move such huge stone blocks.

Use of individual and collectively placed mammoth stone blocks was an art or science long forgotten even by the Hellenistic Age, though the use of such enormous monoliths alone dominated the architecture of the earliest and in many cases still unidentified civilizations. Instead of trying to explain them, the ancient Greeks attributed these constructions to a time of heroes and demigods. Such an attitude is hardly that of an ancient people impressed by something they could not reproduce. It is an attitude many share today.

This is not to say that these mysterious cultures or, to be possibly more accurate, science displayed the intricate engineering knowledge of the Greeks. It is that their desire was for meglo-grandeur and they collectively could bring it about without building on the acquired knowledge of previous civilizations. It is true what Sir Isaac Newton said when assessing his own accomplishments: "I stand on the shoulder of giants." But for the earliest civilizations of mankind we have certainly found none before our own prehistory upon whose shoulders they could have balanced themselves. They did not hew stones to perfection, this is true. Yet they did not shy from selecting the largest natural stones of their desire, sometimes weighing hundreds of tons, then equally unknown to us move the blocks, erect them, and then chisel fine joins to seal them together. If their technology was lacking, their ambition was not.

Despite our great science, we are nevertheless a techno-intricate society, in many ways like the Hellenistic Age was an optically intricate society, its engineering dependent on minute and precise physical beauty. Both of our societies, however, reflect no ability or mental disposition for the grandeur of physical marvels which so permeate the earliest civilizations. Neither the Greeks nor we today can move such enormous blocks that weigh hundreds of tons, and yet such monuments and fortifications (for lack of any other readily apparent interpretation) still exist from a time we classify as prehistory or certainly the earliest time of our own parent civilizations in Sumeria around 3100 BC, a mere 5,000 years ago.

It is the collective ambition, the almost megalomania, that seemed to be natural and undaunted in this first mysterious culture in remote antiquity that is as fascinating to contemplate as much if not more than the stupendous edifices that were the result of it; a trait we admire or marvel at because we seem to have lost it for our shrunken world of mass production and convenience or, worse, because of our shrunken mindset.

Another paradox is encountered in any assessment of the westward march of European civilization. Mass migrations of ancient mankind, in their tribes, can be gauged from the vantage point of our Greco-Roman background as coming from the east. The Indo-European peoples spread out from some central point north of the Middle East, and pour into Europe in various waves, occupying the most temperate areas around the Mediterranean. This continued for millennia, with the later migrations of the Celts underscoring the paradox the most. The Celts do not seem to be firmly in place in Europe until 500 BC, a time considerably after the golden age of the Mycenaean and Minoans cultures, and a time already after the destruction of the temple in Jerusalem by the Babylonians. They came to dominate Western Europe, from modern day Austria, Switzerland, France, and into Spain and the British Isles. Paradoxically, however, in their westward expansion they came across the huge monoliths of Carnac, France, and then across the channel in Britain the mysterious site of Stonehenge. Modern archeology has confirmed that Stonehenge and the monoliths of Britany were in place around the time of the great pyramids or around 2,500 BC, long before the Celts, and may have replaced an earlier wood construction that dated to prehistory, one that reflected considerable science of astronomy.

For *any* westward moving people before or during the Indo-European migration to continue moving westward through open land, to then encounter at the western extremes of Europe the astounding megalithic sites is like the analogy of a modern archeologist digging to the lowest layer of a city's habitation to discover not the most primitive artifacts but those that seem superior even to our own civilization today. Unlike the analogy, however, the westward drive of mankind and the discovery of the megalithic but mysterious culture on the fringes of the Atlantic is fact and not fantasy.

To assume the megalithic builders had immigrated from the east like the other Indo-Europeans is to propose they passed up the choice lands of Europe to live on the farthest reaches of the known world, there to build stone structures that still matched, in magnificence if not in specific style, those of the earliest civilizations far removed from France and Britain but which also used cyclopean stones.

The dating of megalithic culture, as it is called, is also piquing because its coincidence is with that early ambitious time in the cultures with which we are familiar, such as Egypt. In fact, it seems the further west civilization traveled the more it adopted the use of mastering heavy loads and stone blocks, something seen in Egyptian pyramids but not in Sumerian fired clay ziggurats to the east.

From our Judeo-Christian perspective this does not fit. All mankind spread out after the Flood from some central location around Ararat, the location from which even the European grapevine originates. Civilization then began in Mesopotamia, along the two major rivers Tigris and Euphrates. Here mankind built huge cities of mud brick.

A westward and eastward movement of civilization from Mesopotamia or north thereof is so evident from our perspective it is taken for granted, each pocket of it arising around major rivers, like the Nile, Indus, or in the Mediterranean on significant islands or advantageous isthmuses, as in Greece, each preserving legends of a past golden age, and each equally recalling a past global destruction out of which they emerged. Judging from the migration pattern we always assumed this parent civilization was somewhere in the Middle East, the fabled Babel, which in legend thinly preserved the destruction of some one-language, cohesive and yet vast civilization.

Yet it is the furthest from legendary Babel, in the most outlaying edifices in the west, where the buildings were composed of stupendous sized stones. From an engineering perspective it is actually much more accomplished to build in small stone than in monoliths. But these megalithic structures still fit the theory that these civilizations were built by survivors of an early advanced super-civilization that was destroyed. The builders of cyclopean edifies did not have the engineering skills of Mesopotamia, but they still had the desire or need to erect huge monuments, and seem to have done so with what abilities they had.

Even more interesting is the possibility that the Gigantija on Malta, considerably further west than Egypt, is actually the first free-standing stone building. It too is circular like Stonehenge, which is not a feature of Egyptian architecture, and made of huge megalithic blocks. The distinguished professor of Archeology at Cambridge University, Colin Renfrew, notes the paradox when he observed that "In the Near East at about this time, 3,000 BC and perhaps even earlier, the mud brick temples of the 'proto-literate period' of Sumerian civilization were evolving: impressive monuments in themselves but something very different from the Maltese structures."

Megalithic sites and the mysterious culture that built them remained an oddity and their builders distorted by fancy mythologies until within the last 500 years when the mystery grew more complex than the myths. With the discovery of the civilizations of the New World the same paradoxical progression was uncovered. As stupendous as Mayan, Toltec, and Aztec cultures were, and those societies upon which they themselves had built, the oldest civilization in the Andes which preceded them all show a preoccupation with and ability to move huge stones and make organized cities from scratch that are predesigned to accommodate tens of thousands of inhabitants. The ability to do this is even more mysterious at Tiahuanaco in Bolivia because the air is so thin the usual explanation of mass labor to move the megaliths seems to evidently fall short.

There is also a strange similarity in many of the artifacts in the abandoned megalithic sites on both sides of the Atlantic that is seen most clearly in the megalithic sites of Britain and France and in "medicine wheels" in North America. It seems as if at one time in the remote past some cohesive civilization occupied some area around the Atlantic and was dispersed, elements gaining a foothold on the western approaches to Europe, with perhaps a smaller group accessing and influencing the westward pinnacle of Middle East civilization in Egypt with stone cutting and moving technology, where it was then modified to conform to the neat symmetry of mud brick architecture, only on a grander scale; another retreating down the isthmus to the high Andean plains, and others, those compromising the less technological, influencing the North American cultures with similar henges as Stonehenge in Britain but not possessing the technology to take it to megalithic stones, though their wood henges reflect a similar knowledge of astronomy leftover from the same civilization of the past.

Legends and even glyphs of the Maya speak of a great destruction in the east; in other words, across the Gulf of Mexico, and glyphs depict volcanoes erupting, buildings tumbling into the sea, and survivors escaping in canoes.

Naturally, all of the above conjures legends of Atlantis, devotees of which remind us that *atl* is a common word in Amerindian linguistics and that a variation of it even means "water—" thus drawing a thin connecting strand between Old and New World knowledge of such a civilization. Despite the concept of Atlantis being fringed with paranormal crystal power today, it is nevertheless a fact that there appears to have been an "Atlantean" civilization otherwise it is hard to explain the similarities in the various megalithic sites around the Atlantic and their distinct difference with Sumer and Egypt. Their builders mastered and hauled stones we ourselves cannot transport and they did so in ways of which we cannot be entirely sure. And even if our concepts of their crude wood sleighs and use of river passage is correct, none of this explains their ambitious mindset, one that required massive cyclopean architecture and the cohesion of an entire populous state.

Between the two extremes of megalithic sites— those in western Europe and those in America— are the seas of the Bermuda Triangle, where the Bahama banks have sparked interest in the lost continent or island of Atlantis or remnants thereof since they are the only large, shallow banks in the world that could represent huge islands if the water table of the Atlantic was only 50 feet below its current level.

Plato, of course, exaggerated Athens glory, indeed simply added it to the tale, but his tale of Atlantis in his *Timaeus* dialogue reflects that pieces of it came from many sources, some which outright knew of the American continent and that large islands were situated before it. Since Egypt was the custodian of ancient knowledge (in Platonic Greeks' eyes), to give his story credibility Plato's tale is told by an Egyptian priest to Solon, one of the Seven Sages of Greece. The glory of Athens is declared, then the rapine arrival and unprovoked attack by the Atlanteans into all the cultures of the Mediterranean ("Asia and Europe").

> . . .This power came from the Atlantic Ocean, for in those days the Atlantic was navigable; and there was an island situated in front of the straits you call the Pillars of Hercules [Straits of Gibraltar]; the island was larger than Libya and Asia put together, and was the way to other islands, and from these you might pass to the whole of the opposite continent which surrounded the true ocean; for this sea which is within the straits of Hercules is only a harbor, having a narrow entrance, but the other is a real sea, and the surrounding land may be most truly called a boundless continent.

There is little reason to read Plato literally, however sincere the philosopher may have been. Many who favor a more literal translation of the epic wish to believe that perhaps the Mid-Atlantic Ridge, of which the Azores are merely mountain tops, was once much higher or the ocean levels much lower, as it would be before the ending of the last glaciation 12,000 years ago. Yet soundings prove there never was an island so large in front of the Atlantic side of the Straits of Hercules, but then puny Athens was never in a position to put down such a large scale invasion into Europe and Asia. Taking the tale as an embroidered composite, a literal substitute for Atlantis, for the island at least, can be found not in mid-Atlantic but in the Bahamas. The descriptions of the Atlantic found in the tale much more believably describe the Bahama banks, when they were huge islands, and considering their position they were and remain "the way to other islands, and from these you might pass to the whole of the opposite continent."

By a strange twist of fate, the idea that the Bahamas represented a major portion of Atlantis, though it was an Atlantis that was in a remarkably different vein than our Platonic traditions, was first proposed in occult circles, starting in the 1930s due to the psychic "readings" of clairvoyant Edgar Cayce, who through his many trance readings constantly spoke of Atlantis as a past super-civilization and, surprisingly, that the Bahama banks represented the last part of it to sink and take with it fabled technology, which included mind power, crystal generated levitation, and even the ability to transport ships in the sea, under the sea, and then into the air. He called the banks Poseidia, and said it sank about 12,000 years ago and there ended the last intact portion of this past super-civilization, except for the remnants built by its survivors on both sides of the Atlantic. Over successive generations and attacks by our more primitive ancestors the remnants of this civilization finally had its light extinguished; eventually the Atlanteans being bred into us.

While the psychic readings of Edgar Cayce are of more interest to the occult, and even to those who try and blame the disappearances in the Bermuda Triangle on latent forces of

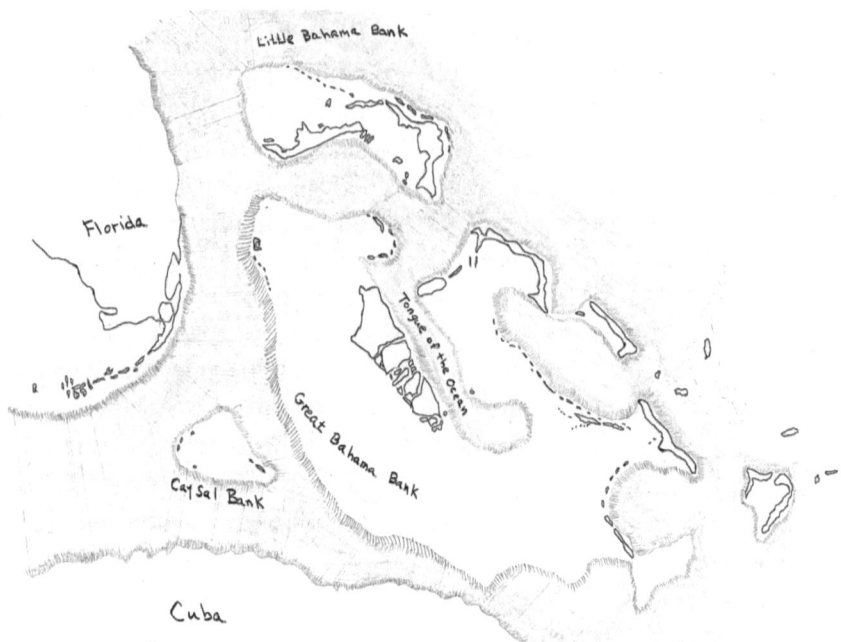

The Great and Little Bahama banks would form 2 huge islands if the Atlantic was shallower by only 50 feet. They are surrounded by deep submarine gorges.

Atlantis now buried beneath the sea, the possibility of a buried and tangibly accessible past civilization is of more interest to archeologists, adventurers, explorers, and to the observer.

Since the details of the Caycean Atlantean theory can be found published within *Into the Bermuda Triangle*, they do not need to be repeated here. A few things need to be underscored, however, before we can proceed with more recent and more tangible discoveries in the Triangle. For it is certainly true that Plato's Atlantis must have come from a variety of sources, and it is equally true that some of them knew of America. Thus thinly the Bahama banks may hold the remains of a civilization that helped inspire the tale. Told perhaps to Phoenicians by Amerindians, who then brought it back to the Mediterranean, its destruction and the stories they brought back may constitute the kernel of truth behind Atlantis.

An intriguing report in 62 BC by the Roman consul Metellus Celer of what appears to be Amerindians washed ashore in Spain in a large canoe may be only one record of many cases where Amerindians were cast upon Europe— yet another possible avenue by which the story was brought to the Americas by seagoing early Americans. In any case, the stories of a sunken island may go back to a time when the banks were themselves huge islands before they were swamped by the Atlantic's rising levels— in others words, to a time of prehistory.

The idea that there is more in the Bahamas than psychic myth gained credence on Labor Day 1968 when Dr. J. Manson Valentine discovered what is now called the "Bimini Road" off the small island of Bimini in the Bahamas. It is a huge 1,200 foot long road-like set of stones, some cyclopean in size, now pillowed and their once neatly fitted joins weathered though still attesting to how they all once fit together with the amazing precision of the most ancient megalithic stonework.

The reason why the discovery was greeted with relative sensation is also the reason for its greatest misfortune. Back in 1933 Cayce had predicted that a part of Poseidia, including a temple and somehow connected with it the vast knowledge of this Atlantean super-civilization, would be discovered near Bimini. In another prophecy, in 1940, he said that the Poseidian part of Atlantis would rise again in 1968-69, the very time period in which Dr. Valentine discovered the Bimini Road. Adherents to Cayce immediately put these separate readings together and proclaimed the Bimini Road a partial fulfillment, and since that day the road's study has remained more the purview of the occult rather than hardened archeology.

Arguments over the Bimini Road do not revolve around its existence but whether it is a natural formation of beachrock formed by the surf or whether the natural beachrock was cut locally and then built into a long ceremonial road or boulevard to access some ancient sacred site. Enough studies today indicate the latter. For instance, the general topography reveals the structure is not in line with the coast and some parallel placements are perpendicular to the coast, nullifying the idea the intricately joined blocks were cut by erosion of the encroaching surf.

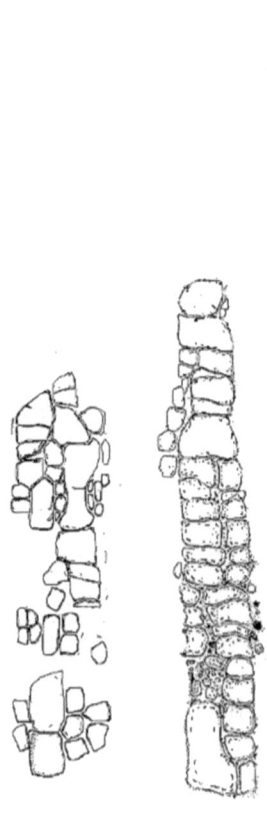
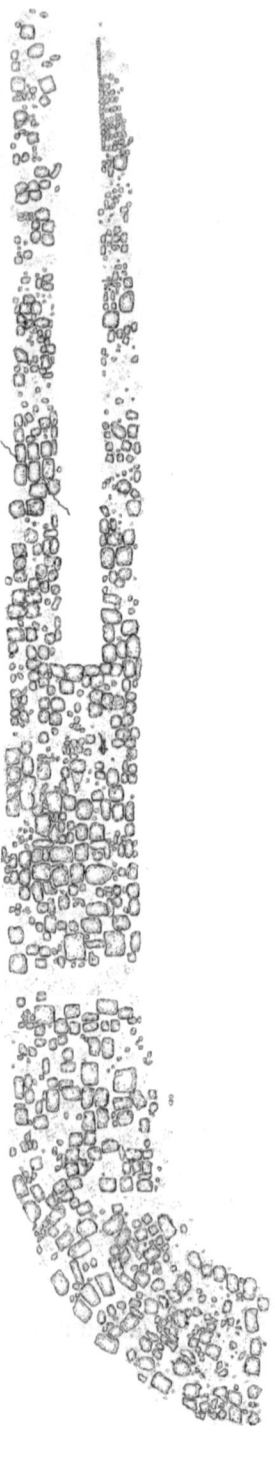

The Bimini Road and two parallel sections (not to scale).

The main Bimini Road is an inverted "J" in design, so that if it was a natural beachrock formation we would have to assume the original one piece of beachrock or reef was unusually shaped to begin with and had oblique and long formations alongside it but separate to it.

Tests of individual and adjacent bocks, however, have revealed they are pieces of beachrock formed at different times and at different areas of the island. Again, this would indicate each piece was cut and moved to the location to form a manmade structure.

Dating, of course, now becomes a problem. The above indicates that Bimini was already basically an island when the formations were built. This unwelcome proposal is refuted by those who wish to link it to Atlantis. They quickly note that the Gigantija and other megalithic island structures were built on high spots and knolls, areas that would become their own islands if the larger island (Malta in this case) sank.

Regardless, if Bimini does date to the early era of our own histories, it would still represent that unknown Atlantean (for lack of a better word) megalithic culture. The similarities are striking. Seven huge megaliths form an impressive section in one of the parallel lines of "roads" or fallen walls. Their joins are so exact as to mirror the dazzling cyclopean work of the Maltese structures of 3100 BC. The presence of several polygonal stones with angles and corresponding joins in the adjacent stone "roads" is particularly reminiscent of Incan walls.

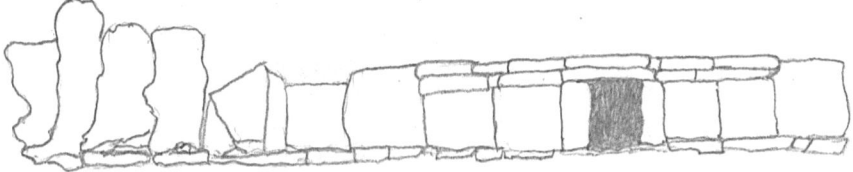

Walls of the Hagar Qim, above, and Gigantija, below, on Malta.

Civilization in America reflects the same paradox embodied in the migration of the Celts. We have declared that the Amerindians migrated over the Bering land bridge at some ancient time and then continued south to temperate zones. But it is a fact that the first monumental cities, including those with step pyramids, were built in the Andes. This would mean that the first migrant peoples passed up the finest land to start building cities in harsh altitudes in South America.

Caral in Peru is, in fact, the oldest city of the Americas, dating to the time of the Great Pyramids of Egypt around 2500 BC— an odd place, at the very least, for the first city of America to begin, considering the theory of migration from Alaska; and an unbelievably coincidental, far too coincidental, time period for civilization to bud in America.

One impression is unshakable. America's first civilizations mirror the Old World's beginning— cities with step pyramids beginning around 3100 BC in unlikely places and traces of an older and mysterious culture specializing in cyclopean stones that largely built on islands and coastlines. The Bimini site is in a way the American Malta— only submerged.

The wonder the Bimini Road instills in those who observe it underwater (something easy to do since local glass bottom boats ferry out loads of tourist to see "Atlantis Rising") must pale by comparison to the structure having been seen on land before it was plunged into the surf and the huge cyclopean boulders pillowed and flattened by the effects of the ocean.

A suggestion that this was beheld on land in relatively recent times, and indeed marveled at, comes from the artwork on the Piri Reis Map, one of the earliest maps showing the New World. Formerly residing in the Sultan's palace at Topkapi, Constantinople, it was discovered from the writing on it that it dated to 1513 AD. Along the distortion of the American coastlines, typical of early maps, a large island can be seen. Its importance is noted by its disproportionate size to the coast and it even dwarfs Hispaniola or modern Haiti/Dominican Republic. Whether this can be taken as a much larger Bahama island because the Great Bahama Bank was not yet submerged as it is

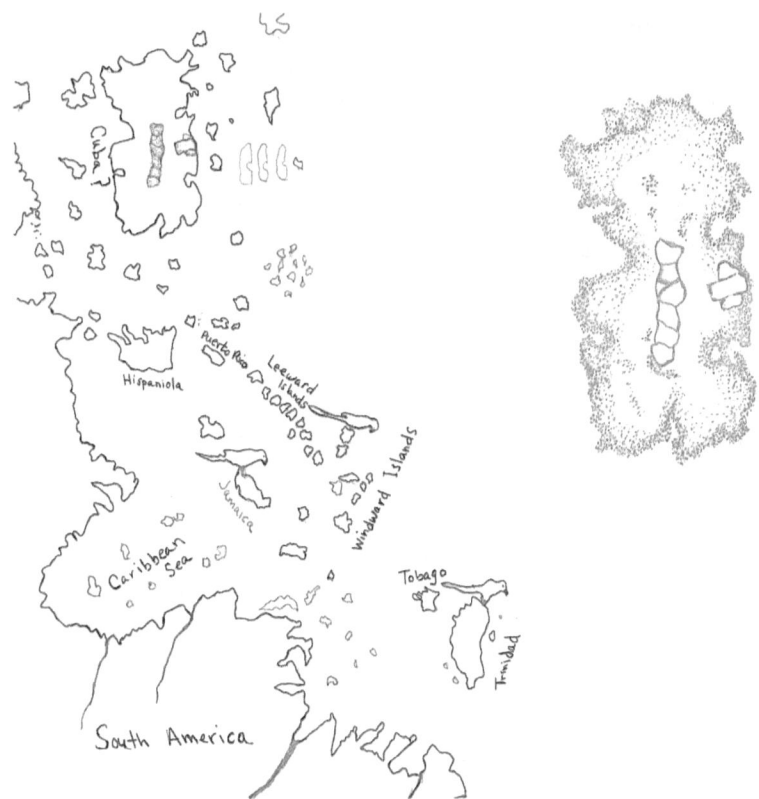

A tracing of the relevant part of the Piri Reis Map with the large island at top. The inset shows the island more clearly marked with two stone structures, a road and perhaps ruins of a temple, arch, or pyramid.

to its present extent, the large island is marked by a noteworthy feature considered, in the art of cartography, to distinguish it as unique to the area. This feature is a row of cyclopean, polygonal stones neatly fitted together. And if it does not represent the Bimini Road, it must represent other edifices on the Great Bahama Bank of similar design though now equally submerged and no longer visible.

Overflights of the Bahamas after Manson Valentine had discovered the Bimini Road consistently spotted more tracings of what appear to be constructions, megalithic sites, perhaps even henges and cities. Although the idea that pyramids have been seen remains fanciful, the overall scene is one of a vast urban development.

Corings have proven the stone *is* local beachrock, meaning that like with the megalithic sites on Malta the society did not transport material from long distances but came to the area already possessing their skills. More than being a megalithic site, the Bimini Road may be a part of a greater urban complex. If the latter, then there could be many more artifacts underwater, perhaps even a vast network of cities buried beneath the shallow banks' current swept bottom sands.

While the idea that pyramids and more complex dwellings on the Bahama Banks or at the bottom of what seems the unnaturally formed Tongue of the Ocean strikes one as sensational, proof of their existence might be a chance dive away considering recent discoveries off Cuba.

The existence of a complex sunken city off the coast of Cuba gained enough recognition from a number of archeologists that an expedition was funded from a surprising source— the National Geographic. The location of this sunken city at the very western tip of Cuba is especially intriguing in light of Mayan legends of a cataclysmic destruction of a city to the east. To traditional archeology this could indicate the sunken city was a Mayan colony, but the discoverer herself, Paulina Zelitsky, initially endorsed a prehistoric date for the city, inspiring those who seek Atlantis to believe they have found the first largely intact stepping stone to their quest.

Sonar tracings of formations on the bottom so strongly suggest the symmetrical layout of an Amerindian city that it was impossible to believe they were artificial. At the same time, however, their depth of 2,200 feet would place the city's construction back before the melting of the last ice age 12,000 years ago, coincidently the time in which Cayce said the last remnants of Atlantis sank in the same general area of the Bahamas.

Believers in Atlantis note that the first appearance of Mayan culture was in Yucatan, the closest landfall to the west from the tip of Cuba, and perhaps this sunken city is a remnant of Cayce's fabled Atlantis and the Mayans mere colonists or survivors. On the other hand, orthodox Mesoamerican scholars note that Mayan culture arises in the Yucatan relatively late in history within the last 2 and a half millennia, not a time commensurate with 12,000 years ago.

For believers in Cayce's Atlantis this does not matter. The process of moving from the Great Bahama Bank to Yucatan may have been a slow one with Cuba used as a stepping stone. The city could have plunged much later and the rest of the culture on the island was decimated by earthquakes. The sunken city could remain a crucial link to Atlantis. In this context it is interesting to note that Cuba does not appear on the Piri Reis Map unless it and *not* a Bahama island is the large island marked by polygonal stones. This would indicate there were great ruins found on Cuba which have since vanished.

Of all the Mesoamerican civilizations, the Maya were distinct, being the only culture to fully develop a hieroglyphic script. To believers in Atlantis this indicates they were closest of all the cultures to the original Atlantean super-society.

Specifically as it relates to the sunken city off Cuba, the controversy involving prehistory would be removed if it could be proved that the city had plunged and therefore there is no reason to suggest a prehistoric date commensurate with the melting of the last glaciation. Seismic plunging could have happened at any time and this would make the existence of the city a little more palatable to the current mindset we have about the past history of mankind, though it would add quite a dynamic to Mesoamerican studies.

Zelitsky herself has endorsed plunging, first in May 2001, causing confusion as to why she adheres to a prehistoric date for the site.

She has observed:

> The area has been seismically active for thousands of years. And what we find on the ocean bottom are fractures from which the magma and volcanic ash came out. From these structures we were able to delineate a configuration of the land that sank because you can see them clearly. The land that sank is very obvious from our image of the ocean bottom. And you can see bays, like harbors, and it's all at the depths of 900 and 700 meters.

Based on various sonar scans and artistic renderings, this is what the sunken site looks like. Zelitsky has described the structures as sitting on a huge plateau, presenting the clear images of "an urban development partly covered by sand...the shapes resemble pyramids, roads and buildings."

Samples of rock taken by Zelitsky's undersea robot were given to Havana's Dr. Manuel Iturralde-Vinent for testing. When the results were finally returned, Zelitsky declared: "Samples that we recovered from the ocean bottom have justified our structures that we call megalithic structures. The samples are granite stone, completely polished, with some incrustations of fossils: fossils of organic creatures that normally live on the surface, not on the ocean bottom. This is very interesting because this is evidence that the whole surface sank to the depth of 2,297 feet, or about a half mile down."

As if the existence of 20 square kilometers of a sunken city is not controversial enough, the existence of the granite conveys a high degree of trade, as granite is not native to Cuba or Yucatan. Because it is smooth, it also reflects a high degree of workmanship, both naturally expected in a culture capable of building such an urban society.

Nevertheless, more proof has not come in 15 years since the first discovery despite the potential knowledge that remains to be found. Money has been short, and though National Geographic helped fund some subsequent robotic searches nothing in the way of clear photography has been produced to help identify the structures, giving rise to the skepticism that there may simply have been too much initial interpretation on Zelitsky's part despite her dogmatic statements above.

Even if she hasn't endorsed Atlantis, Zelitsky has nevertheless fanned the flame of the most controversial aspect— the dating to prehistory. She offered that the area could have plunged 15,000 years ago, unquestionably making this a city representative of a prehistoric civilization of which we have no record. Critics point out that the structures on the readouts, if the interpretation they are a city is accurate, clearly reflect a Mayan city, a layout that is radically different from the isolated megalithic sites of the Mediterranean, France and Britain. The theory of plunging is acceptable, but if so there is no reason to opt for such a prehistoric date.

In truth, it could be that Zelitsky has discovered a great Mayan colony. Peninsula Guanahacabibes, the area of Cuba to which the sunken portion once belonged, would not have been far from Yucatan. A colony seems far more reasonable than that the Maya came from Cuba, else it is hard to explain why any civilization, even 15,000 years ago, if it had begun in Cuba, did not leave any other massive cyclopean ruins extant on the lush island. However, if the sunken city was a lone colony, then the lack of finding other ruins on Cuba would make sense, and its submergence therefore must be placed in far more recent history. The stories of this city's destruction would be pointless to the overall narrative of Atlantis, and yet ironically it could be that modern "Atlantologists" have cannibalized it to promote it as evidence of a shared recollection of the destruction of the continent of Atlantis that comes down to us from Plato.

Even if the sunken city should be proved, it would not help in fitting the Bimini Road into any civilization of the Americas, not as an outpost, not as a colony. Its style is megalithic and it

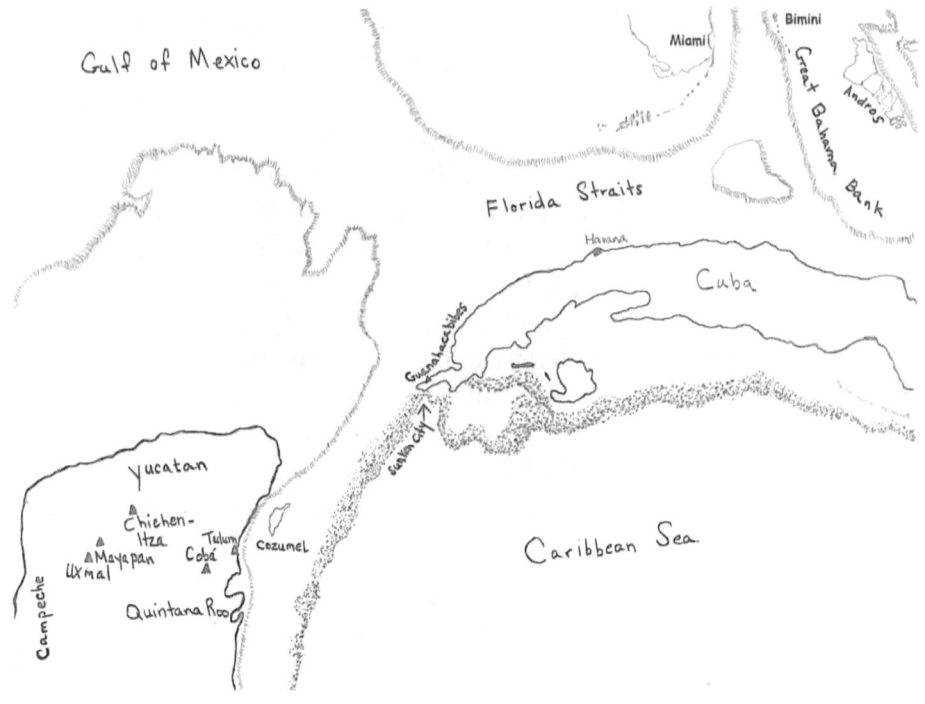

The relationship of the sunken site to the coast of Yucatan.

matches the Maltese architecture of colossal polygonal stones. The Mayans would not have built this as an outpost, and their architecture does not reflect any evolution from this style. If the Bimini Road was built by an Amerindian society it would be hard to fathom why such a tiny island would be deemed relevant to an Amerindian culture so far away and why such a cyclopean style was still used.

Les Hemingway, the brother of Ernest Hemingway, was an avid boater and publisher of *Bimini Out*, a boating newsletter in Miami. He was a strong supporter of the idea that a cold fresh water well on East Bimini was a healing well. Therapeutic cures had been reported by many people who had ventured through the shallow estuary of its flow (about 300 yards) and found the smoothly drilled well in the island's limestone. Skin cancers and other growths have disappeared from bathers who have soaked at least three times in the subterranean fountain. Hemingway has soaked there himself, noting the calming effect.

Flanking the estuary are two mounds etched in the sandstone. The meanings of their shapes are hard to interpret, but on nearby East Bimini three more mounds exist, one with the clear definition of a shark. Another is likened to a whale, and a third looks like a cat or sea horse. Like the vivid images on Peru's Nasca plain, they are designed to be seen only from the air. The existence of these mounds, especially those flanking the healing well, indicates a very early holy site for the gods or for offering to the gods, possibly because of the healing nature of the water in the well.

Tests have confirmed unusually high lithium content to the water, a mineral which is known to cause calmness in humans, and is even a proscribed anti-anxiety drug. If the mounds and style of architecture of the Bimini Road can place the Bimini culture to the era of the Inca or Maya, the very fact Amerindian cultures knew of it indicates they had more exploratory journeys through the Gulf and Atlantic than was first thought, and explored the islands in detail else they could not have found the

Stone glyph, variously credited as from Coba in the Yucatan or Copan in Honduras, showing a Mayan fleeing a city tumbling into the sea by exploding volcanoes.

well to begin with in order to appreciate its unusual benefits.

One discovery on Bimini, though often used to support the Atlantean theory, actually better supports the theory the Bimini Road was made in much more recent history. The beachrock of which it was made was indeed quarried locally, an indication that Bimini was already an island and not just a low hillock on the Great Bahama Bank when it was a huge island in prehistory. This may not make it prehistoric or Atlantean, but like the Maltese and other megalithic sites it nevertheless remains mysterious. It could date to the beginning of history, around 3100 BC, and therefore represents a fragment of that early, ambitious civilization of which we know so little.

Despite orthodox dating of Amerindian civilizations, probing into their past reveals the same paradox discovered in Old World civilizations. The further back one goes, the more ambition one encounters that must have been lost by the subsequent civilizations.

Blocks at Ollantaytambo weigh over 100 tons, with 6 of them appressed to each other with such precision it is hard to conceive how each side was made flush before any kind of fitting was attempted. Stones of the various courses of the fort at Sacsahuaman tower 12 feet high and are intricately cut and joined with adjacent blocks, some that have over a dozen sharp angles, and yet all these smaller stones are sealed to them by a hairline of beveled joins. The Gate of the Sun at Tiahuanaco is carved from a single block of stone weighing 10 tons while other standing stones in the various temple complexes weigh 100 tons each, such as at Puma Punku, all of this put in place in the thin air of 12,500 feet.

Traditionally, the dating of the beginning of Tiahuanaco is over 2000 years after the first civilizations in Sumeria and nowhere near to prehistory. It could be therefore that the first civilized men anywhere in the world naturally preferred colossal stone, leaving them natural for lack of engineering skills to hew them into perfect squares. Instead they hauled huge natural stones, left them in their raw state, and only chiseled them enough to get them to join together. Thus the existence of similar monuments over the world utilizing this same general

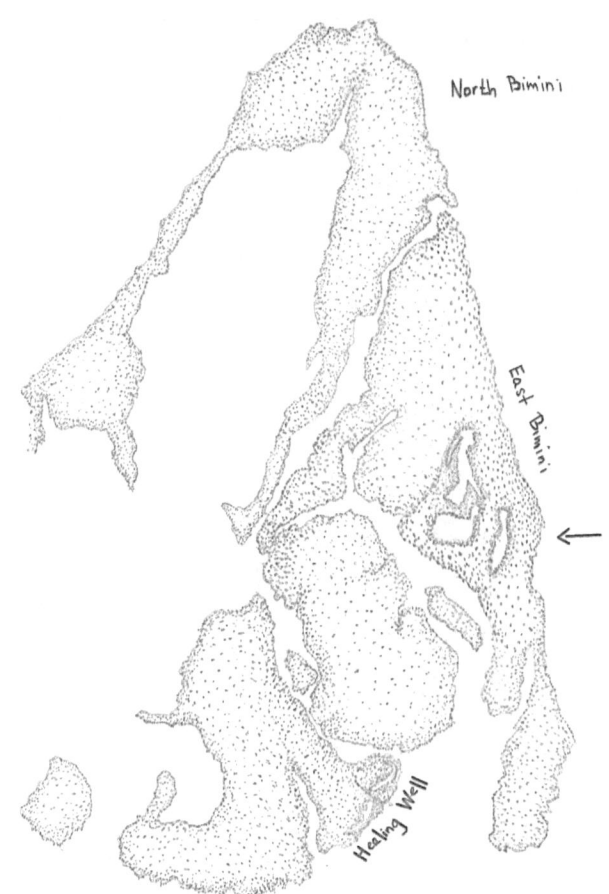

Part of North and all of East Bimini. Aside from the three mounds, the lithium well is also flanked by curious mounds.

architecture does not reflect the existence of a single prehistoric civilization, but the natural course of progress in handling and using stone for buildings. This would also explain the startling similarity in the most ancient Egyptian stonework, as seen in temples and walls at Khafre's pyramid complex (circa 2,500 BC) and in Tiahuanaco over 2,000 years later.

It takes considerable engineering skill to erect a tall building using small, square stones or bricks compared to organizing megaliths and then on top of these placing smaller stones in courses to extend the structure upwards. This would translate to Sumeria representing a higher form of engineering and scientific knowledge over the erectors of the megalithic sites much further west, though clearly the builders of the megaliths spent considerable effort to haul enormous stones, reflecting that curious ambition to build permanent and colossal monuments.

Yet it is true that the greatest megalithic sites seem to ring the Atlantic. No matter how one slices it, it seem the sunken city off Cuba and the stones on the sunken Bahama banks remain controversial and potentially capable of rewriting Mesoamerican history and, to the hopeful in Atlantis, to begin the writing of prehistory, into which so many civilizations since the beginning 5,000 years ago have desired to gaze, beyond the legends of a golden age lost to cataclysm.

Atlantis as a legend survives not just because Plato's *Timaeus* and *Critias* dialogues discuss its existence and destruction. It exists and remains vibrant today because we as civilized men have existed only for a short 5,000 years. It exists because the earliest buildings mankind erected reflects an ambition and a lost art of grandeur. It exists because the greatest megalithic sites seem to move inland from the Atlantic, into the Mediterranean, eventually into Egypt, and into America at Yucatan and down along the Andes. And there appears to be one on the Great Bahama Bank that in style appears to be far more ancient than any civilization in America.

Whether or not it should turn out that the Bimini Road and the mounds or any other structures thereabouts were built by an Amerindian people to mark a healing site as sacred, the existence of such structures in the Bermuda Triangle remain a curious part of its legend of a lost civilization.

We must accept that the Bermuda Triangle is more than its enigma. It is a geographic location, and the alluring topography at its surface is more than matched by the natural wonders and scars at its bottom. Possible manmade edifices have joined themselves to the discussion because of a strange coincidence or by true psychic gift from a clairvoyant who decades before spoke of a make-believe world of a super-civilization to vanish in the area. Edgar Cayce gave us only one real prophecy— Bimini— and a very unbelievable context: Atlantis; an Atlantis of novel power sources which Cayce said operated vehicles in the air and then under the sea, long before witnesses reported UFO and USOs in the area doing the same thing.

But there is something more certain about the depths of the Bermuda Triangle, one less subject to interpretation than the buried stones and one far less subject to the devotion of occult believers. No discussion of the Triangle and its enigma can leave out its place on this globe, its depths and shallows and the forces that must have created this unique mixture of sea and sky, visible order and perhaps invisible chaos.

Chapter 10

A Saga of the Earth's Past

Even before precise details were given to us by modern imagery it was evident just by eyesight, and then underlined by echo-sounding, that the area of the Bermuda Triangle had one of the most tortuous pasts on the Earth. In fact, it is even more evident today that the entire topography of the Triangle is not the result of local catastrophe but the result of past global upheaval.

The neat continental shelf edges of the Americas' eastern coasts and the western continental coasts of Europe and Africa are not to be found in the Bahamas and Caribbean. Islands are scattered about, some like Cuba broken off from the main continental body. Entire chains of islands are the tips of mountain ranges thrust up from the sea bottom. The entire Great Bahama Bank appears equally thrust up from the depths rather than a piece of the Americas broken away as the continents cataclysmically moved apart in ancient times. Titanic forces alone can account for such risings and fallings of land and for the exponential movement of the continents. Explosive scars like the Mid-Atlantic Ridge tell us where the Atlantic's birth began, but this scar itself is only a symptom and not the ultimate cause.

Meteors have been a favorite thing to blame in the modern age, after mankind accepted that such things as stones fell from the sky. A huge ancient impact is more than just a guess. It is an informed opinion. Nothing else imaginable could so fracture the original "mega-continent." Mercury displays a similar fracture, apparently from a meteor that struck the small planet on the opposite side and sent such a jolting force through it that it cracked open on the other side. Ancient legends speak of a time when God or the gods rained down destruction from above, notably on that one great civilization of one language that existed when the earth was one continent.

Noted "Atlantologist" Egerton Sykes took it far enough to explain the Bermuda Triangle. "You don't get this type of collision frequently. But it has, nevertheless, happened in the past. Perhaps the Bermuda Triangle should be called the Bermuda Crater. A massive meteor, driven ten or twelve miles into the surface of the Earth might, over the years, be causing the aberrations."

Readouts of the Atlantic's seabed, however, reveal no massive crater in the heart of the Bermuda Triangle, a location where few disappearances happen anyway. Rather the seabed in the heart of the Triangle is the bottom deserts called the Hatteras and the Nares Abyssal plains. Elsewhere, especially to the east, the Atlantic's seafloor is peppered with volcanic seamounts, each one thrust up in response to the cataclysmic scar which is the Mid-Atlantic Ridge. The Bermuda seamount is a rare exception in the western North Atlantic. In essence it seems all the pressure of the cataclysm vented itself through and around the Ridge and the sea bottom thereabouts, leaving the bottom of the Triangle sunken and caved in.

The Ridge is a massive lattice work of crisscrossing fracture zones and deep rift valleys. The distance between the continents is directly linked to the width of the Ridge. It is widest in the North and South Atlantic and narrowest at the equator where the continents of South America and Africa are closest.

An asteroid may have struck what is now the Pacific in ancient times, but there is no real evidence remaining to suggest such an impact.

No one, in fact, is certain exactly why the Earth burst open along here for 10,000 miles and broke apart the original "mega-continent" or Pangea, but the resulting effects were phenomenal. It must have been at this time that the Earth heeled over on its axis by as much as 26 degrees before coming back to its present incline. This incline is one of the most influential factors on the creation of our modern world. As the Earth heeled over on its axis it had the potential to not only affect the direction of movement of the continents but the toll spin itself. (If the mantel moves in one direction, the crust must move in the opposite direction.) The result is a cataclysmic upheaval of the continental landmasses, the buckling of the sea bottom and the thrusting upward of volcanic seamounts and undersea ridges.

The end result is the Earth as we know it today— the seasons and interactions of the weather, the heat of summer and the cold of winter and the winds that come with them. But the Atlantic remains the most unstable and tortured part of this planet. Positions of land and the rotation of the globe have intermixed to create the powerful and unique Gulf Stream currents, and their location on an inclined Earth here has given them unique potential on the weather no other network of currents in the world can possess.

Oceanic currents are the most volatile in the Triangle due to the subtropical location and the funnel-like effect of the deep Florida Straits between Florida, Cuba, and the Bahama banks. Here the Gulf Stream, issuing out from the warm Gulf of Mexico, attains its fastest speeds, near to 4 mph, and then with its warmth still relatively intact plows forward into the colder North Atlantic off North Carolina.

The sum of this effect can be seen most vividly in the North Wall Phenomenon off North Carolina and over the northern part of the Triangle. This is where the warm waters of the Gulf Stream collide with the colder air and currents of the North Atlantic. Astounding effects include rogue waves at the surface

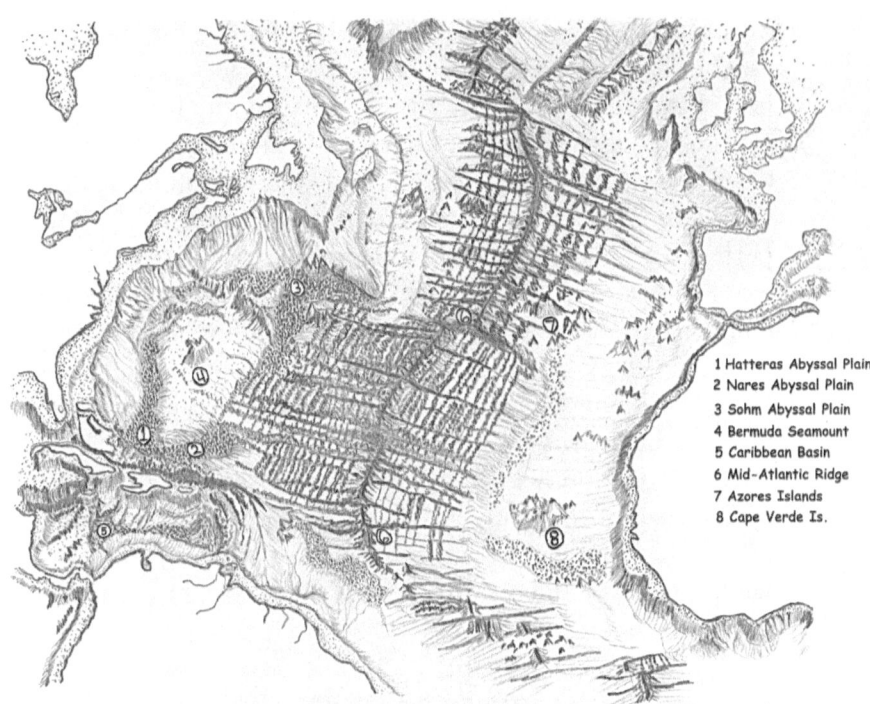

The Mid-Atlantic Ridge dominates the Atlantic sea bottom, a place of fractures zones over 2 miles wide, shifting bottoms and thousands of earthquakes per year. The bottom appears sunken and collapsed off the US coast.

that can damage or sink ships, to sudden and violent up- and downdrafts that can rock an aircraft to pieces or slap it into the sea. The phenomenon can be so powerful that it was officially considered as a possible explanation for the disappearance in 1980 of the 520-foot cargo ship *Poet* north of Bermuda. It has no doubt played a hand in the capsizing of some of the derelicts found, perhaps even those that were found as far away as the Azores, as anything capsized northwest of Bermuda would continue to drift in the current to the Azores. It is certain that rogue waves have sent smaller boats to the bottom quickly.

While the area's unique currents have been extensively used to explain the lack of flotsam being sighted or recovered after a boat or plane vanishes due to the potentiality that all debris is quickly dispersed over the Atlantic, a more intricate view of the interactions and their potential effects is warranted in order to explain some of the Triangle's enigma of electromagnetic anomalies. Along with the visible weather forces tied into this area of the planet, there must be the invisible forces of electromagnetism that are inherent in all matter. Logically, like basic weather we take for granted they too must lay dormant until the right factors collide to create invisible effects and perhaps, on occasion, visible symptoms.

For example, there is or should be no question that the incline and rotation of the Earth are key factors in the creation of such massive vortices as hurricanes and monsoons. They strike along the same latitudes and longitudes on the exact opposite side of the world— the Triangle and the South China Seas. Warm and tropic winds and moisture interact along the Tropic of Cancer, but only in these two locations do the worst storms occur. Basic weather exchanges cannot explain it or hurricanes would happen all over the Earth. Obviously, hurricanes are not the result of the topography of submerged continental shelves, fast oceanic currents, and warm and cold fronts. Like gravity, hurricanes are a natural phenomenon created as the byproduct of many factors, not least of which is the Triangle's location on an inclined planet.

At its quickest stretch the Gulf Stream is subject to eddies, where currents become circuitous. This is the product of the edge of the fast Stream bouncing along the edge of the slower currents of the Atlantic. Just like eddies at a river bank, only far bigger, these are a visible example of what is going on underwater. In a river, the currents are violent along the bottom, churning and tumbling about, like the rip of the ocean tide. Add to this equation the much greater volume of the Gulf Steam, its depth and the currents tumbling against slower currents and a volatile combination has been created for electrical currents. Some currents turn clockwise whereas some turn counterclockwise. The same rings true of the currents over the Bahama banks, only here like a river it is the swift currents tumbling off the shallow bottom.

This has often been called a "state of flux"— a term the Coast Guard even uses. Although they meant it physically— a condition in which shifting bottom sands and tangential currents could erase signs of catastrophe— one should wonder if the conditions are not just as suited for an electrical state of flux. Almost every electromagnetic phenomenon could be transiently created and then wisp away.

A curious evolution of the Triangle phenomenon actually supports the theory that the currents are responsible for some of the unusual electromagnetic aberrations. This is the phenomenon of derelict vessels. Obviously they do not occur today in near the same numbers as in the 19th century when hundreds existed within only a 7 year period. And most certainly mainline cargo freighters are not being found derelict today, the counterparts to the cargo packets found so often derelict over a century ago. There is only one major difference today. Steamships are only a fraction of time in the Triangle— a couple of days compared to a couple of weeks by sail. There is therefore less probability that steamships will encounter a bizarre natural phenomenon over these currents like the *Mohican* did. Derelicts today are the smaller sailboats. Like their 19th century predecessors they are weeks in the Triangle and therefore more likely to encounter an unchancy fate.

While if proven this would crack away at the enigma of the Bermuda Triangle, it would do so only for those areas of the Triangle encompassed by the powerful Gulf Stream unless it can be shown that the currents electrically affect the air and sea around them. Electronic fog has been reported the most over the Bahamas, which are adjacent to the Gulf Stream at a right angle.

Electronic fog is the most irrefutable and frightening of the Bermuda Triangle's enigmas. It too seems tied to the area, the embodiment of small vortices that generate around a plane or ship. But if it is not set in motion by Wilbert Smith's invisible magnetic vortices (also probably unique to the area due to the incline and rotation of the planet), what causes it and intensifies it? So far, the cause remains a major mystery, but its solution may help solve much of the Bermuda Triangle's enigma, at least the one astounding visual phenomenon there is in the Triangle.

Hurricane formation may help us to understand electronic

fog. In a sense, they are the exact opposite. Like a tornado, the hurricane whips into violent vortex motion the storm cells, but at its center or eye it is clear. On the other hand, "electronic fog" seems to mark the center of invisible vortices. The planes and ships that have experienced it are in the center of its eye, the fog forming around the aircraft and giving us a visible phenomenon. It is, of course, far less powerful than a hurricane but the same principle may be involved— electromagnetism and atmospherics. Keen observations by Bruce Gernon and others have revealed that the fog surrounds the aircraft like a donut. It is therefore going hand-in-hand with some form of invisible magnetic vortex.

The vortex origin of electronic fog seems certain. Bruce Gernon's description of the inside of the tunnel through which he flew echoes the witness testimony of Roy Hall in Texas concerning the interior of a tornado. Hall described bluish lights and even streamers that appeared to be glowing vapors, which seem to some extent to constitute a glowing "electronic fog" long before the term was coined by Bruce Gernon who seems to have conducted the fog while in the cloud tunnel. Also like Roy Hall, Gernon noted the dual vortex makeup of the tunnel. While inside the tunnel he noted the wall was spinning counterclockwise. Yet after he spit forth from the tunnel and looked back he noticed it had closed and the slit that represented where it had been was rotating in a clockwise motion.

At present we must accept the electronic fog does not have an easy answer. It can form more ways than one. Aircraft and boats should be able to dispel electric buildup and no fog should be able to cling to them. Repeatedly, however, each witness has confirmed they could not shake the "fog." This again indicates the plane or ship is at the center of the electromagnetic vortex.

The failure of prosaic and established theories to explain the disappearances is all too exemplified by the open failure of the old theory of the Agonic Line, the meridian or central pole of the Earth's magnetic field. In the 1970s, when the Bermuda Triangle was such a hot international topic, the US Coast Guard issued an official opinion, a chit handed out to all inquirers, in which it listed this factor as the most significant of the theories.

. . .The majority of disappearances can be attributed to the area's unique environmental features. First, the "Devil's Triangle" is one of the two places on Earth that a magnetic compass does point towards true north. Normally it points toward magnetic north. The difference between the two is known as compass variation. The amount of variation changes by as much as 20 degrees as one circumnavigates the Earth. If this compass variation or error is not compensated for, a navigator could find himself far off course and in deep trouble.

To help put such a statement in perspective, there needs some clarity. There is True North (North Pole) and Magnetic North, which is located about 1,500 miles away at Prince of Wales Island in the far reaches of Canada. It is to Magnetic North that a compass needle will point. Being 1,500 miles away from true geographic north (the North Pole), a navigator must make certain adjustments to compensate for the difference. The compass always points to Magnetic North. It is only incidental that it points to True North in the Triangle because True North and Magnetic North are briefly in line here.

Since the writing and issuing of the chit, however, the Agonic Line, the narrow corridor where there is no compass variation to calculate, has slowly moved westward, again due to vagaries in the rotation of this inclined planet. It is no longer in the strict Triangle off the east coast of Florida between the coast and the island of Bimini. The Agonic Line is now in the Gulf of Mexico where no appreciable numbers of disappearances occur, making it impossible that simple, poor navigation was ever a factor between Bimini and Miami.

In fact, the Agonic Line is so narrow that when it was still within the strict Bermuda Triangle (in the 1970s) using it as a cause for most of the disappearances was a poor excuse. At Bimini, only 60 miles away from the east coast of Florida, there was already a 4 degree variation in the compass between True North and Magnetic North. The brief moment the compass had no variation was, in fact, so brief, that a pilot could never get lost by not compensating, since only minutes away in any direction are familiar landmarks.

As it now stands the Coast Guard opinion is minus the

theory of the Agonic Line. They do not touch on any esoteric theorizing, of course, but they also do not even forewarn of the very real hazards of piracy. The chit as it reads today:

> The "Bermuda Triangle," or "Devil's Triangle," is a mythical geographic area located off the southeastern coast of the United States that is noted for an apparent high incidence of unexplained losses of ships, small boats and aircraft. The apexes of the Triangle are generally accepted to be Bermuda, Miami, and San Juan, Puerto Rico.
>
> In the past, extensive but futile Coast Guard searches, prompted by search and rescue cases such as the disappearance of an entire squadron of TBM Avengers shortly after take-off from Fort Lauderdale, Florida (1945), or the sinking of the Marine Sulphur Queen in the Florida Straits (1963), have lent credence to popular belief in the mysterious and supernatural qualities of the "Bermuda Triangle."
>
> Countless theories attempting to explain the many disappearances have been offered throughout the history of the area. The most reasonable seem to be citing human errors and environmental factors.
>
> The majority of disappearances can be attributed to the area's unique features. The Gulf Stream, a warm ocean current flowing from the Gulf of Mexico around the Florida Straits northeastward toward Europe, is extremely swift and turbulent. It can quickly erase any evidence of a disaster.
>
> The unpredictable Caribbean-Atlantic storms that give birth to waves of great size as well as waterspouts often spell disaster for pilots and mariners. The topography of the ocean floor varies from extensive shoals to some of the deepest marine trenches in the world. With the interaction of strong currents over reefs, the topography is in a constant state of flux and breeds development of new navigational hazards.
>
> Not to be underestimated is the human factor. A large number of pleasure boats travel the water between Florida's Gold Coast (the most densely populated area in the world) and the Bahamas. All too often, crossings are attempted with too small a boat, insufficient knowledge of the area's hazards and lack of good seamanship.
>
> Many explanations have cited unusual magnetic properties

within the boundaries of the Triangle. Although the world's magnetic fields are in constant flux, the "Bermuda Triangle" has remained relatively undisturbed.

It is true that some exceptional magnetic values have been reported within the Triangle, but none to make the Triangle more unusual than any other place on earth.

While it was well-intentioned, the errors in the chit must be noted. Largely it is just a re-write of the 1970s' chit with the addition of that interesting concession at the end admitting to "exceptional magnetic values." Paramount of the errors is mentioning that the Earth has "magnetic fields" when the planet only has one magnetic field. In any case, the unique electromagnetic phenomena reported in the Triangle could have nothing to do with the overall magnetic field readings in the Earth. They are localized, spontaneous, and then fade away, making testing them and predicting them near to impossible. They are, like gravity, a phenomenon, which means they are the product of many factors. Along with the other unique attributes of the area, the "exceptional magnetic values" may be capable of contributing to alarming results.

One wonders if more information comes in on the electronic fog, also probably not a product of the overall magnetic field but of what must be a combination of many factors locally, if the Coast Guard will amend their comments on the unusual magnetic readings just as they had to drop the Agonic Line theory.

The process of any unsolved mystery is evolution— the process of elimination that finally brings us closer to the essence and from there one step closer to the solution. Via this method it has taken "electronic fog" decades to finally receive popular recognition. The next step is to figure how to reproduce and then nullify its effects.

Practical attempts to learn from some of the mysteries of the Triangle have not been limited to attempts at unraveling "electronic fog," though because of its visibility, albeit briefly, this factor is probably the reason why it is the one phenomenon that has been pursued seriously. Some conservative geophysicists accept that Bruce Gernon briefly flew through a horizontal tornado of sorts, but that he was not truly propelled through time. The reason why such little forward momentum was felt may be because of the lack of gravity which is associated within the core of a vortex, as in the eye of a hurricane.

Still, a forward and momentous propelling, without drag, without any resistance, is a significant step in understanding that the principle of engineered travel of this nature is possible, and even if Time was not breached a rare moment of traveling through a vortex has only reinforced the benefits of using warp bubbles both in atmospheres and in outer space.

It occurred here in the Triangle probably because of the area's unique place on this equally unique orb, and this is the result of the area's unique, tortured past. Blaming "basic weather" or "environmental" factors is an excuse that is used to minimize mystery when it comes to disappearances. But the Triangle has matchless and very visible weather patterns, and just because they are visible, such as the super cell cloud Gernon encountered, does not mean they do not generate at times very sensational *invisible* powers.

The formation of this planet sounds very physical—explosion of molten material, centrifugal force, and then the acting upon itself of the electromagnetic energy inherent in all matter until the planet condensed to form sufficient mass. But look at what a planet creates— a magnetic field, the bending of space, gravity, and so much other phenomena including adjusting the Time Continuum. To minimize the potential of the unique weather patterns of the Triangle is to blind oneself to the forces that created them and in turn may be created by them in ways that we still do not understand. It is to deny the unique geography of the Triangle, its place on this globe, and the chaotic topography below the surface of the sea.

Within the physical universe we have made great strides. Alcubierre's warp bubble is a giant step. But we still need to conquer the concept of hyperspace and dimensions. Alcubierre's bubble will prevent the slowing of Time by preventing the bending of space around a spaceship. It will give us speed even beyond that of light. In order to conquer the galaxy, we must infinitely surpass light speed, lasso hyperspace, or slip through wormholes.

Still harder to comprehend are multi dimensions of multiverses. Doubtlessly disappearances may help us to finally understand them, especially those disappearances in the Bermuda Triangle because they are more commonplace than the rare disappearance elsewhere in the world. It isn't required that one of the aircraft or ships actually slipped into another dimension. What matters is that their disappearances have been so intriguing, in circumstances now so well-documented, that the disappearances remain incomprehensible. It is this quality that continues to incite our minds to ponder the possibilities. Einstein said that logic only takes us from A to B, but imagination takes us everywhere. All that has happened in the Triangle continues to excite our imaginations, as mystery always does, and contemplating them may inspire us to great discoveries.

The unique geography of the Bermuda Triangle in itself, self-contained, and in its juxtaposition on the globe around us, has created both a mystery and a challenge to be overcome. Like the forming of this planet, the Triangle's creation seems purely physical. But beyond the face of the Triangle there may lay pathways to hyperspace, Time, and pathways to other universes we can hardly comprehend. It is not a mystery to be shunned or to be given form only by tabloids. It is not that the Bermuda Triangle is a final frontier on this planet that requires it to be conquered. It is because the most puzzling cases may provide us with the first step into the final frontiers of space, time, and other worlds.

There are more things in Heaven and Earth, Horatio, than are dreamt of in your philosophy.

Bibliography

For a fuller account of all sources significant to understanding the Bermuda Triangle phenomenon the bibliography of Book I (*Into the Bermuda Triangle*) by the author is recommended. Those sources most significant to this volume are listed below.

Air Force Mishap Report, SAC B-52G, 15 October, 1961; Kirtland Air Force Base, New Mexico.

Air Force Mishap Report, MATs C-119G, 5 June 1965. Air Force Safety Center, Norton Air Force Base, California.

Air Force Aircraft Mishap Report, C-133A, 27 May 1962; Kirtland Air Force Base, New Mexico.

Air Force Aircraft Mishap Report, C-133A, 22 September 1963; Kirtland Air Force Base, New Mexico.

Air Force Aircraft Mishap Report, KB-50K, 8 January 1962; Kirtland Air Force Base, New Mexico.

Air Force Aircraft Accident Report, MATs C54G BuNo 45-539, Atlantic Ocean, Kindley Field, Bermuda to Morrison AFB, Florida, 3 July 1947. Maxwell AFB.

Air Force Accident Report Summary, KC-135A BuNo 61-0319,

600 NM NE of Homestead AFB (29.00N, 69.57W); KC-135A BuNo 61-0322, ditto, 8-28-1963. Kirtland AFB.

Arnold, Kenneth, and Palmer, Ray   *The Coming of the Saucers*,
        privately published by the authors, 1952.

Berlitz, Charles,   *The Bermuda Triangle*,   Doubleday, 1974.
--   --   *Without A Trace*, 1977, Doubleday.
--   --   *Atlantis: The Eight Continent*, 1983, Putnam.
--   --   *The Dragon's Triangle*, Wynwood, 1989.

Board Of Investigation into the five missing TBM airplanes and one PBM airplane convened by Naval Air Advanced Training Command, NAS Jacksonville, Florida, 7 December 1945, and related correspondence. Naval Historical Center.

Cayce, Edgar Evans   *Edgar Cayce On Atlantis*,
        A.R.E. Paperback Library, 1968.

Computer Search of the Records of the National Transportation Safety Board for all aircraft posted missing from 1962 through 1992 as requested by the author on May 12, 1993.

Disappearance of the S.S. Marine Sulphur Queen on or about 4 February, 1963. Marine Casualty Report; U.S. Coast Guard.

Eckert, Allan W.   "The Mystery of the Lost Patrol"
        The American Legion, April 1962.

Factual Investigation Report: Missing aircraft between Fort Lauderdale, Florida and Havana, Cuba, September 21, 1978 Douglas DC-3 N407D. National Transportation Safety Board Report via National Technical Information Service, Department of Commerce, Washington D.C.

Factual Aircraft Accident Report: Near St. Thomas, U.S. Virgin Islands November 3, 1978 Piper PA-31-350, N59912.

--   --   --   --: Missing between Fort Lauderdale and Bimini, Bahamas, Cessna 402B, N44NC, March 31, 1984, MIA-84-F-A126.

--   --   --   -- Unknown - Missing Aircraft, February 11, 1980, Beech BE-58, N9027Q.

--   --   --   -- Near Puerto Rico, June 28, 1980; Ercoupe 415-D, N3808H.

Fawcett, Lawrence & Greenwood, Barry,
         The UFO Cover-Up, Prentice Hall, 1984

Flight Mishap Report, 10 September, 1971, F-4E Aircraft #67-0310. Air Force Safety Center, Norton Air Force Base.

Gaddis, Vincent,   *Invisible Horizons*, Chilton Books, 1965.

Good, Timothy,   *Above Top Secret*; Quill, 1988.

Gould, Rupert T.   *The Stargazer Talks*, 1944.

Halvorson, S. Report of Assistance on Gloria Colita, 1940. National Archives and Records Administration.

Hill, Paul R.   *Unconventional Flying Objects* HR, 1995

"In The News" —Bulletins of the US Coast Guard.

Aug. 19, 2009: Coast Guard suspends search for missing Pasco County man (Portus); Sept 20: Coast Guard searching for missing female boater near Anclote Key (Migliorni); May 14, 2013: Coast Guard crews search for missing boater near Key West, Fla. (Rydberg); Sept 13, 2009: **Update** Coast Guard suspends search for missing boater (Schermerhorn); July 16, 2010: Coast Guard suspends search for missing boater near Sanibel Island (MacQuarrie); May 8, 2008: Miami man missing after leaving Key West, Coast Guard searching (Garcia); Dec. 21, 2013: Coast

Guard suspends search for missing man near Jupiter Inlet (Porcaro); June 24, 2003: Coast Guard suspends search for missing boaters (Leone); Jan 13, 2016: Coast Guard searches for missing boater bound for U.S. (Trindade); May 26, 2008: Coast Guard Suspends Search for Missing Boater Near Bahamas (Steenburg); Feb. 6, 2009: Coast Guard searching for missing man (Franklin); June 19, 2008: Coast Guard Suspends Search for Missing Boater Near Soldier Key (Arguelles); Jan 3, 2013: Coast Guard crews search for missing person off Elliot Key, Fla. (Myhre); Oct 19, 2007: Coast Guard Searching for Missing Sailor (Didier); July 10, 2012: Guard suspends search for missing Sarasota man Key West, Fla. (Van der Hoven); Dec 23, 2004: Search Suspended For Lone Fisherman (Rodriguez); Oct 11, 2009: Coast Guard searching for 3 men aboard overdue vessel off the west coast of Puerto Rico (El Seco Area); June 22, 2009: Coast Guard suspends search for 3 overdue fishermen in waters off Piñones, Puerto Rico; April 21, 2008: Coast Guard Suspends Search For Missing Fisherman In U.S. Virgin Islands And Puerto Rico Waters (Don Chepo); Oct. 2, 2007: Coast Guard Suspends Search For Missing Boater (Extra Labor); June 30, 2011: Coast Guard suspends search for overdue boater near Boca Raton, Fla. (Randall Ward); Date: Aug. 25, 2010: Coast Guard suspends search for possible missing boater in Madeira Beach St. Petersburg, Fla. (Makin Waves); July 04, 2010: Coast Guard suspends search for missing North Carolina man off coast of Myrtle Beach (Heads or Tails); Oct. 22, 2011: Coast Guard Searching For Overdue Boater (Know Patience).

Investigation into the circumstances surrounding the loss of AB 524 (BUNO 149945) and the subsequent death of LT. Paul T. SMYTH, USN, --- -- ---- and LT. Richard W. LEONARD, USNR, --- -- ---- at about 1437R, 22 Feb 1978. Navy Mishap Report, Office of the Judge Advocate General.

Keyhoe, Donald E., *Flying Saucers From Outer Space*, Henry Holt & Co., 1953.

Marx, Robert F. (with Jennifer G. Marx), *In Quest of the Great White Gods*, Crown, 1992.

M/V SOUTHERN CITIES: Sinking with loss of life, Gulf of Mexico, 1 November 1966. U.S. Coast Guard Marine Board of Investigation Report and Commandant's Action. U.S. Coast Guard.

Report of Court (No. 7952) s.s. "Samkey" O.N. 169788. Department of Transport, London.

Report of Independent Investigation Of Major Aircraft Accident Involving R7V-1 BUNO. 128441 At Sea On The Great Circle Route Between Shad Intersection (Lat 37-40N; Long 73-00) And Lajes Airport, The Azores On 31 October, 1954. U.S. Navy, Navy Safety Center, Norfolk, Virginia.

Report of the Court investigation of the accident to the Tudor IV. Aircraft "Star Tiger" GAHNP on 30th January, 1948, held under the Air Navigation Regulations, 1922. His Majesty's Stationary Office. Air Accidents Investigation Branch

Report on the loss of TUDOR IVB "STAR ARIEL" GAGRE which disappeared on a flight between Bermuda and Kingston (Jamaica) on 17th January 1949. Ministry of Civil Aviation. Department of Transport, London.

Ruppelt, Edward J., *Report On Unidentified Flying Objects*, Doubleday, 1956.

Sanderson, Ivan T., *Uninvited Visitors*, Cowles, 1967.
-- -- *Invisible Residents*, World, 1970.

Sigsbee, C.D. *Wrecks and Derelicts of the North Atlantic, 1887-1893 Inclusive.* US Hydrographic Office.

Spencer, John Wallace, *Limbo Of The Lost*, Phillips, 1968.

Steiger, Brad, editor, *Project Blue Book*, Ballantine Books, 1976.

Stone, May, Letter to author from New York Historical Society, New York, March 9, 1993, re: schooner Ellen Austin.

Titler, Dale M. *Wings of Mystery*, Dodd, Mead, 1966.

Waters, John M. Jr., *Rescue At Sea*, Von Nostrand, 1966.

Winer, Richard, *The Devil's Triangle*, Bantam, 1974.
-- -- *The Devil's Triangle II*, Bantam, 1975.

Zink, David, Ph.D., *The Stones of Atlantis*, Prentice Hall Press, 1978, 1990.

www.ingramcontent.com/pod-product-compliance
Lightning Source LLC
Chambersburg PA
CBHW030136170426
43199CB00008B/90